SINGLE ROPE TECHNIQUES

Swallows circling in Sotano de las Golondrinas, Mexico. The pitch is 333m.

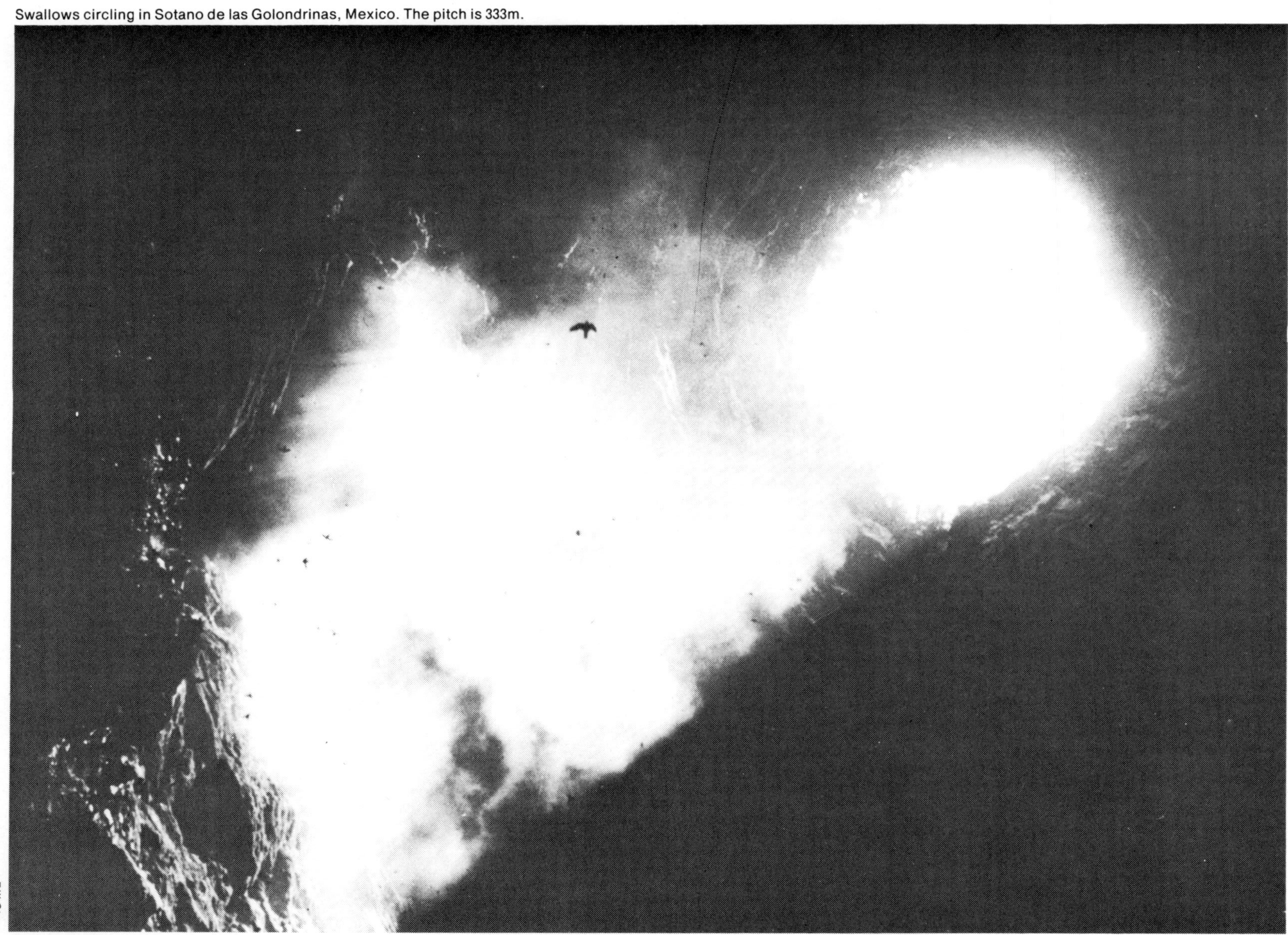

Bill Stone

SINGLE ROPE TECHNIQUES

a guide for vertical cavers

by Neil R. Montgomery

assisted by Donna Mroczkowski

sketches by the author

Sydney Speleological Society Occasional Paper No 7

The Sydney Speleological Society
Sydney
1977

SINGLE ROPE TECHNIQUES
a guide for vertical cavers

Sydney Speleological Society Occasional Paper No 7

First published 1977 by
The Sydney Speleological Society
P.O. Box 198,
Broadway, N.S.W., Australia, 2007

National Library of Australia Card Number
and ISBN 0 9599608 3 x

cover design by the author

Other Occasional Papers by the
Sydney Speleological Society —

No 1. RDF Equipment, New Caledonia Expedition
No 2. History of Colong Caves, New Guinea
No 3. Chillagoe Caves
No 4. Bungonia Caves
No 5. Australasian Map Index No 1
No 6. Timor Caves

Printed in Australia by
Lakes Printers
34 Railway Street, Wyong

CONTENTS

INTRODUCTION

> "Hastily abandoning our packs, we climbed the low ridge above the joya and suddenly found ourselves on the edge of a true precipice. We could not contain our excitement. People were carefully running from one vantage point to another, exclaiming at the voluminous, wonderful pit but not really comprehending the immensity ... not at first anyway. Organise and drop rocks was foremost. The watch was ready, the rock was ready, and when the first 13 second free-fall resounded previous excitement seemed minor."
>
> Raines (1972) on the exploration of El Sotano in Mexico.

Most of the world's highest mountains have been conquered, but as for the deepest caves, who knows? In the last decade more than three quarters of the world's hundred or so known caves over 500m deep have been bottomed. In the last three years the world depth record has been broken three times and is now pushing towards 1500m. Vertical caving is in its golden age — and this is largely so because of the common acceptance of single rope techniques (SRT). Originally devised for mountaineering, SRT has been taken into caving and is now recognised as the best general method for shaft exploration. It is used by the speleologist and sport caver alike.

Single rope techniques are methods of descending and ascending a single fixed rope. The technique of descent is called an abseil (or rappel) and involves winding the rope through a friction device or around parts of the body. For the ascent, or prusik, mechanical rope clamps called ascenders are generally used. There are numerous methods of prusiking in common use today. Nearly all make use of two or three ascenders which connect the climber to the rope. Upward progress is made in small increments by moving up the ascenders one or two at a time.

In taking this lead role in technique, SRT has replaced the use of caving ladders, which had been at the forefront of cave exploration for most of this century. Before the 1950's, SRT had been only an adjunct to ladder climbing, partly because safe, reliable ropes and abseil/prusik equipment were not then readily available. But during the 1950's, and particularly the 1960's, mountaineers improved their equipment and techniques. Some cavers recognized the potential of mountaineering methods for vertical caving and adapted the equipment and techniques for cave exploration. Mountaineers had long used abseiling as a method of mountain descent and, with the invention in 1931 of the Prusik knot (named after its inventor), modern cave exploration was on its way (up, of course!).

This book is a complete guide to SRT and includes equipment and techniques from many countries. The sources of information are numerous. My experience of Australasian vertical caving and association with cavers here has naturally formed a major element, but in addition, much knowledge was gained from cavers in Europe and North America while caving abroad in 1975. Research in the speleological literature broadened this knowledge. Being also a rockclimber my experience and reading in this area has proved invaluable. The book was written in mid-1977 and up until publication date I have tried to keep informed of the latest developments in this rapidly evolving subject. There are still key areas where further development is certain to take place, such as ropes, for example. Any new information (and comments on this book) are welcome for a future edition.

There is still a wide variety of techniques and equipment shared by both the above and below ground enthusiasts, and with each being keen experimenters and writers, the methods and equipment are forever changing. My task would have quadrupled if I had attempted to cover all the material on SRT that has been published in newsletters and books. Instead, the emphasis is on SRT as it is commonly practised at present, and only scant reference is made to techniques which have either become unpopular or never achieved popularity. In addition, the writing is essentially non-academic, which means that, for example, detailed discussions of how abseil and prusik devices work have been omitted. Where possible, references are given for articles on such subjects.

The book is intended for people with some experience of caving. There is no information on such basics as lighting, clothing and footwear. It is advisable for people who have never been caving, or vertical cavers who have previously used only ladders, to gain some experience on cliffs on the surface first and then in easy vertical caves having short pitches. Abseiling and prusiking will probably be learned quickly, but anchoring and rigging techniques never are. In this area, one is constantly learning as every pitch presents its unique problems. The Chapters on anchors and rigging should be viewed as the most demanding in the book.

A final note. It is hoped that all readers will be strongly aware of the need to conserve, to the greatest extent possible, the delicate and sensitive cave environment which is the heritage of everyone.

Neil R. Montgomery
18 First Avenue
Epping, NSW, 2121
Australia

August, 1977

FOREWORD

Caving is a widely pursued activity participated in by a large cross section of people throughout the world.

It has the elements of adventure as speleologists seek "new vast innumerable caverns".

Often to explore the unknown, the descent and the inevitable ascent of long pitches has to be undertaken.

Over the years various methods of ascending and descending have been used with flexible ladders being the main stay. But with the need to ascend quickly, safely and with equipment requiring the minimum of personnel, as is the case of multi-pitch caves and expedition caving, Single Rope Techniques (S.R.T.) are fast becoming the vogue.

The equipment used in S.R.T. is being continually improved to satisfy new techniques and to make the equipment more "fail safe".

The author Neil Montgomery has been a member of the Sydney Speleological Society for more than ten years. During this time he has caved extensively both in Australia and overseas, chasing "the deepest cave in the world" where S.R.T. is of paramount importance. He is as a consequence fully conversant with the latest techniques and equipment.

In writing this book he set out as completely as possible all the important information pertaining to S.R.T. as well as his own personal observations that can only be gleaned from experience.

The Sydney Speleological Society in publishing this book hope that both beginners and experts will benefit from the effort the author himself has extended in writing it and the various people who helped in the publication.

We feel an understanding of the limits and benefits of the techniques as set out in this publication is a very important contribution to safe caving.

B. S. Nurse
President
Sydney Speleological Society

ACKNOWLEDGEMENTS

I would like to acknowledge the assistance of all cavers who have discussed techniques with me over the years, and especially Julia James and Andrew Pavey with whom I have pondered SRT since I did my first prusik.

Many people have helped with this book. Thanks to —

Donna Mroczkowski for editing and typing the manuscript.

Kitty Dunn, Julia James, Donna Mroczkowski, Andrew Pavey, Philip Toomer and Bruce Welch for reading the manuscript and making many valuable suggestions.

Keith Dekkers, Malcolm Handel and Andrew and Geoff Montgomery for similar help with Chapter 1.

Paul Caffyn, Harold Coleman, Julia James, Bill Stone, Donna Mroczkowski, Andrew Pavey and Geoff Montgomery for photographs.

Geoff Montgomery for all photographic prints except for the ones on pages 1, 14 and 75, and to Andrew Pavey for those.

Cheryl Kanaley, Randall King, Robyn and Geoff Montgomery, Donna Mroczkowski and Margaret O'Shaughnessy for modelling some of the sketches and photographs.

The Petzl brochure for Figures 73, 101, 114 and 128.

Jim Chester, Ross Ellis, Chuck Pease and the Shining Mountains Grotto for the use of their libraries.

Ross and Christine Ellis, Randall King, Geoff Montgomery, Donna Mroczkowski, Ben Nurse and Philip Toomer for proof reading; Ross Ellis and Ben Nurse for help and advice with publishing, and the Sydney Speleological Society for publishing.

Neil R. Montgomery

1: ROPES FOR ABSEILING AND PRUSIKING

The abseil-prusik rope is the centrepiece of SRT. It, alone, must support the entire weight of each caver as he goes down or up a pitch. Therefore, it **must not fail.** This places stringent demands on cavers to choose ropes with high safety factors and protect them from damage both above and below ground. The caver's choice is complicated by the lack of any international standards such as those set up years ago for mountaineering ropes. Whereas companies all around the world make climbing ropes to meet the requirements of the Union Internationale des Associations d'Alpinisme (UIAA), to the author's knowledge, only one company (Blue Water Ltd in the USA) manufactures ropes especially for vertical caving. Cavers can hope that in future years more companies will manufacture caving ropes and that international standards will be set. For the present, however, cavers need to be aware of the demands SRT places on their ropes so that they can make a safe choice. In any event, such an understanding helps cavers appreciate what a vulnerable item the rope is and just how much careful attention it needs.

This chapter does not give any lists of rope brands and their test data. Such information may be obtained from manufacturers, supply shops, and caving literature. This chapter does, however, give guidelines for rope selection on the basis of fibre type, rope construction and rope diameter. It is felt that a suitable rope can be chosen by paying careful attention to these factors and then by rigorous rope testing in actual cave use.

DESIRABLE PROPERTIES

By varying rope fibre type, construction and diameter, manufacturers produce a wide range of ropes with varying properties to suit different purposes. Cavers need to decide which properties are desirable in a vertical caving rope and then attempt to determine the fibre, construction and diameter best able to give them. It isn't simple because a lot of compromises need to be made. For example, thick ropes are generally stronger than thin ones, but they are also heavier, so that strength needs to be balanced against weight. Keeping in mind that many rope properties are related, it is useful to list and discuss them individually.

Right: Caver prusiking the Drum Pitch (50m), Bungonia, NSW, Australia.

Andrew Pavey

TENSILE STRENGTH

The strength of a rope is usually determined in a laboratory by applying a steadily increasing load on the rope until it breaks. The load at breaking point is called the tensile strength. Minimum strength requirements can be calculated by roughly determining the maximum loads cavers are likely to place on ropes, and then multiplying this figure by say five, to safely allow for knots and wear in the rope, each of which can reduce strength by a factor of two. The two most taxing uses of vertical caving ropes are tandem prusiking (two cavers on a pitch at one time) and the holding of any slight falls which may occur if the rope gets snagged on ledges or under flakes and then suddenly gives way. It seems that forces equivalent to tensile loads of about 300kg could readily be applied in either case so that a tensile strength of 1500kg can be taken as a safe minimum for ropes for general use (tests by Patten 1966 on tandems).

With discretion, weaker ropes may be justified on short drops of only 5m or so, where falls are improbable and tandems out of the question. Be cautious of manufacturers' strength figures if they seem extravagant. In tests done in Britain, Eavis (1974) found that strength (while adequate) often deviated from stated figures.

ABRASION RESISTANCE

High abrasion resistance is a very important property for a vertical caving rope. The greatest single danger in SRT caving is that of abrading the rope against sharp rock edges while abseiling or prusiking. Another subtler form of abrasion is due to the rubbing of dirt particles against the fibres inside the rope, an unavoidable situation in caving. Some rope types are far tougher than others in both these respects.

STATIC STRETCH

The property of static stretch determines how much the rope will extend when a caver's weight is applied to it. It is important when starting a prusik because it controls the amount of prusiking which needs to be done before actually leaving the floor, or water if one happens to be swimming at the time. Stretch starts to get annoying when it is greater than about 2% under body weight (2m stretch on a 100m pitch).

A more important concern is that the motions of prusiking (and sometimes abseiling) cause a yo-yoing bounce in the rope. Since while prusiking one does not normally load the rope much above body weight, the amount of bounce experienced relates closely to the static stretch of the rope. The higher the static stretch is, the more bounce there is and the higher will be the risk of abrasion against sharp edges (Eavis 1974). Further, under conditions of high bounce, the fibres flex markedly against each other, provoking grit abrasion as well. Low static stretch is a very desirable property.

ENERGY ABSORPTION

For their sport, rock climbers emphasize the importance of using ropes which stretch considerably in the event of a fall and so absorb the energy of a fall without placing excessive stresses on the body. In a far less important way, a capacity for energy absorption in vertical caving ropes will be of use to cavers in the unlikely event of a snagged rope giving way and causing a fall while abseiling or prusiking. The need for energy absorption, however, must be carefully balanced against the more important need for low static stretch. Ropes of low static stretch should be chosen, but the need for energy absorption should be kept in mind and efforts made to have it as high as possible. No low stretch rope should be used for rock climbing. A heavy fall could seriously injure the climber, even if the rope did not break.

FRICTION

The friction offered by a rope's surface is a major determinant of the amount of control given by an abseil device and the ease of pushing up an ascender while prusiking. Good abseil control and low resistance to the movement of an ascender are important rope qualities. The friction of a rope largely depends on its construction (page 5).

HANDLING QUALITIES

The handling qualities of a rope include such factors as flexibility, grip, ease of packing and susceptibility to kinking or tangling. For the most part, these variables are hard to define and only become apparent under actual cave use. However, it is worth singling out the tightness of a rope's construction as a major determinant of its handling qualities (page 6). Very tight or very loose ropes do not handle well.

WEIGHT

Lightness is an advantage, provided one is not skimping on essentials such as strength and abrasion resistance.

WATER ABSORPTION

A rope's capacity to absorb water depends mainly on the amount of open space between the rope fibres. This is determined by the construction of the rope (page 6). Low water absorption is desirable to keep down weight when carrying wet ropes.

COST

Cost works in the same way as weight. While cavers are notoriously poor, it would be foolish to buy inferior ropes just because they are cheap. Cost only becomes a factor when choosing from a selection of ropes which are all safe.

CHEMICAL RESISTANCE

It is an obvious advantage to buy ropes which are resistant to chemical attack since, through carelessness, ropes may come in contact with household chemicals and battery acids or alkalis. However, all rope fibres in use today are susceptible to certain chemicals, and it is important to know which chemicals do harm the various fibres (pages 3-4).

HEAT RESISTANCE

Heat resistance is an important property. Isenhart (1975) ran a series of tests to see what temperatures abseil devices could reach during abseiling. Ropes must be able to resist these temperatures. Various models of rappel rack and carabiner brake descenders (see Chapter 6) were used for abseils at moderate rates (about 0.5m/sec) on a 100m pitch and most models had heated to around 100°C by the end of the pitch, with temperatures still rising. Faster abseils (about 2m/sec) generated temperatures over 150°C in some cases.

A rope can be subjected to heat in another way as well, which is less conspicuous but more dangerous than the problem of the hot abseil device. During prusiking (and abseiling to a lesser extent), rope bounce can cause rubbing against a rock edge, producing enough frictional heat to weaken the rope and accelerate abrasion. Eavis (1974) has shown that this heat can be especially damaging to the fibres of ropes of low heat resistance, such as polyethylene or polypropylene, so that rapid failure occurs at the edge (page 4).

The softening temperatures of abseil/prusik ropes should be at least 150°C to give security against both these heat sources, unless one is rigging pitches of less than about 10m, where heat problems should not arise. It is important to consider the softening temperatures of ropes rather than their final melting temperatures, since permanent rope damage or complete failure will always occur when a rope softens. Softening temperatures are generally 50°C to 100°C less than melting temperatures.

SUNLIGHT RESISTANCE

Exposure to sunlight slowly degrades ropes causing loss in strength and abrasion resistance (Moncrieff 1970). The deterioration is more rapid in latitudes nearer the equator, at higher altitudes and in the summer months (Smutek 1975). It was once a serious problem but manufacturers have nowadays lessened the effect considerably by using more resistant fibres and by adding stabilizers. It has not been eliminated, however, and some fibre types offer higher resistance than others (see below).

ROPE FIBRES

With a knowledge of the desirable properties of an abseil/prusik rope, the various rope fibres that are available can now be examined. Subsequent sections will treat construction and diameter.

NYLON

Nylon is a tough, stretchy, high strength fibre having many properties which justify its popular use. Nylon is a name for a group of substances (polyamides) which are chemically very similar, but which do vary widely in physical properties. Type 66 and Type 6 (also called Perlon) are the most common ones used in rope manufacture. Nylon 66 melts at 260°C and nylon 6 at 215°C to 220°C, though neither should be exposed to temperatures in excess of 150°C in air. Surprisingly, while nylon 6 has the lower melting point, it is better for normal abseil use as it can withstand higher temperatures than nylon 66 without any damage. However, under extreme cases of abseil heating, nylon 66 would survive longer than nylon 6 without breaking, which is probably more important (Moncrieff 1970). Nylon 6 also has higher tensile strength, better abrasion resistance and better sunlight resistance than nylon 66 (Richard Newell, pers. comm.).

Nylon 6 is the type used to manufacture most mountaineering ropes (a choice apparently based on its elastic properties) and nylon 66, in two varieties, is used for Blue Water ropes. Variety 707 is used in Blue Water II and Super 707 in Blue Water III. Blue Water III has slightly better abrasion resistance and better handling qualities, but gives faster abseils when new (Newell 1976).

The properties of both types of nylon are excellent, in general, though several points require mention.

While chemically very stable, nylon is attacked by phenol, cresol and acids. No foods or drinks and very few household products contain these chemicals in concentrations high enough to cause damage. The only product of great concern is battery acid as used in lead acid caving lights. Nylon ropes should never be placed near these lights. Nylon deteriorates slowly in sunlight, though normal cave wear should force a nylon rope's retirement long before significant weakening occurs.

There are several problems peculiar to nylon ropes. One is their tendency to stiffen with use, a characteristic which affects their handling qualities, but does not seem to indicate any marked deterioration in physical properties (Mixon 1966). Stiffening can be somewhat relieved by washing with a fabric softener (Isenhart 1974d). Another more worrying character of nylon is its response to wetting. Nylon ropes when wet absorb water into the spaces between the fibres and also into the fibres themselves with dramatic effects on rope properties. Saturation is reached in just a few minutes of exposure to water, reducing tensile strength slightly (by about 10%) and roughly halving abrasion resistance (Eavis 1974). While these reductions still leave a high safety factor, extra care is called for on wet pitches. Efforts should also be made to keep nylon ropes dry while moving them through the cave, though this is worthwhile with all ropes anyway to cut down on weight.

TERYLENE (POLYESTER)

Nylon and Terylene vie for the position of top SRT fibre. Terylene is a higher density fibre than nylon and melts at 249°C. It is stable to 175°C in air compared to nylon's 150°C. Nylon has an advantage of greater tensile strength and dry abrasion resistance, but while nylon is adversely affected by water, Terylene is scarcely affected (Moncrieff 1970). As a result, Terylene seems to be a slightly better fibre for wet caving whereas nylon is much better for dry caving. Terylene does not stiffen appreciably on ageing and has a greater resistance to sunlight than nylon. Terylene's resistance is good to weak alkalis and all acids except hot, strong acids. Battery acid has no effect under atmospheric temperatures. The only chemicals of real concern to cavers are strong alkalis such as caustic soda of the concentration found in NiFe cell caving lamps.

Terylene is a lower stretch fibre than nylon. Paradoxically, this is a disadvantage to Terylene since low static stretch can be produced in ropes of either fibre by choosing a suitable construction (page 6). However, energy absorption does depend on fibre type and in this respect, nylon is superior (Moncrieff 1970).

The choice between nylon and Terylene is not clear cut. It depends on the relative importance placed on each of the advantages and disadvantages discussed here. Both fibres are excellent and pricing is similar.

POLYPROPYLENE (ULSTRON AND TENSTRON) AND POLYETHYLENE (COURLENE)

Ropes of these fibres have had some use in SRT. Many of their properties are attractive. They are light, cheap, strong and they float. They have excellent chemical resistances, the only weakness of note being polypropylene's susceptibility to strong oxidants such as hydrogen peroxide. However, they have dangerously low heat resistance. Polypropylene has a higher melting point (165°C) than polyethylene (110°C to 120°C), but neither fibre is safe above 50°C (Moncrieff 1970, Varnedoe and Veitch 1965). As explained previously, this creates an extremely low abrasion resistance and makes melting of the rope by a hot abseil device a strong possibility. A couple of serious incidents have already occurred through the use of 10mm braided polypropylene ropes. They were used by the 1973 British Expedition to Venezuela and on one 45m pitch severe rope melting occurred at the pitch bottom after a fast abseil (Phil Chapman, pers comm). In the 111m Gaping Ghyll shaft in Britain, a caver fell to his death when a 10mm braided polypropylene rope abraded through (Eavis 1975).

Both polypropylene and polyethylene are out of the question as general-purpose abseil/prusik ropes, but, with discretion, they still can be used on pitches under about 10m, where there is usually little danger of abrasion or melting. In an unknown cave where many short pitches are expected, it can be a good idea to carry a length of 50m or so and cut it to length as required. Polypropylene is better in nearly all ways than polyethylene and pricing is similar.

NATURAL FIBRES

Natural fibres such as manila, sisal and hemp once held the foremost place in vertical caving but have now been totally superseded by synthetic ropes which are superior in every way. Indeed, natural fibre ropes of the highest quality may be hard to obtain because of the general decline in their market. Their use should be generally avoided.

ROPE CONSTRUCTION

The manufacture of synthetic rope begins with a chemical process to produce the material (nylon, Terylene, etc).

The material is then melted and extruded through tiny holes in a metal disc to produce long, hairlike fibres which are subsequently cooled and stretched. The actual degree of stretch involved at this stage is critical in determining some important rope properties. High stretching produces a rope of higher tensile strength and lower stretch than does low stretching (Moncrieff 1970, Lucas 1973). This point is generally of little concern to cavers with the notable exception of Terylene ropes. Terylene ropes which have been highly stretched in manufacture may have too low an energy absorption for safe underground use. Such ropes may be labelled with a word such as "prestretched". They are uncommon, but are most likely to appear with a continuous fibre construction (see below).

After manufacture, the fibres are bunched into yarns, using one of two construction methods. To make staple yarns, the individual fibres are cut into lengths less than about half a metre long and spun together. To make continuous fibre yarns, the fibres are twisted or grouped together without being first cut, so that individual fibres run the entire length of the rope (Figure 1). Staple ropes have a fuzzy or matt finish, while continuous fibre ropes appear smooth and shiny. Staple and continuous fibre ropes differ mainly in the properties of friction and water absorption (page 2). Continuous fibre ropes give faster abseils and prusiks because of lower friction between the rope and the abseil and prusik devices. They are often a little too fast on abseil when new, though after the first few uses they roughen a little and become acceptable. Matt ropes generally give controlled abseils from purchase onwards and are only marginally slower for prusiking than smooth ropes. However, thick matt ropes (13mm and 14mm) are often annoyingly slow for both abseiling and prusiking as they are very bulky. They should be avoided. Continuous fibre ropes generally absorb less water than matt ropes.

Nylon is only readily available as a continuous fibre rope; other fibre types appear either way.

Yarns are made into ropes by laying or braiding. Laid ropes are formed by grouping the yarn into three (or more) much thicker strands and twisting them together. Braided ropes, also called sheathed or kernmantel ropes (kernmantel is German for core and sheath), consist of one or two sheaths of plaited strands around a central core (Figure 2). The core generally contributes about 70% of the rope's tensile strength. The core may be itself plaited, but usually it is made of parallel or twisted yarns.

LAID ROPES

Laid ropes are known for their generally good abrasion resistance. The tightly laid nylon varieties such as Goldline hard-lay (from the USA)

Author

FIGURE 1: Enlargement of a staple rope (Marlow 16 plait Terylene, top) and a continuous fibre rope (Blue Water III nylon, bottom).

Author

FIGURE 2: Three types of rope construction. A laid rope (Goldline nylon) is shown at top, a double-sheathed braided rope (Marlow 16 plait Terylene) at centre, and a single sheathed braided rope (Blue Water III nylon) at bottom.

in fact are extremely abrasion resistant. This, however, is the only strong point of laid ropes for use in SRT. Their major drawback is that when using them on a free hanging pitch there is a very disturbing tendency for the caver to spin, because the strands untwist under load. Spinning can make hard going out of what might have been an enjoyable abseil or prusik, and has led to extreme giddiness on many occasions. Spinning does not always occur, only usually. Raines (1968) describes the use of Goldline laid rope on the 333m free abseil into Sōtano de las Golondrinas in Mexico. There was negligible spin. Laid ropes are also stretchy, again because the strands untwist under load. Nevertheless, their abrasion resistance makes them attractive to some cavers and they do find use, particularly on pitches against walls where spin is impossible and on short drops where spin and stretch are not serious anyway. They have no advantage in cost over braided ropes.

Laid ropes are not commonly available in Terylene, so that a discussion of laid ropes for SRT really reduces to a discussion of laid nylon ropes.

BRAIDED ROPES

Braided ropes in both nylon and Terylene have come well to the forefront in SRT and are strongly recommended. They do not contribute to spin, and are available with low static stretch, giving two clear advantages over laid ropes.

The prime point to consider when choosing a braided rope is the tightness of the sheath. Tight sheathed ropes have higher abrasion resistance than loose sheath ones, since they resist grit penetration better and are harder to cut on sharp edges. Moreover, in the unlikely event that a sheath is cut through during a prusik, a tight sheath will barely slip on its core. Sheaths are not connected to their cores and using a loose sheathed rope, it is possible for a caver attached to a cut sheath by his ascenders to uncontrollably slide down the core until the sheath bunches somewhere and stops the fall, or until the sheath slips entirely off.

Using Jumars on a Super Braidline nylon rope (loose sheathed) on the 40m pitch in Dale Head Pot, Yorkshire, a British caver fell about 12m when the sheath severed. The loose sheath concertinad all the way down the pitch until held by a knot at the bottom (Griffiths 1976). A test with Jumars on the tight sheathed Blue Water caused a fall of only 200mm (Newell 1976). Tight sheaths also minimise rope stretch and water absorption, the latter simply because there is less air space to fill. However, a significant drawback of tight sheathed ropes is that they may be too stiff to have good handling qualities. Blue Water is in this class.

Thick sheaths give better abrasion resistance than thin ones. Rope sheaths are designed to be abrasion resistant, but rope cores are not. Once a rope has cut through to its core, it is in a perilous state. Some ropes (e.g. Marlow sixteen plait Terylene) have two sheaths which also gives a high safety factor.

The main point of concern with a rope's core is the contribution it makes to rope stretch. Cores which consist of straight or twisted yarns give less stretch than those which consist of plaited yarns. Newell (1969) showed that a twisted core gives a rope much higher abrasion resistance than a plaited core.

DIAMETER

Rope diameter is an important determinant of strength and abrasion resistance. When buying a rope it is wise to measure the diameter and not just rely on the manufacturer's label. Discrepancies of over 1mm can occur (Eavis 1974).

Experience teaches that 11mm to 12mm ropes are the best general purpose ropes for pitches over 25m. Ropes thicker than 12mm are too heavy, too costly, and tend to jam in climbing devices. Below 11mm the margin of safety is significantly reduced because of lesser strength and, even more importantly, lesser abrasion resistance. Thin ropes have higher stretch than thick ones under the same load, a factor which increases abrasion risk (page 2). They also cut more easily on sharp edges because their individual fibres are under more tension and there is less rope to cut to reach breaking point. A rope abrades slowly at first and then faster and faster as the tension in the remaining fibres increases. When a rope is cut half-way through, it is subject to extremely rapid failure. An extra 1mm or 2mm of diameter gives a huge boost to safety.

Ropes less than 11mm in diameter are best restricted to pitches of under 25m where the risk of serious abrasion is usually slight (not always!) and to free drops, where the rope does not touch the rock. It is interesting to note that in Continental Europe 9mm and 10mm ropes are used extensively on pitches of all lengths by taking great care in rigging pitches as free drops.

THE ROPE MARKET

To summarise, the choice for the vertical caver is narrowed mainly to 9mm to 12mm nylon and Terylene ropes of braided construction. Laid nylon ropes and polypropylene ropes also find limited use.

NYLON ROPES

Of the nylon ropes, Blue Water appears to be the best. It has a lower static stretch than any other nylon rope and is extremely abrasion resistant. Blue Water rope has a diameter of 12mm and is available in two varieties, Blue Water II and Blue Water III. Blue Water III is more flexible and slightly more abrasion resistant than Blue Water II, though it is very fast for abseiling when new. Both varieties are readily available from caving shops.

Static (i.e. low stretch) mountaineering rope is also good, though it has more static stretch than Blue Water and a thinner sheath. It is a tight sheathed rope, but no comparison with Blue Water has been made on abrasion resistance. Edelrid and Interalp are two common brands of static mountaineering rope, available with a diameter of 10mm for SRT. Ropes of this thickness require great care in rigging to guard against abrasion. Nevertheless, static mountaineering rope is probably the most popular rope for SRT in France, where it has been used with an excellent safety record (Paul Courbon, pers. comm.). Most climbing shops sell this rope. The British company, Bridon, make a low stretch nylon called Super Braidline. It is adequate, but has a loose sheath and has been noted to abrade fairly easily (Griffiths 1976, Reckert 1977, Richings 1977).

Laid nylon ropes only receive significant use for SRT in North America. Hard-lay Goldline is the universal choice, manufactured by The Cordage Group and distributed by a number of climbing shops and caving shops in North America. Interested cavers in other countries may be able to import Goldline or find a similar rope locally. It is 12mm in diameter and is of extremely tight construction.

TERYLENE ROPES

Braided Terylene ropes are made largely for yachting and are available from boating shops and some caving shops. They are either of staple or continuous fibre construction. Unfortunately, the continuous fibre types often have a very loose sheath which creates poor abrasion resistance and handling qualities. A tight sheathed continuous fibre Terylene rope (called 1080 H) is being released in New Zealand by Donaghy Ropes, especially for cavers. Initial reports are very favourable (Eavis 1977).

Several fairly tight sheathed staple Terylene ropes are on the market. The varieties by Downs, Marlow and Kinnears have been used with good results, though they do become very heavy when wet. They are available in 10mm and 12mm diameter sizes for SRT. It is difficult to compare these ropes with the tight sheathed low stretch nylon ropes. To the author's knowledge, no caving groups have sufficient experience of both to make a valid comparison. The main difference would seem to be that the nylon ropes have better general abrasion resistance and the Terylene ropes better handling qualities. The Terylene ropes are much easier to stuff into a pack.

POLYPROPYLENE ROPES

Boating shops sell braided and laid polypropylene ropes in diameters of 10mm and 12mm which are good for pitches under 10m. If possible, check that they have been stabilised for sunlight resistance, since unstabilised polypropylene degrades very quickly (Koon 1973).

BLENDS

Several companies produce braided ropes which contain two different fibre types. A Donaghys rope with a loose Terylene sheath and a nylon core is used in New Zealand, but it has poor abrasion resistance. Bridon in Britain markets a rope called Braidline Marina, which has a loose Terylene sheath and a polypropylene core. It is an attractive product since the polypropylene makes the rope light yet is insulated by the Terylene. The rope does have a very low abrasion resistance (Eavis 1974) but possibly a tight sheathed Terylene/polypropylene or nylon/polypropylene rope would be suitable for SRT, should one be made.

Some rope suppliers and manufacturers are listed in the appendix.

CARE OF ROPES

Ropes for SRT are normally bought in lengths of 100m or more and cut to shorter lengths as required. Rope ends can be melted with a match or hot knife to prevent unravelling. (Figure 3).

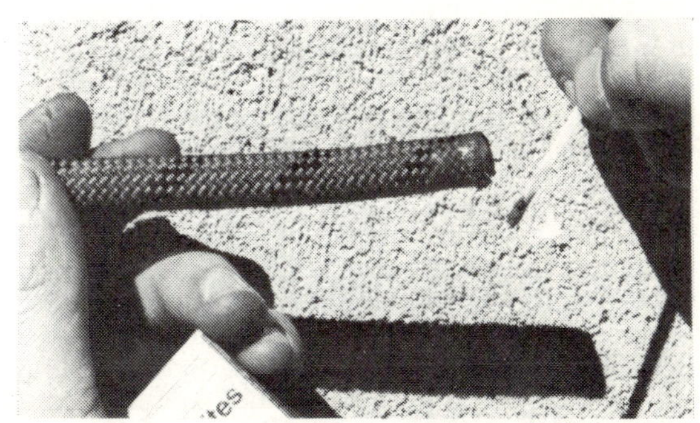

Geoff Montgomery

FIGURE 3: Melting a rope end.

INITIAL TREATMENT

When a new rope is bought it should be washed before use. Washing removes the lubricants that are used in the manufacturing process and remain on the rope. Otherwise, it will give very fast abseils for the first few uses, especially if it is of the continuous fibre type. Washing also shrinks the rope, which tightens its strands. This improves abrasion resistance and reduces stretch (Isenhart 1974d)). Incidentally, ropes should be bought about 5% longer than required to allow for shrinkage. Often the retailer will do this as a matter of course.

MARKING ROPE ENDS

After its first wash a rope will not shrink much more (it will partially restretch if anything) and its length and possibly year of purchase can be marked at each end. An excellent method is to write or punch the information on plastic tape (use indelible ink) and hold the tape in place with shrinkable clear-plastic rope-whip. The rope whip can be bought as a single length of tube from a plastics supplier and cut up (it is known as shrinkable irradiated PVC tubing) or it can be bought ready cut and packaged from boating shops or hardwares at a vastly increased cost. The tube is simply slipped over the rope end with the marker tape underneath and heated with a match until it shrinks to give a snug fit.

ROPE CARE UNDERGROUND

The cave environment is a harsh one. Ropes require careful protection from the dangers of falling rock, sharp edges and grit.

Carrying ropes in packs is very worthwhile (Chapter 8). Ropes are easier to handle in packs; they can be kept cleaner, and the chances of contact with harmful battery acids or alkalis is reduced. Unfortunately, some ropes (e.g. Blue Water) are too stiff to pack well and are therefore often carried in coils.

Before a rope is fed down a pitch, efforts must be made to clear away any loose rocks near the edge of the drop. Otherwise, they may fall on the rope and cut it. If loose rocks are met on lower ledges, the first caver to descend may have to pull the rope up onto the ledge so that the rocks can be thrown down safely.

At pitch tops and bottoms, it is wise to coil up any loose rope and place it out of the way. This reduces the possibility of rope damage due to rockfall, and lessens the chance that someone may tread on the rope. One should avoid treading on the rope since grit may be ground into the rope fibres.

Protecting the rope from edge abrasion while abseiling and prusiking is another vital aspect of rope care which is considered at length in Chapter 4.

After the cave trip, tight knots should be undone since they can cause permanent kinking. Ropes should be packed into a car well away from any batteries and not be left in a closed car in the hot sun. Temperatures may climb high enough to cause permanent damage.

WASHING ROPES

Ropes must be washed when dirty to reduce the effect of grit abrasion on both the rope and abseil/prusik gear. A washing machine does the best job. Ropes can be chained prior to washing to save hours of frustration untangling them afterwards (Figure 4). Nylon and Terylene can

Author

FIGURE 4: Chaining a rope prior to machine washing.

safely stand hot water, though hand warm water (about 40°C) is best for nylon ropes because higher temperatures cause stiffening of their fibres. The rope needs to flex to work the dirt out (Penberthy 1972a). Polypropylene and polyethylene ropes should be washed in cold water. Any detergents (liquid or powder) can be used. Natural soap is not as effective as the more powerful detergents because soap lacks the additives which keep the grit suspended in the water, so that it does not settle back on the rope. Pre-soaks and bleaches are of little value. Bleaching will whiten the rope if one cares about pristine whiteness, but chlorine bleaches must not be used on nylon ropes. Concentrated fabric softeners are useful for increasing flexibility should ropes stiffen with use and as a bonus they help relieve grit abrasion by forming a barrier between the rope fibres and dirt particles (Isenhart 1974d).

Ropes are best dried in the open air, preferably out of direct sunlight. Hot air driers are suitable for nylon and Terylene ropes (not polypropylene) provided the drying temperature is held below 100°C (Penberthy 1971).

Ropes should be washed during expeditions even though one may be remote from a washing machine. Streams or lakes are useful. A good technique is to anchor a descender somewhere near the water supply, soak the rope and then pull it through the descender. This squeezes out the dirty water. If the rope is still dirty, the process is repeated. The descender technique is also useful for partially drying wet ropes prior to carrying them.

STORING ROPES

A dark dry place is desirable for rope storage. Under such conditions, ropes do not appear to deteriorate to any marked degree (Borwick 1974).

INSPECTING ROPES

Ropes should be checked frequently for any serious surface abrasion (mild fuzzing is not serious), burnt, soft or hard spots or regions of reduced diameter. Any irregularity should be treated with suspicion and a decision made as to whether the rope should be cut at this point. A good practice is to feel and look at a rope as it is fed down a pitch.

RETIRING ROPES

Ropes should be retired when they have been subjected to a heavy stress (such as a fall) or when wear becomes serious throughout the entire rope. Laid ropes can be assessed for wear by opening up the rope and looking down at the inner surfaces of the strands. If these surfaces show substantial powdering, the rope is no longer safe. Braided ropes are harder to check because only the outer sheath can be inspected. However, provided good care has been taken of a braided rope, the condition of the sheath will give an accurate picture of what the core is like. It would take an extraordinary set of circumstances to damage a rope's core and leave the sheath intact. Penberthy (1972a) recommends inspecting the yarns of the outer sheath with a magnifying glass (10x is adequate (Figure 5)). When 50 per cent of the fibres in the yarns are cut, the rope probably has lost 30 per cent or more of its original strength and should be retired.

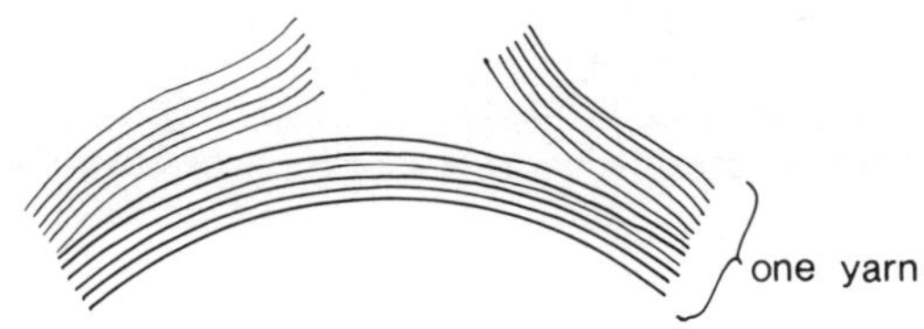

FIGURE 5: A braided rope should be retired when 50% of the yarns of the outer sheath are cut (after Penberthy).

A degree of self discipline is required to retire a rope that has served faithfully for years. It is all too easy to deem the rope safe because it held last time and continue using it. One must make a definite decision at some stage to retire the rope and follow it through. It is only with scrupulous care of ropes and abseil/prusik equipment that the use of SRT can be justified.

2: BASIC ROPE KNOTS

A knowledge of knots and the ability to tie them quickly are essential parts of a caver's repertoire. Many are the times when complete reliance is placed on a single knot. In light of this, it is distressing to find that a great deal of conflicting information is published about knots, probably more than on any other aspect of vertical technique. Some writers recommend that cavers learn just a few basic and versatile knots, while others recommend a host of knots, each having a special purpose. Further, published tables of knot strengths often bear little comparison to each other.

The approach taken in this book is that it is far better to use just a few simple and versatile knots all the time than to use, and worse, teach others to use, a large assortment of specialised knots. The reasons are fairly obvious. In any emergency it may be a life-saver if an adequate knot can be tied without thinking twice. Such an automatic response is more likely if one only knows a few knots. Another reason is that if cavers are taught to use a wide variety of knots as a general practice, the chances of someone mistying a knot are increased.

This chapter concentrates mainly on three basic knots and their simple variations. Certain other knots will be presented later in the book. Chapter 5 treats knots for webbing tape and Chapter 7, prusiking knots.

FEATURES OF A GOOD KNOT

The five features of a good caving knot are versatility, security, strength, ease of tying and ease of checking. Ease of untying is also important, but is not often obtained. Several of these features require comment.

Ease of checking is a quality which often receives insufficient attention. It should be obvious at a glance whether a knot has been tied correctly. Safe cavers generally remember what a knot looks like and check visually after tying that their knots are correct. They also check other people's knots before using them. This should be viewed as a standard safety practice and not an insult.

Security refers to a knot's ability to remain tight after tying. Some knots in their basic forms tend to work loose when not under load. The bowline is well-known for this. Such knots should be finished with an overhand knot to secure them (page 11). In addition, any knot may be prone to slight slippage under load. To allow for this, all knots should be tightened by hand before use and have tail ends protruding by at least 50mm.

All knots reduce the strength of the rope in which they are tied, generally by 20% to 40% of the unknotted strength. The reason is that a knot bends the rope. When a load is applied to the rope, the fibres on the outside of the bends are stressed more than those on the inside, creating a zone of weakness. In fact, a rough estimate of a knot's strength can be made by examining the severity of its bends (Link 1958). Modern caving ropes are sufficiently strong to bear a strength reduction of 20% to 40% safely, except under unusual stress conditions. A knowledge of knot strengths is, therefore, useful, but should be kept in its proper perspective. The other four factors generally carry more weight in choosing a knot for a particular purpose, especially if the rope is to be attached to a carabiner. Bending a rope around a carabiner is likely to cause a greater strength loss than any common knot (Link 1958). For example, the Plymouth Cordage Company (1958) reported nearly a 50% strength loss in their 11mm Goldline rope by bending it over a 9.5mm diameter carabiner.

Unfortunately, it is difficult to obtain reliable and widely applicable data on knot strengths. There are several reasons. One is that different researchers use different test apparatuses, thus making cross-comparisons difficult. Another arises from the practice of stating knot strength as a percentage of unknotted rope strength. A false picture will be given if the researcher relied on a manufacturer's strength rating rather than on a separate test. However, the most important reason is that a knot's strength depends largely on the type and diameter of rope in which it is tied (Borwick 1974).

Knot strength figures only give an accurate picture for the particular rope used in the test. For this reason, exact percentage strengths are not given here. In this chapter, it will only be noted which knots consistently show good test results (tests by American Alpine Club 1967, Borwick 1974, Pope 1972).

END LOOPS

A knotted loop will need to be formed in most rope ends. The loop can be used to provide an attachment point for rigging the abseil/prusik rope, to form a large stopper knot at the bottom of the rope to avoid abseiling off the rope end (Chapter 6), or to make harness connections. The figure eight loop and the bowline appear to be the two best options. They are certainly the most popular.

THE BOWLINE

In its basic form, the bowline is one of the most widely known and used knots (Figure 6). It achieves its best application when a rope has to be made fast around some object, such as an anchor point or the waist. It is very quick to tie in these situations. With a little practice it can even be tied one handed in the dark, a fact which promotes the bowline for emergency use. Another feature of note is its remarkable ease of untying, even after sustaining a load to near breaking point. This may prove useful in rescue work.

Figure 6 shows the correct method of tying the bowline. Always ensure that the loose end lies on the inside of the loop. The bowline is incomplete until the loose end is secured with a keeper knot, preferably an overhand knot.

The bowline also has four or five more complicated versions, which provide more than one attachment loop or cater for some special situation. Some are covered by Smith (1975). Their use can always be averted by making simple arrangements of slings or basic knots.

THE FIGURE EIGHT LOOP

The figure eight loop is more versatile than the bowline and is probably the most popular caving knot at the time of writing (Figure 7). The knot can be tied incorrectly involving a 10% strength loss (Borwick 1974). The correct knot is the one with less severe bending in the standing part of the rope. Borwick's tests on eight nylon climbing ropes found the figure eight loop to be stronger than the bowline in every case, on average by about 10%. The figure eight loop has other advantages over the bowline in that it does not require a keeper knot for the loose end and that it is quicker for tying a loop where the rope does not need to be first passed around the point of attachment. These advantages make it generally preferred for making stopper knots or carabiner attachment loops (in midrope as well as end positions). It can also be used to tie a rope around an object, but not as quickly as the bowline (Figure 8). The figure eight loop is the more difficult knot to untie.

An overhand loop (Figure 9) is a good substitute for a figure eight loop in situations where bulk or speed of tying is critical. For general usage, however, it is not as strong and can prove almost impossible to untie.

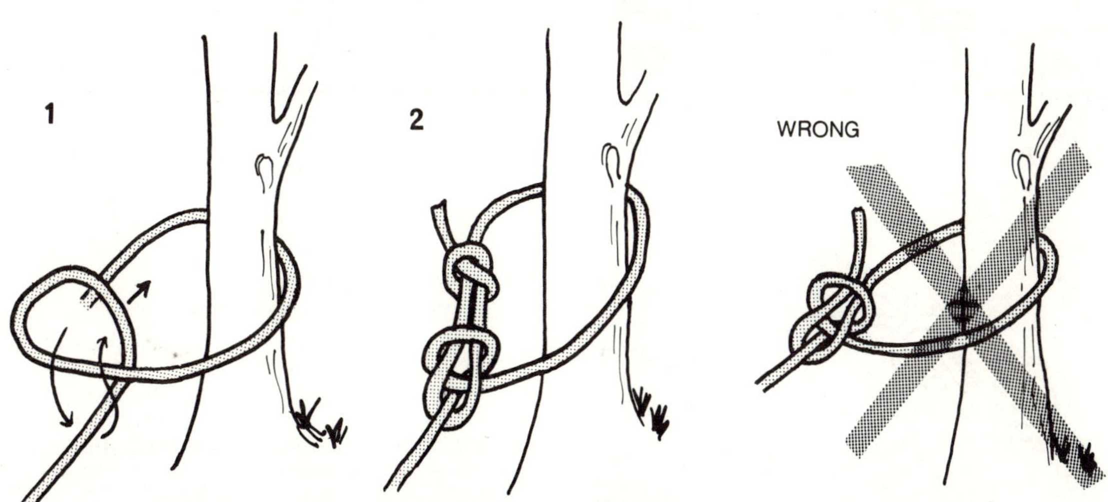

FIGURE 6: The bowline. The loose end should be on the inside of the loop, secured with an overhand knot.

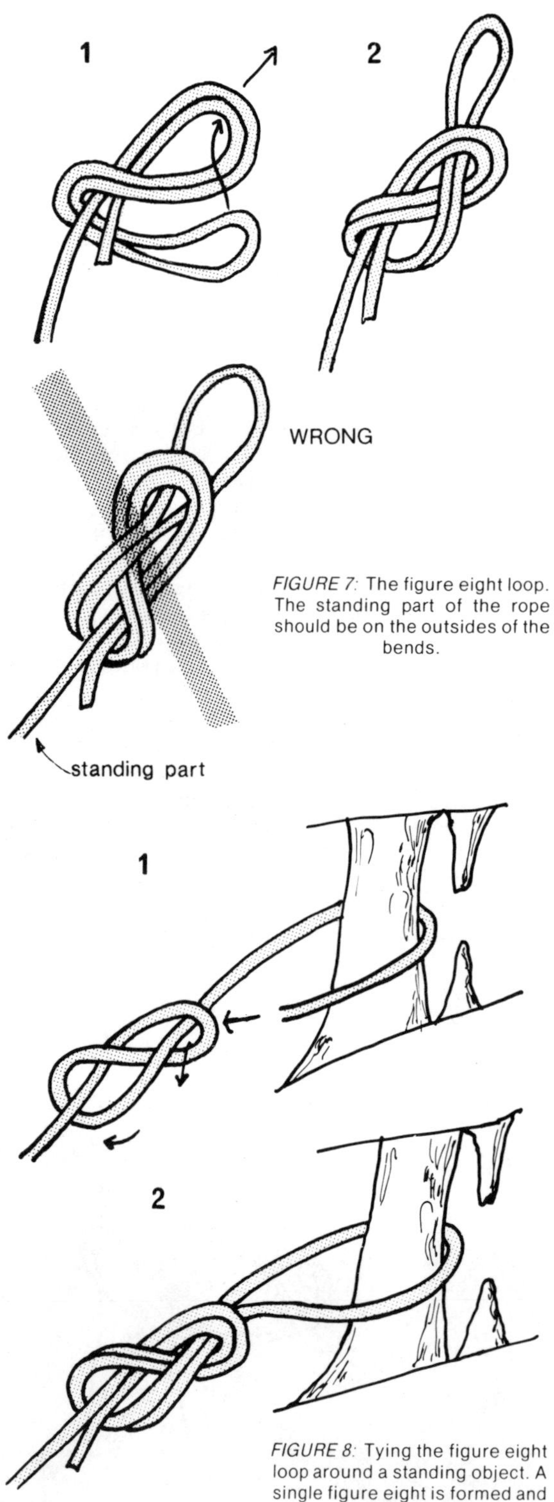

FIGURE 7: The figure eight loop. The standing part of the rope should be on the outsides of the bends.

FIGURE 8: Tying the figure eight loop around a standing object. A single figure eight is formed and the end is woven back through the figure eight.

FIGURE 9: The overhand loop.

MIDROPE KNOTS

In pitch riggings, a rope often needs to be secured to an anchor some distance from the top of a pitch. Both the bowline and the figure eight loop are suitable. The bowline is formed as already shown in Figure 6, but in a doubled portion of the rope (Figure 10). The figure eight loop is tied as shown in Figure 7, and connected to the anchor with a carabiner and sling (Figure 11).

ROPE JOINS

Rope joins are frequently required in pitch riggings and in forming slings. For joining equal diameter ropes, the figure eight bend and the double fisherman's knot are excellent and very similar in performance. For unequal rope diameters, the double fisherman's knot is preferred.

DOUBLE FISHERMAN'S KNOT

The double fisherman's knot takes a little practice to tie, but has an unmistakable, aesthetic appearance when formed properly (Figure 12). Each half of the knot is tied separately and then the halves are drawn together.

FIGURE EIGHT BEND

The figure eight bend (Figure 13) is formed in much the same way as one method already shown for the figure eight loop (Figure 8). A figure eight is formed in one end and then the other end is woven through it. The standing part of each rope should be on the outside of the first bend.

An analogue of the overhand knot is found in the overhand bend (ring bend, water knot) which is faster to tie and less bulky than the figure eight bend, but harder to untie (Figure 14).

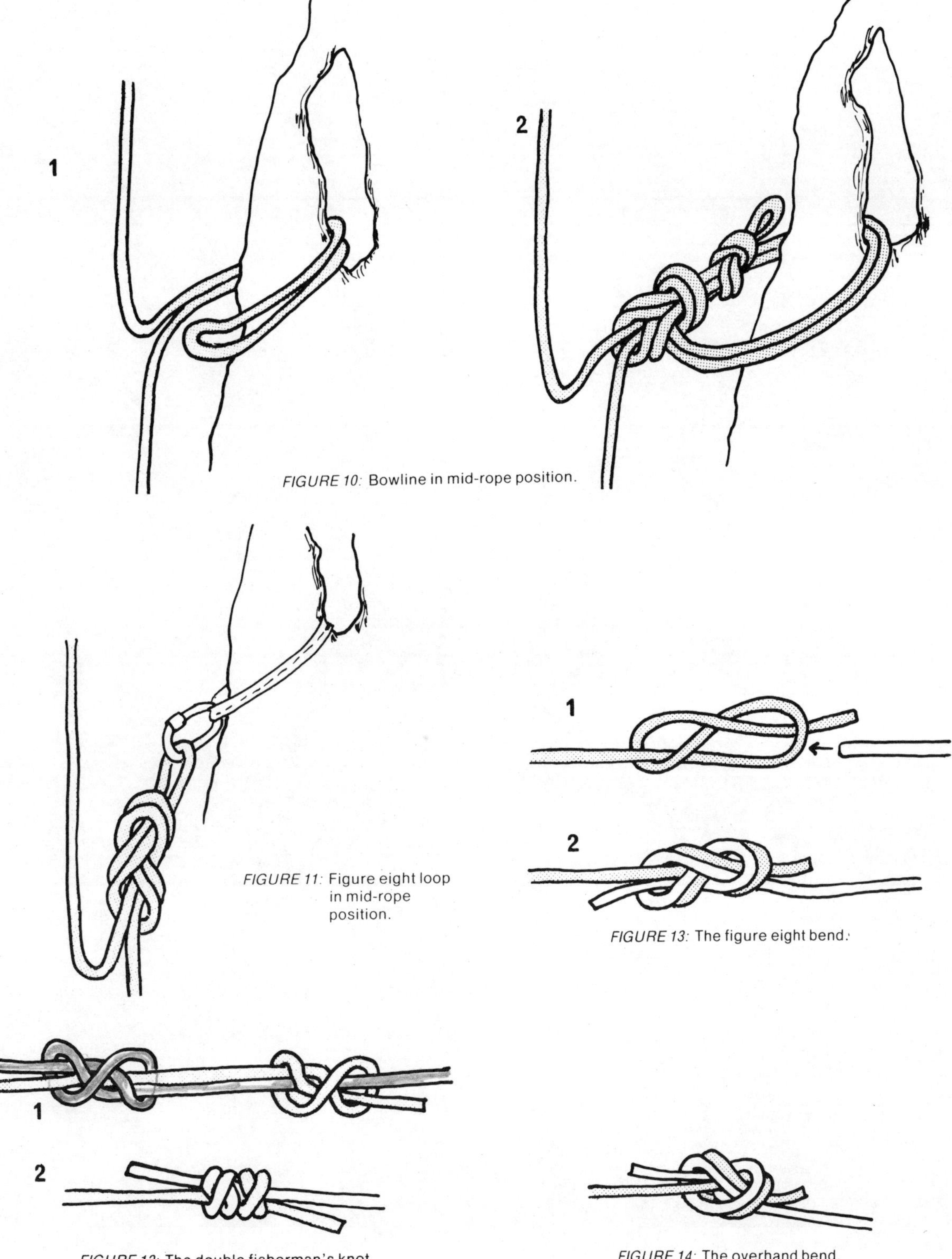

FIGURE 10: Bowline in mid-rope position.

FIGURE 11: Figure eight loop in mid-rope position.

FIGURE 13: The figure eight bend.

FIGURE 12: The double fisherman's knot.

FIGURE 14: The overhand bend.

Jughandle used as an anchor for a pitch in Ulysses Cave, Astraka Plateau, Greece. *Andrew Pavey*

3: ANCHORS

Every rope must be rigged on every pitch in a completely dependable way. This creates a demand for unerring judgment in the selection of anchors. It is a demand which should be valued as an integral part of the challenge of vertical caving.

To be safe, anchors must be both strong and secure. The strength of an anchor depends on the strength of the rock which composes it and the strength of any artificial component which may have been placed, such as a chock, piton or bolt. Its security depends on the method of attaching the rope and applying the load. An incident in Canada illustrates the importance of ensuring security as well as adequate strength. On a 17m pitch in Yorkshire Pot, Alberta, an inexperienced group anchored their rope to a bedrock knob at floor level. All cavers except the last descended safely. While abseiling over the edge, the last man carelessly pulled the rope off the knob, fell to the bottom of the pitch, and sustained serious injuries which necessitated a full scale rescue from this remote and difficult cave. The knob was strong enough, but the rope was insecurely fastened (Shawcross 1973).

While security is a product of correct rigging technique, a high degree of judgment is involved in deciding whether an anchor is adequately strong. In fact, the question: "What is adequate strength," is itself rather subjective. A workable attitude would be to aim to use anchors which are judged to be at least as strong as one's rope (page 2). Modern mechanical components of anchors (carabiners, pitons, etc) should certainly meet this criterion, but with the rock, one is never sure. The solidity and purity of the rock and the presence of possible facture planes are factors to assess. In dubious cases, some idea of strength can be obtained by attaching a foot stirrup to the anchor and hopping up and down in it. Another test is to give the rock a tap with a piton hammer. Unstable rock often sounds hollow or moves slightly. In any event, it is usual to provide each pitch with two or more inter-connected anchors to cover errors of judgment. Then if one anchor fails, another will hopefully hold. After discussing the types of individual anchors, consideration is given at the end of this Chapter to the methods of arranging these multiple anchors, a task which is not as straightforward as it might appear at first.

NATURAL ANCHORS

The same natural processes which form caves also produce a fascinating variety of features (knobs, flakes, etc) which may serve as anchors. The simplicity and aesthetic appeal of natural anchors should promote a search for them before any consideration is given to artificial placements, such as chocks, pitons or bolts. Keen observation, experience, and ingenuity will produce natural anchors for most cave pitches.

In many instances, the rope can be tied directly to a natural anchor using a bowline or figure eight loop (Figures 6 and 8). The tie should be made in the strongest and most secure position possible. This position is usually that where the natural anchor joins the wall, floor or roof. For floor level anchors an additional slip knot can be used to prevent the rope from being easily pulled off (Figure 15). Direct tying is the simplest approach, and the most economical one on equipment. An alternative, common in the USA, is to wind the rope around the anchor several times and tie a slack knot (Figure 16). Provided sufficient winds are

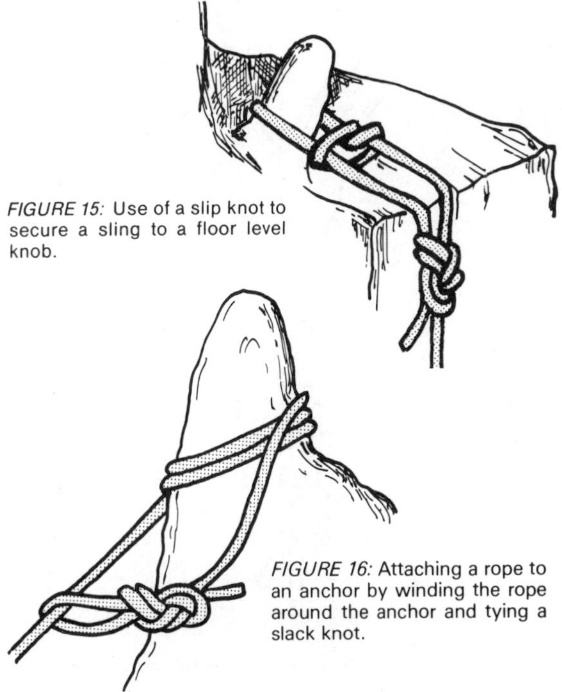

FIGURE 15: Use of a slip knot to secure a sling to a floor level knob.

FIGURE 16: Attaching a rope to an anchor by winding the rope around the anchor and tying a slack knot.

made, the friction between the rock and the rope will hold the load entirely, and the knot will act only as a safeguard. This method eliminates any strength loss due to knotting and will allow the rope to be easily detached from its anchor if a rescue becomes necessary (Isenhart 1974b). However, for most pitches it would hardly seem worth the additional expenditure of rope and time to provide for such a freak pitch accident. The strength argument has little merit, since caving ropes are always chosen to have strength far in excess of actual requirements.

Despite the advantage of tying a rope directly to a natural anchor, safety considerations may make the practice unwise. As a result of solutional processes, limestone surfaces frequently contain minute yet sharp crests and spikes. Unless the rope is padded (Chapter 4), these can cause rope damage. In addition, drastic strength losses may be suffered by the rope if it is passed around abrupt corners. A piton hammer may be a useful tool in such cases. One can look or feel around the rope's entire contact area with the rock and round off any danger spots. If it is impractical or undesirable on the grounds of conservation to round the anchor in this way, then a wire strop can be used, although it still should not be bent around very sharp corners. Wire strops are short lengths of wire rope with swaged loops at each end. The loops are joined with a carabiner. The wire rope should be flexible, rust resistant and about 5mm in diameter (Figure 17).

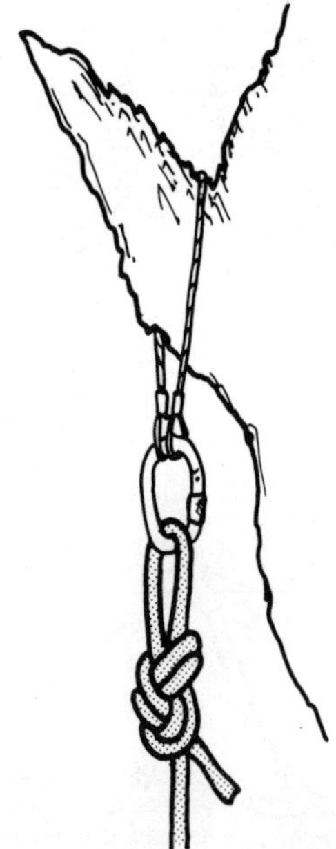

FIGURE 17: A wire strop used on a sharp knob, to save the rope from abrasion.

Another situation which militates against direct tying with the abseil/prusik rope is where a rib, flake or knob is being used as an anchor and it has only a shallow groove or a narrow slot to contain the tie. The rope may roll out or simply not fit. With discretion, a tape sling or a wire strop can often be used to good advantage (Figure 18). A tape sling

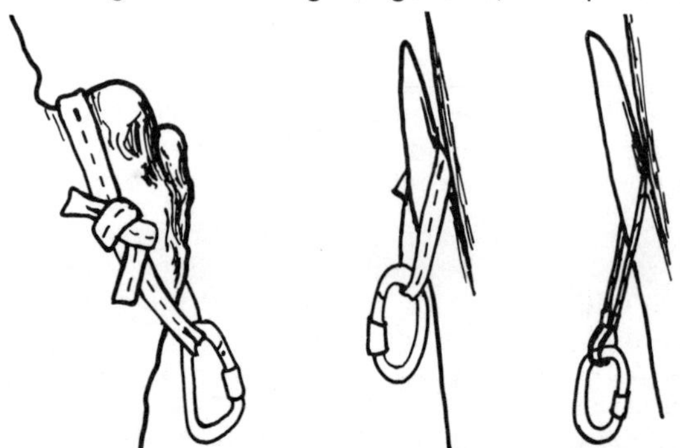

FIGURE 18: Use of a tape sling in a shallow groove (left), and a tape sling and a wire strop in a narrow slot (right).

will be suitable for shallow grooves and tape or wire for narrow slots. In the case of shallow grooves, the tape will prove more secure than rope because it will hug the rock and less readily tend to roll off. Flat tape is preferred over tubular for the same reason (Robbins 1973). Tape is discussed in detail in Chapter 5.

A final precaution with natural anchors concerns the amount of slack with which the rope (wire or tape) is fixed (Figure 19). If the rope is cinched up

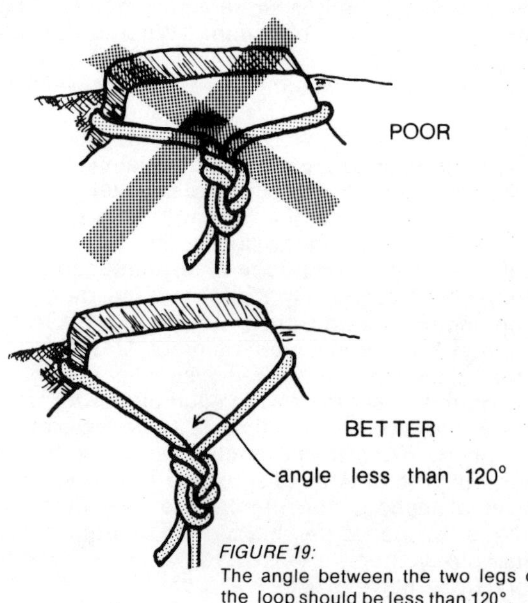

FIGURE 19: The angle between the two legs of the loop should be less than 120°.

tightly around the anchor, forces well in excess of body weight may sometimes be applied to the rope. With some knowledge of physics, this fact can be easily demonstrated, though it is hard to appreciate intuitively (Rohrer 1966). The critical feature is the angle between the two legs of the loop. If this angle is greater than 120°, the loop will be loaded in excess of body weight. At 150° the loading would be almost double body weight. At 165°, about four times. For angles less than 120°, the loading is less than body weight. One should attempt to make 120° the largest angle used. This caution should be particularly noted if a slip knot is tied to give security to a floor level anchor.

Some common types of natural anchors can now be described. It will be impossible to cover all the individual possibilities. What is important is that any natural anchor is carefully inspected, tested and preferably backed up with one or two other anchors.

BEDROCK KNOBS

Knobs commonly protrude from cave walls and floors, more so in some areas than others. Generally, a loop of rope, wire or tape can be passed over the knob to make the anchor. With slender knobs, greatest strength is obtained by tying to the base of the knob. This eliminates leverage on the knob.

RIBS

Solutional action often produces ribs on cave walls which, if suitably shaped, can be used for anchors in the same way as knobs (Figure 20).

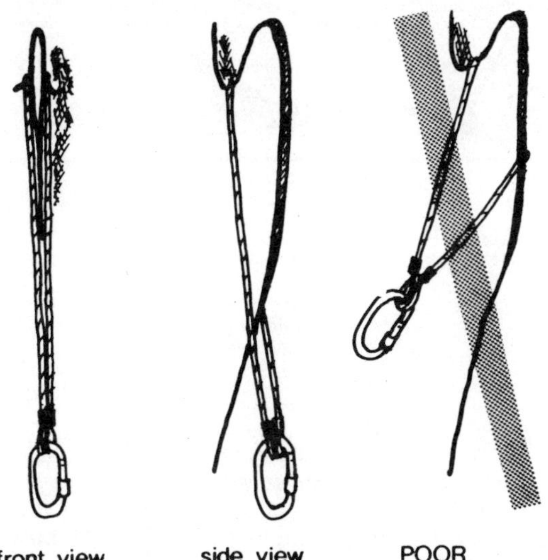

FIGURE 20: Thin ribs can provide good anchors when loaded in the rib direction. A sideways load (shown at right) may snap a rib.

Provided they are loaded in the rib direction, they are generally quite strong. A sideways load may snap off a rib. If a rib lacks any distinct notches to accept the rope, sometimes a shallow notch can be enlarged or a new one created by chipping with a piton hammer. This would obviously not be done if better anchors were available, but as a conservation measure it could be preferable to placing a bolt.

FLAKES

Flakes are thin slabs that lie parallel to the cave wall (Figure 21). Usually, they are formed by solution or fracture along a concordant plane of weakness. Before anchoring to a flake, it is important to gain some idea of the strength of its bonding to the wall. Even large flakes can pull off under load if they are only weakly attached. Tapping with a hammer will usually expose an insecure flake. If the security of a flake still is at all doubtful, it will be best to load the flake in a downwards or sidewards direction, rather than in an outwards direction which might pull it off.

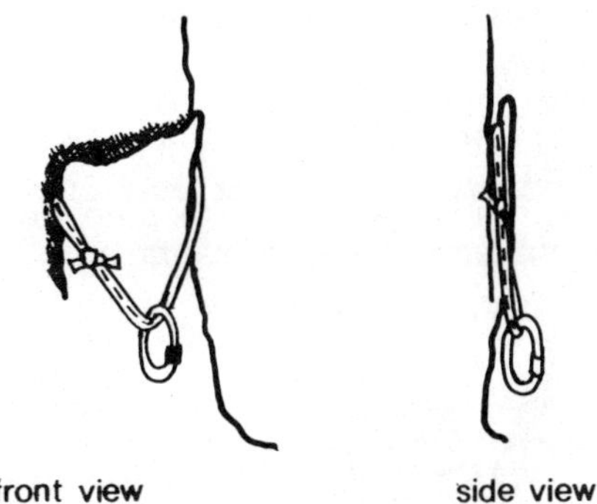

FIGURE 21: A flake anchor. Flakes should generally not be loaded in an outwards direction since they may pull off the wall.

JUGHANDLES

Jughandles (also called threads) are small tunnels or arches in the rock (Figure 22). Strong jughandles make superb anchors because they are totally secure. One should be on the lookout for jughandles in unlikely places. Often the tiniest solution hole will form one. For threading small holes, a wire strop is often useful because of its stiffness.

SPELEOTHEMS

As anchors, speleothems (such as stalagmites and columns) should be treated with caution because they are often not as strong as they look. Their weakness results from their orderly crystalline structure. Even large speleothems can

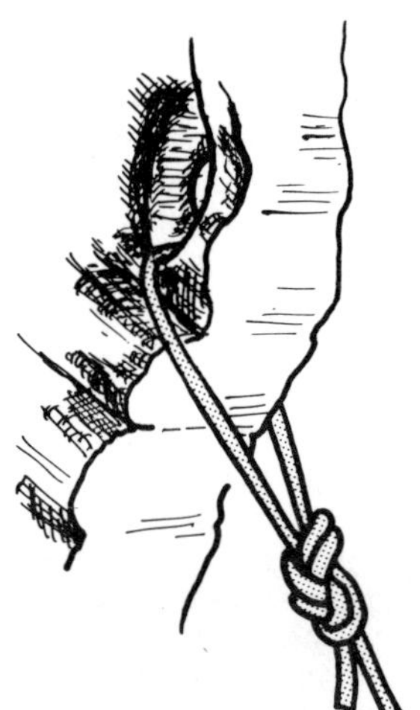
FIGURE 22: A Jughandle

fracture neatly in two along a crystal cleavage plane. A speleothem less than about 70mm thick would be a dubious prospect. Another danger is that speleothems can grow on mud or sand and be easily dislodged. Sometimes the sediment will be treacherously concealed by a thin layer of flowstone (Figure 23). Normally, only a sturdy stalagmite or column founded on rock should be used. Best of all, it should be also set in a mass of flowstone. The rope must be fixed to the base of the speleothem to eliminate leverage.

FIGURE 23: Stalagmite anchors. The lower one is founded on loose sediment and may pull out under load.

BOULDERS

Boulders make good anchors if they are heavy and stable enough not to budge. A stable boulder (ie, one that cannot roll) lying on a flat surface would need to contain at least half a cubic metre of rock to have sufficient weight (about 1 tonne). This volume would need to be larger for a boulder lying on an incline leading down to the pitch top.

It is important to tie to a boulder in a way that will not lever it out of its position (Figure 24). Except in the case of large or very solidly wedged boulders, it is not generally advisable to tie to minor protrusions on the boulder's top or sides. Otherwise, the boulder may twist or pivot and release the rope. The author once had a serious fall when this happened with a boulder of about 1.5 cubic metres. The incident nearly caused a double fatality.

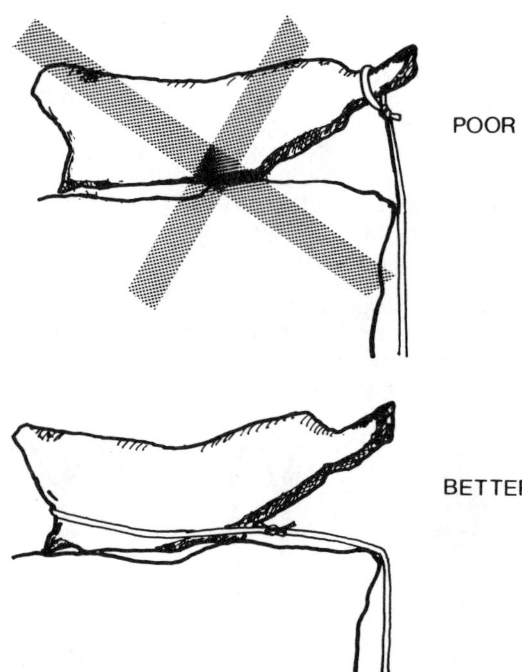

FIGURE 24: When anchoring to a boulder, it is generally inadvisable to tie to minor protrusions on the boulder's top or sides.

CHOCKSTONES

Rocks wedged in cracks are called chockstones (Figure 25). Chockstones used as anchors should be firmly wedged, and of strong, compact rock so that they will not crumble or pull free. Likewise, the sides of the crack must not crumble or fracture. The crack should become substantially narrower in the direction of loading so that the load acts to more firmly wedge the chockstone.

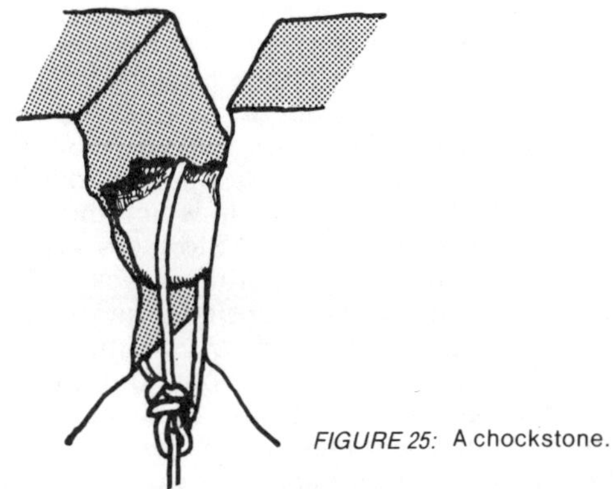

FIGURE 25: A chockstone.

If a suitable crack is available but does not already contain a good chockstone, then a rock can often be picked up off the floor and inserted by hand. Alternatively, a poorly situated chockstone may be repositioned.

TREES

Trees can be used as anchors for surface shafts if they are alive and have well-imbedded roots. Often quite small trees will be adequate, provided their roots are sound and the rope is anchored at ground level. Roots can be tested by shaking the tree. Caution should be exercised with palms, grass trees and fern trees which have a fleshy wood. They are usually too weak.

Dead trees which have washed underground can be used if they are securely jammed and not rotten. Rotten wood is identified by a soft crumbly texture. Trees still retaining their bark will usually be safe.

Sometimes short wooden beams are carried underground and jammed across pitch tops. These are perhaps the simplest types of artificial anchors.

BEAMS

Beams are quite frequently installed in European caves though they have little popularity elsewhere. They usually serve as single anchor points where no natural anchors are available, or they may be used to position a rope away from a waterfall or an area of loose or sharp rock. They are common fixtures in the wet caves of Yorkshire in Britain.

Beams will often repay the initial effort needed to place them, because they are easily inspected and can last many years, even in wet conditions. A good choice of wood is 100mm x 130mm hardwood. It should be soaked in wood preserver. Beams of this quality can serve for ten to fifteen years (Childs 1976, Brook 1974). Metal bars are alternatives to beams but they are not easily cut to size and wedged.

Beams are normally placed across narrow shafts or chimneys. Prior to placing a beam, the site should be inspected and an appropriate length of wood cut. It would be rare to use a beam longer than about 2m because of the effort required to carry it underground, and because a longer beam could bend and break if loaded in its centre (Brook 1972). When a beam is installed, each end should be firmly supported, if necessary, by lashing down or securing the ends with light gauge bolts. In the case of bolts, one could, of course, consider a direct bolt anchor instead (page 26). Where practicable, caving parties who anchor to a beam should tie at the beam ends for maximum strength (Figure 26). Considerably higher forces are imposed on a beam if the rope is attached to its centre.

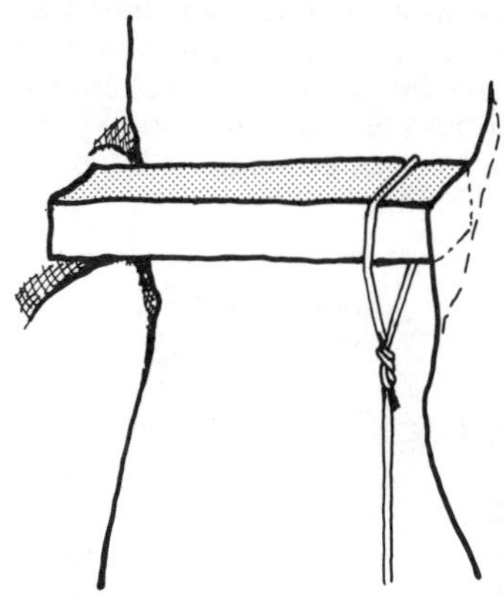

FIGURE 26: A beam. It is important to tie the rope on at one end of a beam.

CHOCKS

Chocks (also called nuts or crackers) are small metal blocks which function as chockstones. They are threaded with wire, tape or cord for attachment purposes. A selection of chocks of different sizes and shapes forms a useful anchoring kit for cavers. Normally, chocks are placed by hand and removed after use. Rarely would they be hammered into place or left as permanent anchors. In rock climbing, chocks are the centre of a major world-wide trend away from pitons and bolts (page 23) and towards anchorage which does not damage the rock. At the time of writing, rapid innovations by climbers are occurring both in chock design and in the techniques of chock placement. It is a fascinating area of equipment and technique; a science and art in itself.

A number of companies manufacture chocks and retail them through climbing shops. They are available in many shapes and sizes (Figure 27). Wedges, hexagonals, tubes and T-sections are common shapes. They range in size from wedges 2mm or less in thickness to tubes about 150mm long. Small chocks are usually marketed with wire loops to make the greatest use of their small thread holes. Thin tape or cord would be too weak. The wire will also be sufficiently rigid to act as a handle in poking the chock deep into a thin crack. Larger chocks have larger thread holes designed to accept tape or cord, though they may still be fitted with wire. Cord is stronger and more durable than tape, but tape will fit through narrower portions of a crack than cord. A good selection would include some on wire, some on tape and some on cord. The thinnest wedges (those with wire less the 3mm diameter) are best avoided because their wire will have only minimal strength for anchoring purposes and the holding power of the chock will be difficult to ascertain anyway. Very large chocks are rather too bulky. A crack requiring a large chock could possibly be fitted with a natural chockstone.

For a number of years a US company, The Great Pacific Ironworks (formerly Chouinard), have headed the field in chock design. This company produces size graded ranges of Stoppers (wedges) and Hexentrics (hexagonals). Figure 28 depicts placements of Stoppers and Hexentrics which illustrate the ways in which most commercial chocks operate. The Stoppers are primarily designed for thin tapering cracks. They are wedge-shaped in both profiles, giving two placement positions. The more versatile Hexentrics have four placement positions and are generally used in larger cracks than the Stoppers. Their forte is near-parallel sided cracks where their holding power depends largely on a powerful camming acting produced by the bias of the sling towards one wall of the crack. Indeed, use of the camming principle in chock design has been the main reason for the dramatic upsurge in the popularity of chocks. Forrest Mountaineering Ltd, Colorado Mountain Industries (CMI), and Clog Climbing Gear all produce camming chocks. In particular, Kirks Kamms by CMI seem to be particularly suited to solutionally rounded holes and cracks in limestone. Also, Clog have introduced a

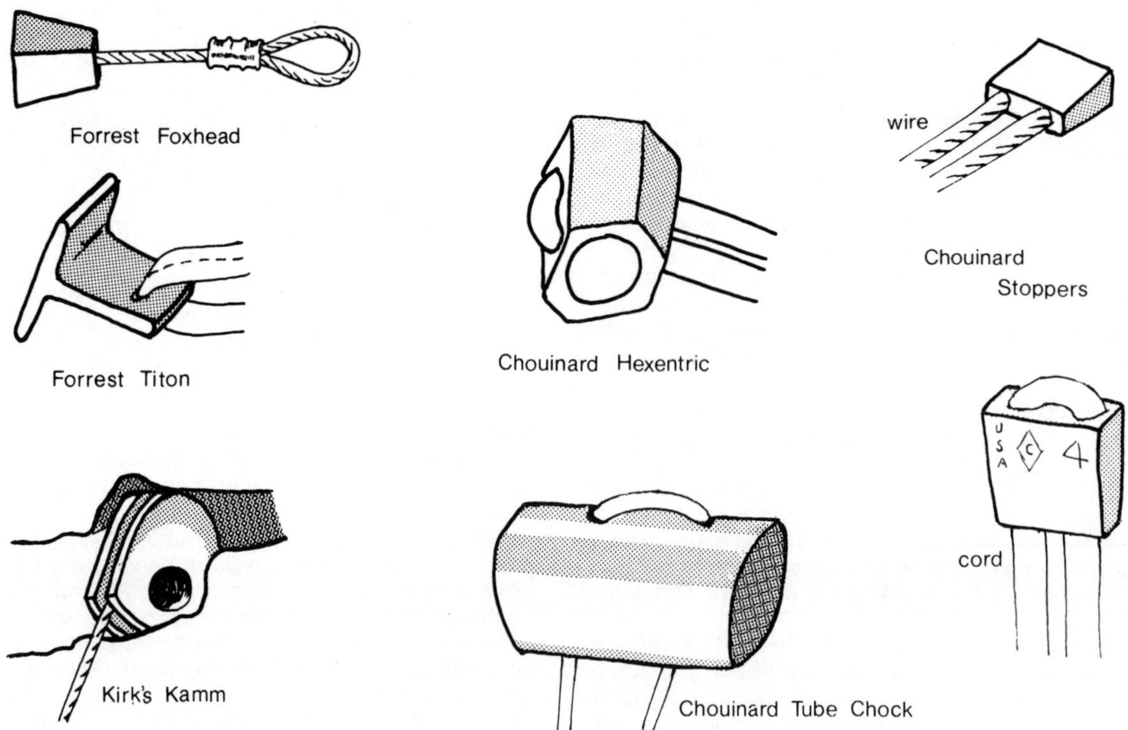

FIGURE 27: A selection of chocks. (After the manufacturers' catalogues.)

FIGURE 28: Typical placements of a Chouinard Hexentric and Stopper (after Chouinard and Frost).

range known as Cogs which are very similar to hexentrics but may prove to be even more versatile (Jamieson and Friend 1977). For experimenters, an excellent Russian design is described by Bertulis (1976).

CHOCK PLACEMENT

As for any anchor, high strength and security are the two fundamentals of good chock placement. A chock should be secure in the direction of loading, but it must also be able to withstand minor tugs in other directions. Often a sideways or upwards tug might be applied when clipping on or off the rope. Of more concern, if the rope forms one pitch in a chain of pitches running down a shaft (page 38), then an upward tug is almost certain to occur while clipping on or off the rope above. All possible forces on a chock must be considered at the time of placement.

Chocks are most often placed in cracks which run parallel or semi-parallel to the direction of loading (Figure 29). Prospective cracks should be closely inspected and a position chosen which narrows in the direction of loading. Strong placements usually feature a large contact area between the metal and the rock. One should avoid placements where the chock is supported by only one or two minor rock nubbins. The nubbins may break under loading, or the chock might pivot out of position. After selecting a likely placement, a suitable chock is inserted by hand and firmly wedged with a sharp jerk on its sling. The chock's security is then tested with light outward and upward jerks. It could also be tested in the load direction by hopping up and down in a foot stirrup attached to the chock.

Occasionally, chocks will not wedge but only wiggle loosely in their placements. Slight rope movements may then unseat them. A common remedy is to fit a second chock in the crack, slotted upwards below the loose chock and tightly connected to it (Figure 29). The loose chock should then be completely secure. Care must be taken not to connect the two chocks in a way which causes excessive loading on the top chock (Pierson 1976). A good method uses a small loop of shock cord (Puckett 1976). Shock cord is a tough stretchy rope with a nylon sheath and rubber core available from hardware and boating shops. It is much easier to obtain a tight connection with shock cord than with normal tape or rope.

Chocks may be fitted in cracks running perpendicular to the load direction although suitable placements can be scarce. The usual site is an area which is narrow at the surface of the crack and wide behind. The chock is slotted into the

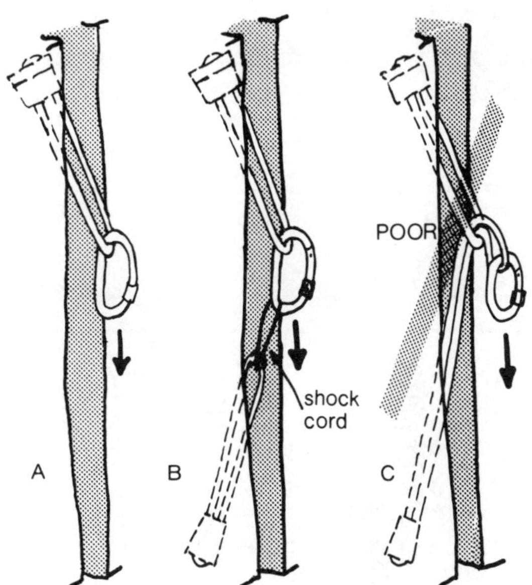

FIGURE 29: Chock placement in a crack parallel to the direction of loading. In A, the chock is firmly wedged in. In B, the chock is loose and is secured with a second chock, slotted upwards below the loose chock and connected to it with a loop of shock cord. Diagram C shows a poor alternative arrangement to B, which results in a force on the top chock equal to twice the applied load.

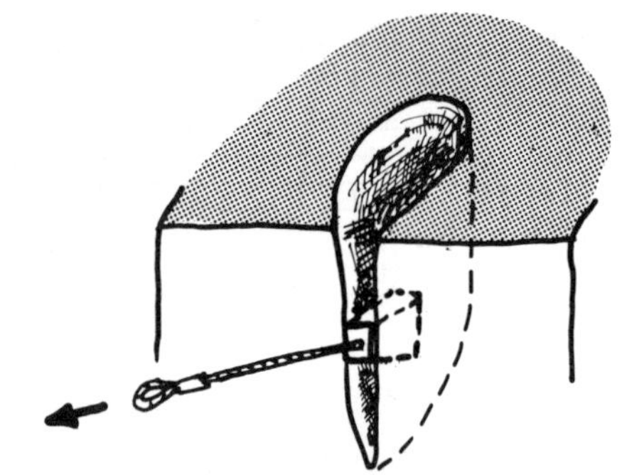

FIGURE 30: Chock fitted into a crack running perpendicular to the load direction.

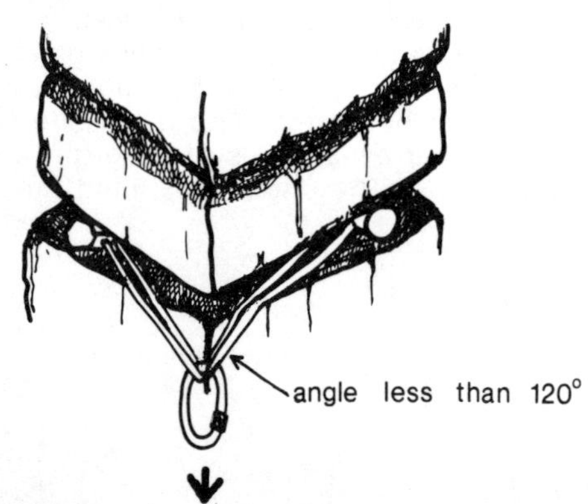

FIGURE 31: Two chocks fitted into a crack running perpendicular to the load direction. Neither chock would be secure on its own.

FIGURE 32: A chock tied off on one side in a shallow crack (after Anderson), and a jammed knot.

crack at a convenient spot and moved sideways into position (Figure 30). A more inventive scheme uses two chocks opposed as in Figure 31. The chock slings must be arranged at angles which avoid excessive loading (page 22).

Limestone offers other possibilities for the alert caver. Often small pockets and solution holes will accept chocks. Shallow cracks can be fitted with chocks tied off on one side. Also, pitons, carabiners and rope knots can serve as chocks (Figure 32). It is only when one becomes proficient at chockcraft that the many possibilities become apparent.

THE STRENGTH OF CHOCKS

Cavers using chocks for the first time usually feel insecure about the strength of a small anchor that is merely inserted by hand. Encouragingly, climbers have found them generally so reliable and strong when well placed that there is really little cause for alarm. In a series of tests by Cal Magnussen, an experienced climber, eighty-two chocks (largely Forrest and Chouinard) were placed and an estimate made of their holding power using the ratings poor, fair, good or excellent. The chocks were then loaded to failure (Smutek 1977). The tests were done in granite, but will be broadly applicable to any solid rock. Magnussen's ratings were generally accurate. Nearly all "good" or "excellent" chocks pulled out at loads of over 1000kg or failed by sling breakage. There were a few notable exceptions, enough to stop one from becoming over-confident. Of particular note is the situation where a chock is placed behind a flake or a detached block. Depending on the taper angle of the chock (Figure 33), the chock will exert an outward force on the flake or block which may be many times greater than the applied load of the caver's body. The smaller the taper angle, the

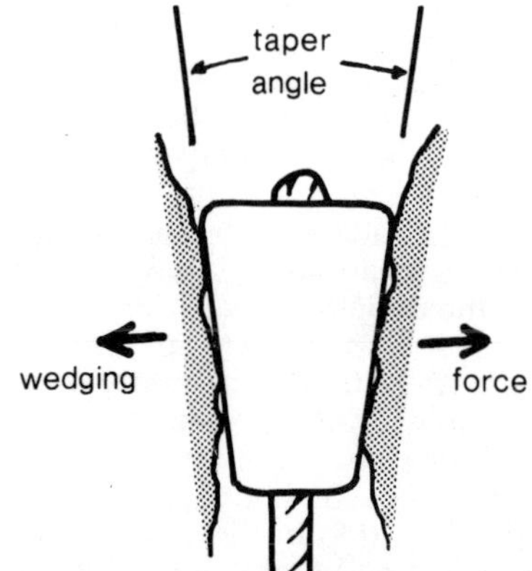

FIGURE 33: Depending on the taper angle of a chock, the chock will exert a wedging force which may be many times the applied load of the caver's body. (after Peters.)

greater will be the force. For example, a Chouinard No 2 Stopper with a taper angle of 8° will in theory exert a force seven times the applied load. A taper angle of 14° (eg No 5 Stopper or No 1 Forrest Arrowhead) will cause a four times load and a taper angle of 20° (No 1 Forrest Foxhead) almost a three times load (Peters 1976). A jerky abseil or prusik on a chock anchor could obviously pry loose quite a large flake or block.

Accordingly, it is not possible to be completely sure about the strength of any particular chock and thus chocks would rarely be used as single anchors. However, a multiple anchor comprised of two, three or even four good chocks should quell any doubts.

CHOCK REMOVAL

Most chocks can be removed with a sharp jerk. Others require thought and patience. Generally, a problem chock can be tackled by considering how it was placed and wriggling it out along the same path. Light taps with a hammer, prods with a long piton or use of a special chock removing tool can all help. Removal tools are usually around 200mm long and have a hook at one end. Some commercial tools are available or one can be easily home-made from bailing wire or thin aluminium plate. A standard shelf bracket will even be suitable (Figure 34) (Bunning 1974, Schaffer 1974, Smutek 1976). Hammers, pitons and chock tools can also be useful for tricky chock placements or cleaning dirt from prospective cracks.

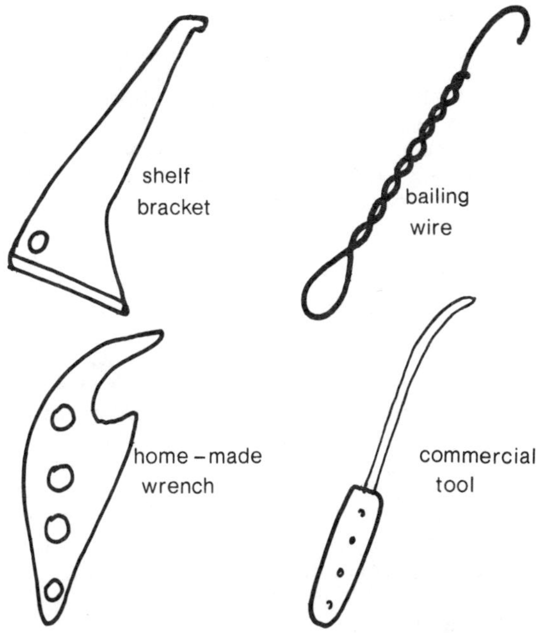

FIGURE 34: Some tools for removing chocks.

LEARNING TO USE CHOCKS

Correct chock placement is of prime importance in any chock anchor and is a technique which certainly requires practice. It is a good idea to begin on cliffs on the surface. Chocks should be placed in many attitudes and tested with body weight. After this apprenticeship, chocks can be used underground, perhaps initially as backups for more certain anchors. Finally, complete chock anchors may be constructed, using at least two chocks.

PITONS

Pitons (also called pins or pegs) are metal spikes which are driven into cracks and holes in the rock. Like chocks, pitons came to caving by way of rock climbing. During the 1940's, 1950's and 1960's, piton technology flourished, reached an impressive standard, and formed the basis of major advances in climbing. That period is now over. Chockcraft has arrived, with its emphasis on not damaging the rock. Very little new piton design work can now be expected from climbers. Piton manufacture has sharply declined and some makes will doubtlessly disappear. This is to the loss of cavers since pitons are fine tools for underground use. They can serve in many cracks unsuitable for chocks. The growing needs of cavers are unlikely to regenerate a dying market and cavers might do well to buy up stocks of pitons while they are still available.

Probably the greatest advance in piton technology came in 1947 when John Salathe developed hard steel pitons in America (Robbins 1971). Pitons were formerly made of mild steel. Mild steel pitons bend to the shape of the crack into which they are driven. They have poor durability and often only minimal strength for anchoring purposes. They can be considered totally obsolete. Particular care should be taken not to use old pitons with welded rings or poorly placed eye holes (Figure 35) (Armitage 1966). Most pitons are

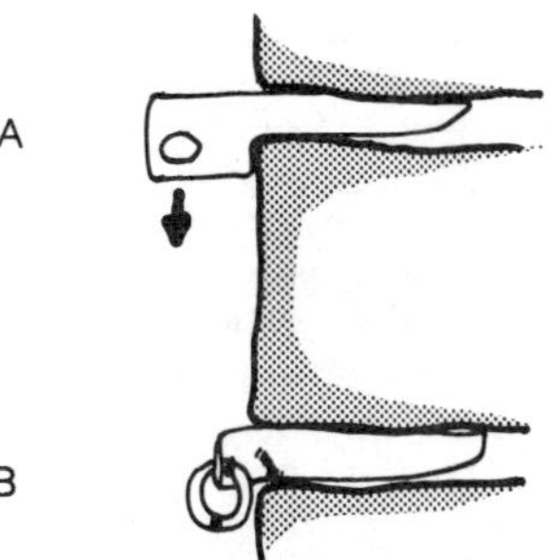

FIGURE 35: Old pitons with poorly placed eyeholes (A) or welded rings (B) should be avoided. In A, the eyehole is placed so far from the piton shaft that the piton would bend under load.

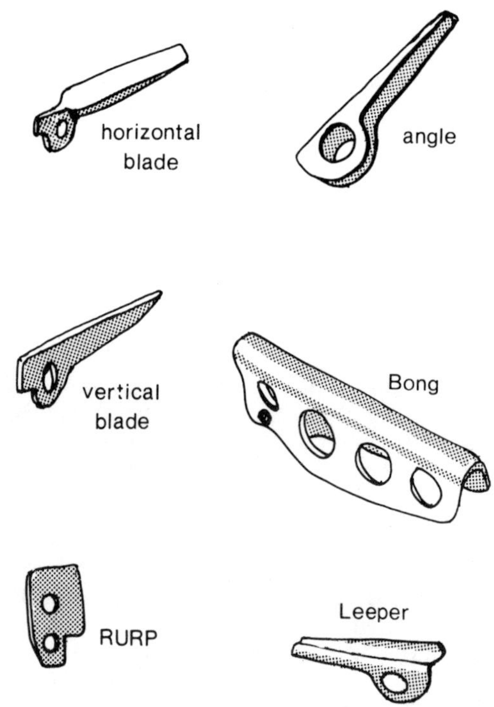

FIGURE 36: Some types of pitons. RURPS and vertical blade pitons should be avoided. A carabiner is clipped into the piton eye for rope attachment.

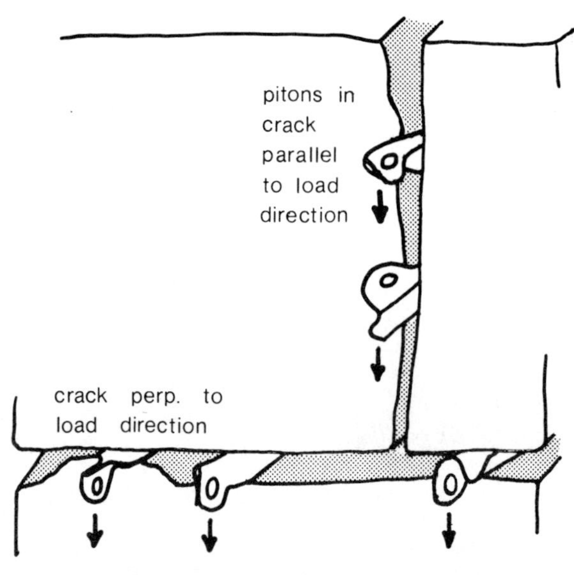

FIGURE 37: Placement of pitons in cracks running parallel and perpendicular to the load direction (indicated by arrows). It is important to orientate the eyes in the way shown to achieve the greatest mechanical strength from the pitons. Angles, for example, lose roughly half their strength if placed upside down in a crack perpendicular to the load direction (Armitage 1966).

now of hard alloy steel, commonly known as chrome-moly steel. These bend little and are very reliable.

Pitons are available in numerous shapes and sizes (Figure 36). A good selection for caving would be comprised of intermediate sizes, concentrating on angle pitons and Leepers. While a few blade pitons can prove handy, they are generally of limited use because cracks in limestone are usually somewhat enlarged by solutional action. Vertical blade pitons are not worth carrying. The very small pitons called RURPS should never be used because of their low holding power. Large Bongs would be too bulky to carry underground for general anchoring purposes. When placing any piton, one should ensure that the piton eye is in its correct orientation (Figure 37).

PITON PLACEMENT

Pitons are inherently secure because they are driven into place with a hammer. Therefore, the prime feature of a good piton placement is high strength. High strength is usually attained in cracks which run perpendicular to the direction of loading (Figure 37). In such cracks, the piton cannot rotate or pull out of position under load because it levers solidly against the walls of the crack.

Pitons may be placed in cracks parallel to the load direction, but the crack configuration must be suitable. A close inspection and skilful placement will be required. Cracks which have interior tapers, twists, bumps or nubbins are best because they may allow a placement where rotation of the piton under load is impossible. In contrast, smooth, parallel sided cracks are generally poor prospects because the piton may easily rotate and pull out at low loads. In general, angle pitons and Leepers resist rotation much better than knifeblades, and long pitons are better than short ones (Armitage 1967).

Placements which cause a direct outward pull on a piton should be generally avoided, though

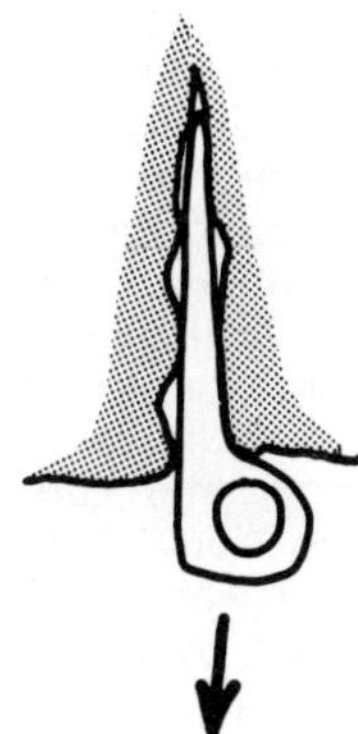

FIGURE 38: A piton placement causing a direct outward load. Such placements should be generally avoided.

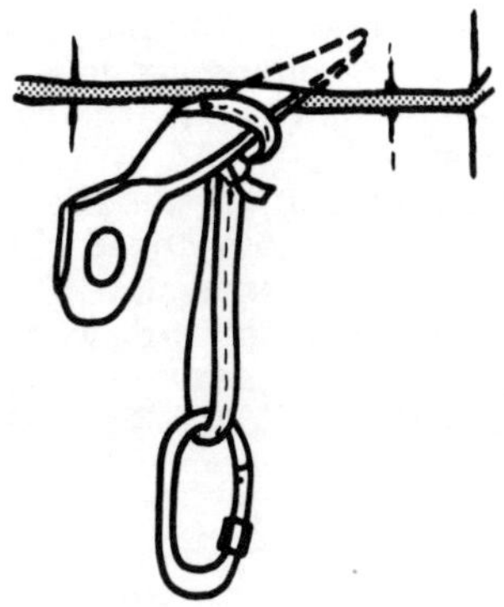

FIGURE 39: A hero loop attached to a piton which could not be driven in fully.

they can be safe if the piton is long and well driven (Figure 38).

A general method of driving pitons is presented by Chouinard and Frost (undated).

> "First, select the piton size for the crack and then locate the section of the crack that best fits the piton. (Depending upon its length and taper, the piton should normally allow one-half to three-quarters of the blade to be inserted into the crack before driving.) Pound the piton in only part way, then give one or two light downward blows (vertical crack assumed) on the head to see how well it is in, and how well it resists shifting. Then drive more according to the results of the test, and retest with another downward blow until the piton appears adequately solid in its resistance to shifting. Restrain the urge to give it that one extra blow — this is the one that will make the piton difficult to remove and cause it and the rock to become unnecessarily damaged in the process. If, however, a perfect placement is not possible, then the best security can of course be obtained from a really hard-driven piton, particularly in vertical cracks."

Chouinard and Frost's comments apply to pitons that will be removed after use. For a permanent placement, often desirable in popular caves, pitons should generally be hard driven. Permanent pitons should be inspected for strength and security before use by each subsequent party. Rust is a particular hazard.

Contrary to common belief, listening to the note made by a piton as it is driven is of little value in assessing the piton's holding power. Extensive tests reviewed by Armitage (1967) show that a high ringing note does not reliably indicate a good placement, nor does a dull thud indicate a poor one. Judicious placement and testing in the way suggested by Chouinard and Frost are of greater value. However, if the note which is made suddenly goes dull and hollow then fracturing of the rock can be suspected.

An occasional possibility which is unique to caves is the driving of pitons directly into porous flowstone without the presence of any obvious cracks. Possible sites are any nooks in the flowstone which identify points of weakness or any grooves where two separate flows have merged. A strong knife blade piton should be used and checks made during driving to see that the flowstone does not fracture. Obviously, conservation ethics severely restrict the extent to which this technique can be used.

Ideally, a piton should be driven fully in to avoid any bending of the piton blade when a carabiner is attached to the eye and load applied. Bending will greatly reduce the strength of a piton and possibly even snap the blade (Armitage 1966). If a piton cannot be fully driven, then it should be provided with a sling snugged against the rock instead of the usual carabiner. These slings are called hero loops (Figure 39).

Proficiency in piton placement should be gained in much the same way as was suggested for chocks (page 23). Even when one is proficient, rarely would total reliance be placed on a single piton. Instead, a piton should be combined with other pitons, chocks, bolts or natural anchors.

PITON REMOVAL

Pitons can be left as permanent anchors but often they will be removed at the conclusion of exploration. The usual technique is to bash the piton with a hammer as far in one direction as it will go, give it one more hard blow and then hit it fully back the other way. The process is repeated if necessary. Since pitons are tapered, they will usually work themselves out. The slender end of the hammer should be used with blows directed as close as possible to the surface of the rock to avoid damage to the piton head. Stubborn pins may require extra persuasion. Two common approaches are to pull outwards with a sling while bashing or intersperse bashings with prying of the piton using a beaked piton hammer (Errington 1972). Probably the piton will then pop out unexpectedly and thump you in the face. Hard steel pitons will serve for years if removed with care. However, cracks or stretched areas will eventually appear in the head region and at this stage the piton should be discarded.

BOLTS

A rock bolt is placed by drilling a hole in solid rock and then pounding the bolt in by hammer or setting it with a spanner. A hanger is then fitted to the bolt for carabiner attachment. Most bolts have an expansion mechanism to cause them to grip securely in the hole. Bolts are an emotive subject. On the one hand, they are the ideal anchors since they can be situated almost anywhere and are strong and secure when properly placed. On the other hand, they are ugly. Even though small, a bolt is an unsightly piece of metal in an otherwise natural environment. Bolts also can remove one of cave exploring's main technical challenges: that of constructing safe, well-positioned anchors using the natural features of the rock. The bolt-oriented caver may never see the inobvious jughandle or crack which only close scrutiny will reveal. Bolts are the easy way out.

Ethically, bolts are only justified in the absence of a suitable alternative anchor (the question of what makes a suitable anchor is considered at length in the next Chapter). Cavers exploring a known cave generally do not have an ethical problem since if a pitch is not already provided with a bolt, then a suitable anchor should present itself upon looking. An exception is in caves which formerly had been descended using wire ladders. The danger of rope abrasion in SRT demands that ropes be more carefully placed than ladders so that some ladder anchors would be unsuitable. A bolt may then be desired.

The main ethical problem confronts cavers exploring a new cave. If the cave is in a remote expedition area and will be only infrequently descended by experienced groups, then the most ethical approach is to use a minimum of bolts and contrive anchors with pitons and chocks when no suitable natural anchors are available. However, caves in popular areas require more thought. One cannot expect all other parties to be proficient in piton and chock placement. If it is judged desirable to make a provision for subsequent, less experienced groups, and it is undesirable to leave pitons or chocks, then a bolt could be placed.

Even after deciding to place a bolt, the ethical problems are by no means over. A decision needs to be made on the bolt diameter and only after that, on its type and length. The decision again depends on the anticipated popularity of the cave. Light bolts about 6mm in diameter are available in a number of varieties for insertion into rock. They are convenient to carry and quickly placed (maybe ten to fifteen minutes by hand), but are not very suitable as permanent anchors. Leeper (1963) performed extensive tests on six common types and brands of 6mm bolts placed in unweathered granite. They were loaded in the normal way bolts are in caving, ie, close and parallel to the rock (called shear loading) (Figure 40). Load was steadily increased to the point of failure. At best they held 1500kg. At worst, less than 600kg (these brands, called Star Pin Grips and Star Dryvins, will not be mentioned further). Limestone is generally mechanically weaker than granite and when this fact is combined with the possibilities of shock loading, of rust and of metal or rock fatigue, the deficiencies of 6mm bolts should be obvious. Bolt replacement every one or two years could be warranted; in most cases leaving an unsafe bolt or a scar each time. Six millimetre bolts find their best use in very remote caves where another visit would not be expected for many years.

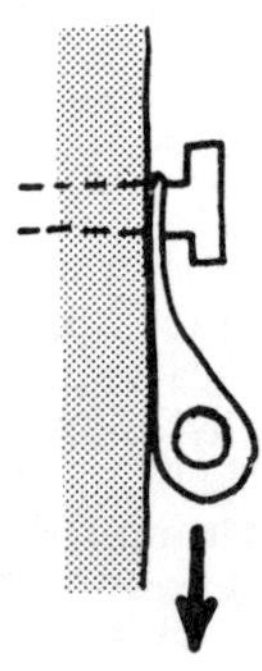

FIGURE 40: Shear loading of a bolt.

In more popular caves it is certainly worth the effort to place a 10mm to 12mm bolt. There are some excellent brands available. For example, the Rawlplug Company makes a 12mm diameter bolt called the Rawl G6 (page 29), which can hold a shear load of about 3500kg when placed in concrete (Childs 1976). When well serviced with grease a bolt such as this should last five to ten years, and can be replaced without drilling a new hole (Brook 1974).

Any readers who view the above approach to bolts as conservationist in the extreme would do well to consider the case of some caves in Continental Europe where bolts have been very commonly placed as anchors for many years. It is not unusual to see pitch heads spiked with five or six light bolts placed by different expeditions, often in plain view of perfectly adequate natural anchors. Sometimes bolts have even been placed in natural anchors.

TYPES OF BOLTS

By far the most popular type of bolt nowadays is the self-drilling anchor. It is available from several different companies, with minor variations. Self-drilling anchors have a toothed casing which itself

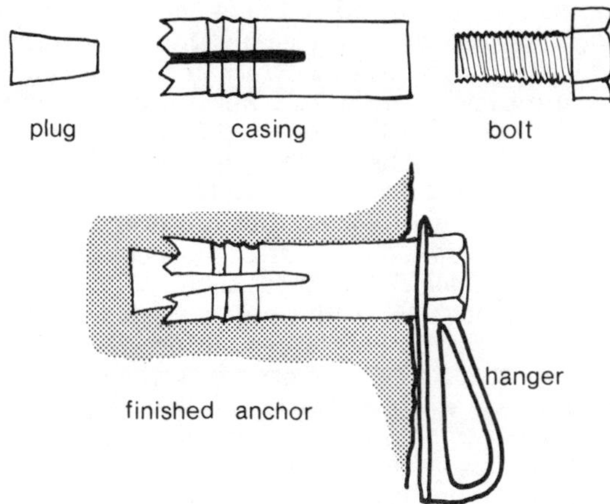

FIGURE 41: Self-drilling anchor. The toothed casing drills a hole under hammer blows. The bolt is set with a spanner. In use a carabiner is clipped into the hanger.

drills the hole (Figure 41). A driver is screwed firmly into the casing and pounded with a hammer while being frequently turned clockwise by hand. The casing must be regularly removed and cleared of rock flour. When the end of the casing is about 2mm under the rock surface, it is removed, an expander plug inserted and then the casing is hammered home. The plug expands the inner end of the casing, causing the teeth to bite into the rock. After hammering, the driver is unscrewed leaving a well placed casing flush with the rock surface. A high tensile bolt and a hanger are then fitted. An excellent feature of self-drilling anchors is that they gain their strength from the end of the hole where the rock is usually less weathered and therefore probably soundest.

Sometimes when driving the casing, the rock fractures away entirely leave the casing jammed on the end of the drive. The whole kit will then be useless unless a pair of pliers is handy.

Self-drilling anchors are commonly available for bolt diameters between 5mm and 10mm. Unfortunately, they are generally less than 40mm in length so they should not be used in limestone which is badly weathered to this depth. In good rock, the 10mm sizes are suitable as permanent anchors. An essential precaution, with any self-drilling anchor, is to use a high tensile bolt. Hardened alloy steel cap screws with an Allen socket head are the strongest. Some kits are complete with bolts and some are not.

Bolts requiring a hole to be separately made with a rock drill are also in common use, though their market is declining because of competition from the self-drilling types. Self-drilling anchors have the advantage that a fresh drill is necessarily used each time. Drill breakage is also less of a problem. Reusable drills need to be sharpened regularly and replacement bits must also be carried.

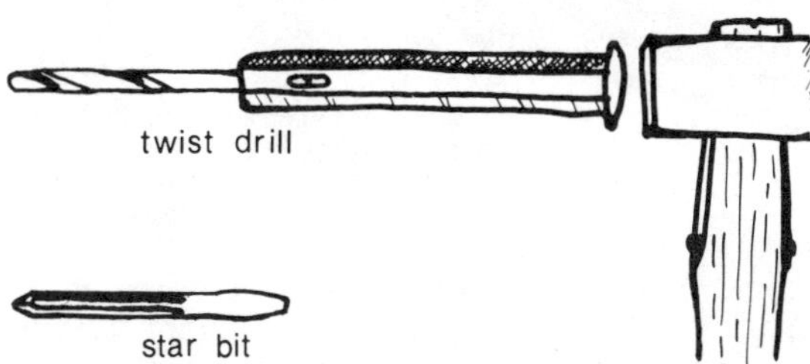

FIGURE 42: A drill holder with replaceable twist and star bits. The drill is pounded with a hammer while being turned clockwise by hand.

There are two basic types of rock drill — twist drills and star drills (Figure 42). They consist of a holder and a replaceable drill bit. To insert a new bit in the event of breakage, a wedge is needed to remove the broken bit. Breakage usually results from carelessly bending the drill as it is being hammered or not hammering it straight. Twist drills seem to perform better in limestone than star drills. Users of star drills will need to carry a length of rubber tube to blow out rock flour during drilling or else the rock flour tends to pack down into the hole. Holes made with twist drills clear themselves of rock flour and there appears to be no time saved by blowing them clear (Leeper 1963, Frank 1975).

All else being equal, speed of drilling varies with the hole diameter, its depth, and the quality of the rock. In good rock, ten to twenty minutes is an average time for a hole about 6mm diameter to be drilled about 40mm deep to accept a light bolt, while a 24mm diameter hole drilled 115mm deep to accept a 12mm expansion bolt could take four hours (Brook 1972). Speed of drilling and the sound made by the hammer blows are good indicators of the quality of the rock. If a hole is made very fast and the drill sounds dull, then the rock is probably poor. If a lot of bolting is to be undertaken such as on an artificial climb, then a more powerful drill could be considered. Two types of mechanical rock drill are described by Isenhart (1976) and Standing (1972). Electric drills are good if a battery or generator is made available and supplied with a suitable length of cable. Such systems make it possible to plant many bolts with very little effort. They should be used with great discretion.

There are several types of bolts that can be inserted into pre-drilled holes. Australian rock climbers initiated the use of standard high tensile steel bolts, hammered into holes drilled with bits about 1.5mm thinner than the bolts (Figure 43).

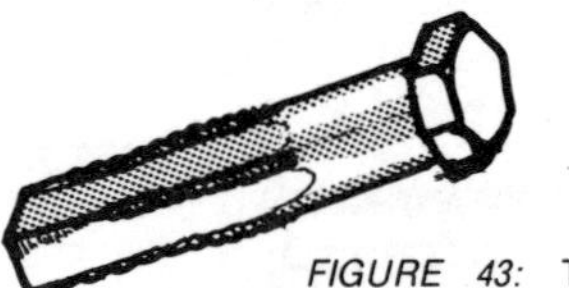

FIGURE 43: The Australian rock bolt. A standard high tensile steel bolt which has been ground flat on four sides leaving four thin ridges of thread which bite into the rock.

Eight millimetres and 10mm are the common bolt diameters. Eight millimetre bolts 30mm long are suitable for non-permanent anchors in good rock. Longer ones are required for soft rock. A 10mm diameter bolt 75mm long makes a good permanent anchor, as testified through fairly extensive use by Australian rock climbers (Caffyn 1974, Davis 1969, Montgomery 1974). Normally, the bolts are ground to a square cross section, leaving only four ridges of thread which bite into the sides of the hole. However, in soft or porous rock an unground bolt may be better and a few should be carried in the kit.

Australian rock bolts have not been well tested to establish failure loads. From appearances they will be good under a shear load but possibly not under an outward load. However, outward loads are not advisable for any bolts (page 30). Unlike the self-drilling anchors, the bolts are obviously non-removable after being driven. A hanger will therefore need to be left on each bolt, unless a keyhole bracket is used (page 29). When the bolts become old and unsafe, they can be broken off with a stout hammer blow or sometimes screwed out or broken with a spanner.

Two commercial rock bolts popular in the USA are the Rawl Stud and the Rawl Drive. They are identical except for their head (Figure 44). These bolts headed the field in Leeper's tests, surpassing even the Phillips self-drilling anchor. Six millimetres and 10mm are the popular diameters.

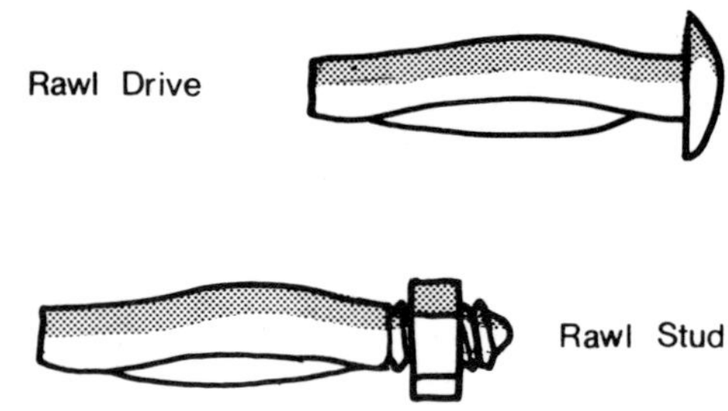

FIGURE 44: Rawl Drive and Rawl Stud (after Leeper). These bolts gain their holding power from compression of their split middle sections.

Lengths vary from 25mm to 75mm, the longer ones being preferred for soft rock. Rawl Drives and Studs gain their holding power from outward pressure exerted by a split section of the bolt. Since this section is towards the middle of the bolt, the rock must be sound in this region.

While the Rawl Drives and Studs have excellent strength when well placed, they perform poorly in holes that are drilled too wide or too shallow. They are more sensitive than most other bolts in this respect (Leeper 1963). In Leeper's tests, where Rawls bottomed in their holes during driving and then were struck several more times with the hammer, they lost a large degree of holding power. A further problem is that the metal in the split section fatigues with age, often causing the bolts to loosen. For these reasons, Rawl Drives and Studs are not particularly good as permanent anchors (Deal 1968).

The best permanent bolt anchors in use today would be the 12mm diameter expansion bolts commonly used in Britain (Figure 45). They require 24mm diameter holes about 115mm deep; difficult holes to drill, but well worth the effort. The exceptional feature of these bolts is that they are set with a spanner and can be similarly removed for inspection, greasing or replacement. The casing is not hammered in, as is the case with self-drilling anchors. Therefore, only one hole need ever be drilled.

Several different types and brands are described by Childs (1976) and test results given. A basic choice is between a projecting bolt type and an eyebolt type. The projecting bolt requires a hanger to be fixed, whereas the eyebolt has the advantage of direct attachment for the carabiner or rope. However, the eyebolt is inherently the weaker of the two since a shear loading on the eye (which is the normal type of loading in caving) causes a bending force on the bolt shaft. In Child's tests where bolts were rigidly fixed in a metal plate and loaded to destruction, the Rawl

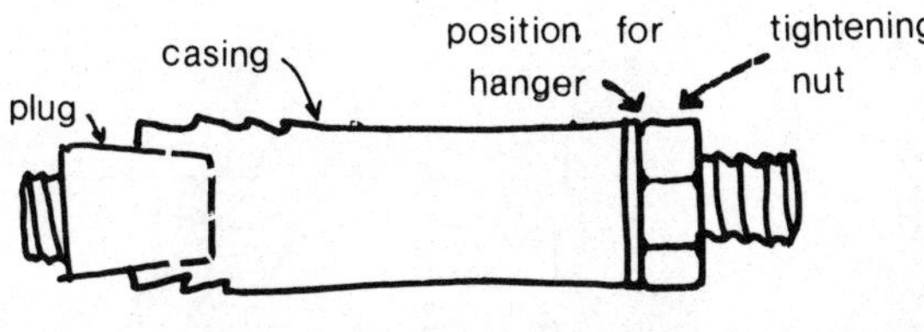

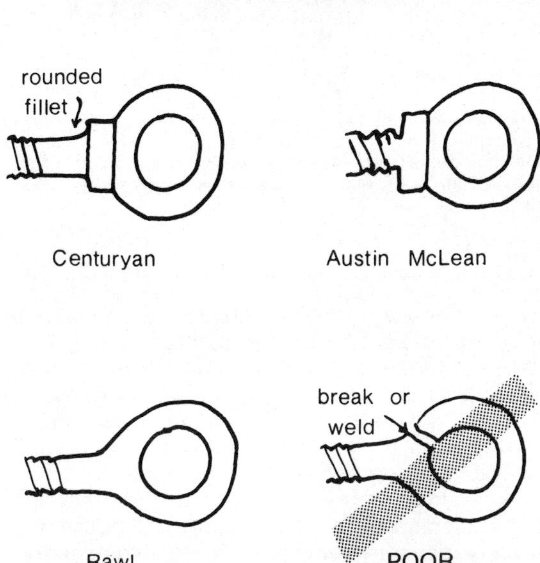

FIGURE 45: Twelve millimetre diameter expansion bolts. The bolts are set in a pre-drilled hold by tightening a nut at the front of the casing. The nut pulls an expander plug into the end of the casing. The bolts may be of the protecting type or eyebolt type (after Brooks and Childs).

brand of eyebolt broke at under 1000kg, which is less than could be expected from a well placed 6mm bolt. The Rawl G6 projecting bolt could be expected to hold over 3500kg in the same test. Only eyebolts with solid forged eyes (rather than incomplete or welded eyes), and a strong eye neck should be used. The best brands tested by Childs were the Austin McLean B.S. 529 and the Centuryan. Both have a collar at the base of the eye, and the Centuryan has a rounded fillet as well. The Centuryan broke at about 4000kg, the Austin McLean at about 1800kg.

Eyebolts should be placed with the eye as close as possible to the rock surface to reduce bending forces. As well as setting the tightening nut with a spanner, the eye must be screwed in with a bar.

HANGERS

With the main exception of eye bolts, every bolt is fitted with a metal plate called a hanger to provide a secure carabiner attachment (Figure 46). There are many commercial brands, most of them made from aluminium plate about 3mm thick. They can also be made in a small workshop, provided a suitable alloy is chosen.

Figure 46 shows some common designs. The best do not cause any bending forces or outward forces which may serve to break or loosen the bolt. Hangers of a simple bent plate design may cause such forces. They should be avoided, with the exception of keyhole brackets of good design. Keyhole brackets are retrievable hangers for non-permanent bolts lacking a removable head, such as the Australian rock bolt and Rawl Drive. With a carabiner attached, keyhole brackets are completely secure, but once the carabiner is removed, the hanger can be slipped off by aligning the carabiner hole with the bolt head. Keyhole brackets of good design (Figure 46) cause slight (if any) outward or bending forces.

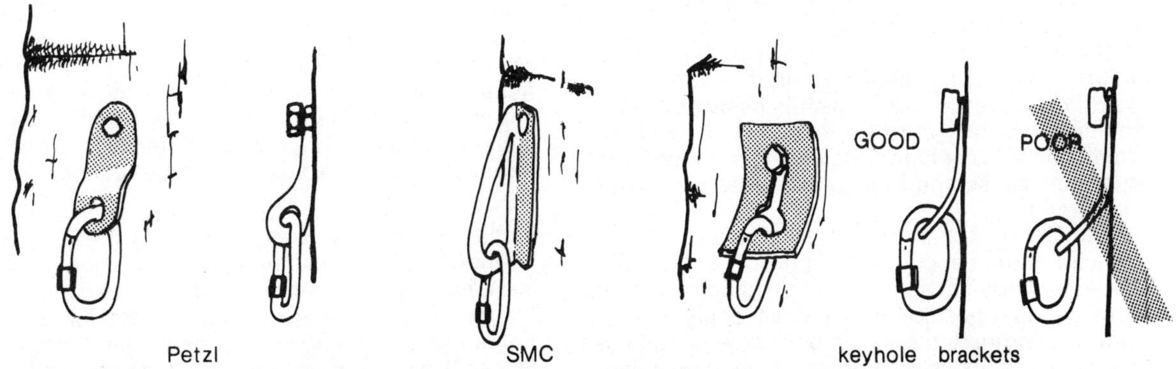

FIGURE 46: Examples of bolt hangers. The SMC and Petzl models do not normally cause any outward or bending forces on a bolt. Bent plate hangers, such as the keyhole bracket, may do this, if of poor design.

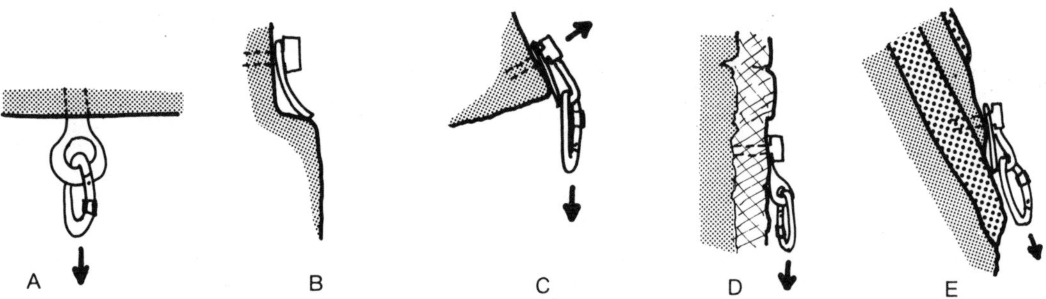

FIGURE 47: Poor bolt placements. A illustrates a placement causing a direct outward load. Any loosening of the bolt could cause it to pull out. In B, no allowance has been made for attaching the carabiner. The bolt in C is too close to a rock edge, creating a possibility of the rock fracturing and, furthermore, loading of the bolt causes an outward force on it. D shows a bolt in badly weathered limestone, and E, a bolt in thinly bedded limestone. In both cases fracturing of the rock is very likely. Bolts should be placed on flat areas of sound rock and shear loaded.

PLACING BOLTS

All the small items of equipment (bolts, spanners, etc) required to place a bolt are normally carried in a small bag or pouch which is attached to the waist while bolting. The hammer and gloves (useful to protect the hands from stray blows) can be carried separately. A precaution while bolting is to tie the hammer and driver to the waist with thin cord to prevent an embarrassing loss in case they are dropped.

Bolts are usually placed in the cave walls or floor to ensure that they are shear loaded. A direct outward loading, as might be obtained from a roof placement, should be avoided (Figure 47). Bolts are very strong in an outward direction when properly placed and new, but any loosening of the bolt with age or use could cause it to be pulled out. Other factors requiring careful attention are the quality of the rock, the position in which the rope will hang (see next Chapter), and the ease of actually drilling the hole. One should be comfortable while drilling or a poor hole will probably result. Concerning the quality of the rock, mechanical strength and the presence of possible facture planes must be considered. It is wise to avoid flowstone and rock which is shaley or badly weathered, or has individual beds less than about 50mm thick. Sometimes, however, a weathering crust can be scraped away to reveal solid rock underneath.

After choosing a general location, the exact drill site can then be chosen (Figure 47). The site should be fairly flat so that the bolt hanger will not be placed in a position where it will apply an outward or bending force to the bolt, or else make it impossible to attach a carabiner. One should also keep at least 100mm away from any edge to minimise the possibility of rock fracture.

Holes should be drilled horizontally or angled slightly downwards into the rock (about 5°). Then if the bolt loosens, it will not pull out under load. The drill should be held steady to produce a straight, even hole, and the hammer blows should be as heavy as possible without causing drill damage. Leeper showed that, in granite, heavy blows are much more effective than frequent light taps. The same will probably apply to limestone. A corollary is that the hammer should also be heavy. If a lot of bolting is envisaged, then a 1kg lump hammer could be carried. Otherwise, a piton hammer is the usual choice.

When a hole is finished, it should be inspected for any fractures and blown clear of rock flour. The bolt or casing is then driven, again keeping a careful watch for rock fracturing. The sound made by the hammer blow during driving is a good indicator here. If the note suddenly goes dull and hollow, fracturing can be suspected. A good bolt will go in just far enough to allow the hanger to be fitted snugly against the rock. A bolt which stops moving before it is fully driven in should not be pounded excessively as this will only reduce what holding power it does have. A bolt such as this can still be used if it is provided with a hero loop instead of a hanger (Figure 39). It would, of course, need to be combined with other, better anchors.

Once a bolt is inserted, its protruding portion should be liberally coated with thick grease if it is intended as a permanent anchor. A 12mm expansion bolt should, in addition, be greased along its length prior to insertion, but a bolt for a self-drilling anchor must not be, as it may then work loose. The expansion bolt is always tightened with sufficient force to prevent it from easily working loose because of greasing.

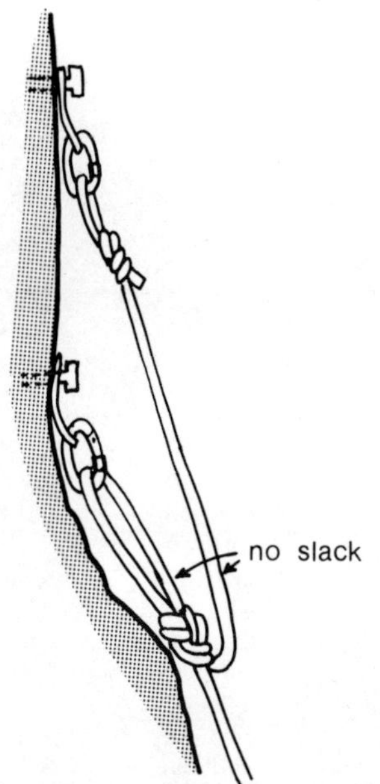

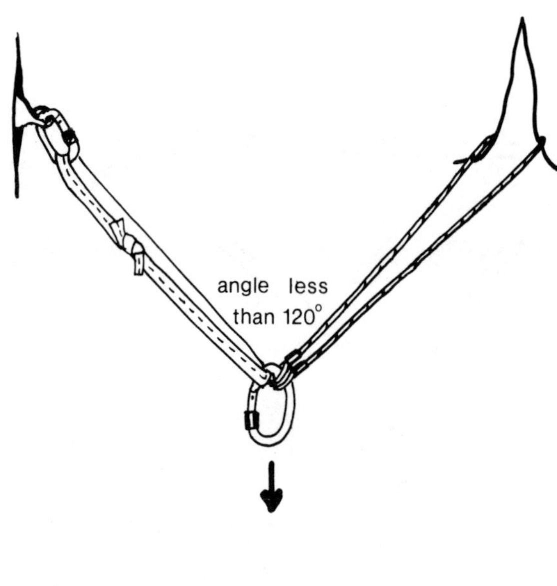

FIGURE 48: Good methods of connecting two anchors. On the left, two bolts have been aligned in the load direction. If one fails, the other will be subjected to only a small shock load. In the arrangement on the right, if one anchor failed the load would pendulum onto the other, but the shock load would still not be great. Three or more anchors can be connected using extensions of the same methods. Figure 49 shows some poor alternative arrangements.

BACK UPS FOR BOLTS

Some cavers mistakenly view a bolt as an absolutely reliable anchor. In reality, it is just as fallible as any individual chock or piton. Every bolt should be backed up with one or two other anchors.

Bolts which have been positioned with the prime purpose of achieving a good rope hang can often be backed by natural anchors, pitons or chocks in less suitable positions. However, in situations where the bolt was placed because no alternative anchors were available, it is wise to place two bolts. They should not be situated too close together since every bolt stresses the rock immediately surrounding it. If the second bolt is placed in the stress zone of the first, then the rock may facture. The size of the stress zone will depend on the quality of the rock (larger for better rock) but a spacing of over 300mm should always prove sufficient.

It is best to align the two bolts in the proposed direction of loading. If one bolt fails the load can then be immediately transferred to the other. Methods of connecting the two bolts to enable this are considered in the section on multiple anchors, which now follows.

MULTIPLE ANCHORS

Complete confidence should rarely be placed in a single anchor, especially if it is a chock, piton or bolt. One should always attempt to use two or more connected anchors to cover errors of judgment. In constructing these multiple anchors, two important points require attention.

The first point concerns the angle between any two sling legs in the multiple anchor (Figure 48). The danger of making this angle too large has already been mentioned in the discussion of natural anchors (page 16). The angle must be less than 120° or one or both of the slings will be stressed in excess of the applied load.

Secondly, it should be determined what will happen if one of the anchors fails. In the event of failure of one anchor, the rope must not pull free or another anchor should not be subjected to a severe shock load. Figure 49 illustrates some tempting arrangements which ignore these fundamentals.

Asking the question, "What will happen if . . .?" is a habit which every vertical caver would do well to acquire.

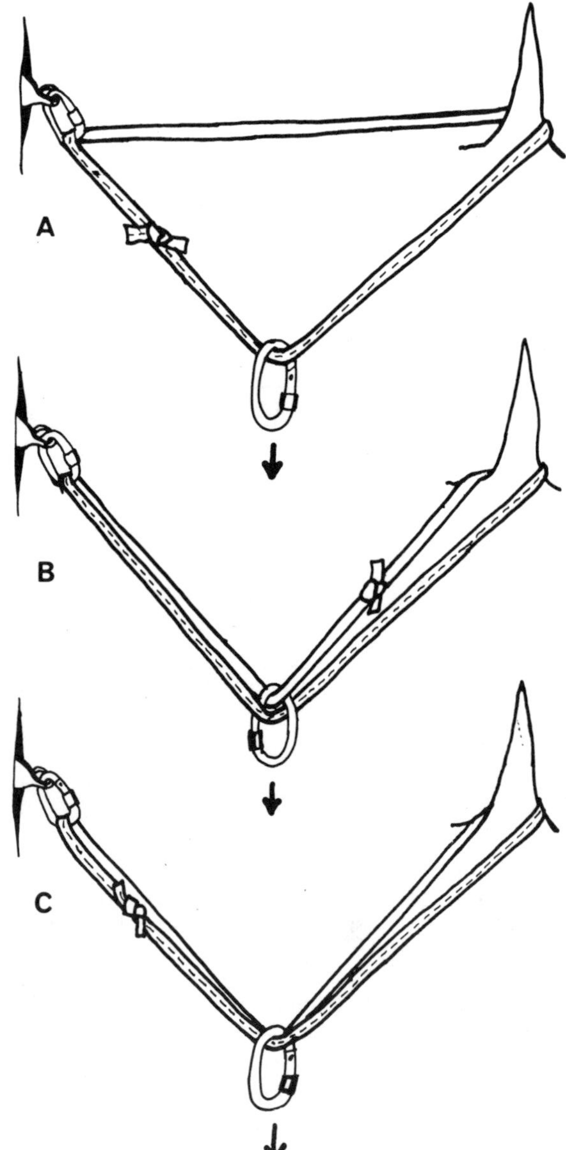

FIGURE 49: Some common, but poor, methods of connecting two anchors. In A and B, if one anchor fails the other will be subjected to a substantial shock load. Such arrangements may be useful for sharing the load between two weak anchors in rock climbing, but they have no place in SRT. Arrangement C is even worse — if one anchor fails the central carabiner will probably slide entirely off the sling.

Andrew Pavey

A caver makes her way off the top of a pitch in the deep New Zealand cave, Gorgoroth. A bolt has been placed to hang the rope free of the rock.

4: RIGGING

Rigging ropes on pitches is a very demanding area of vertical technique. For every pitch a rope must be selected, anchored and arranged in a way which permits each caver to make a safe descent and ascent without danger from rope abrasion, rockfall or water.

ROPE LENGTH

The first task in rigging is to make sure that a rope of sufficient length is available. In descents of known caves this is done before going underground. Normally, a map would be consulted to obtain pitch lengths, but the party must take care to carry sufficient rope to tie to the anchor as well as cover the length of the pitch. Before rigging the rope, it is important for the party to check that it is actually at the correct drop. Maps can be misread.

In an unknown cave, an estimate will need to be made of pitch length. This is usually done by looking over the edge, dropping a rock, and measuring the time which elapses until the rock is heard to hit bottom. The method is most applicable to free drops.

FREE DROPS

Except for long free drops the approximate formula

depth in metres $= 5t^2$

can be used, where t is time in seconds. Unfortunately, when t is greater than about 5 (ie, pitches over about 125m) large errors start to appear because the time taken for the sound to travel up the shaft becomes significant, as does air resistance on the rock. While allowance can be made for the speed of sound (about 340m/sec) air resistance depends on the shape of the rock. Roughly spherical rocks are best, but they by no means eliminate the problem. On a very long drop the formula could cause an overestimate of more than 100m. It is better to go by experience. As a guide, 200m drops take about 7 seconds, 300m drops about 10 seconds (Raines 1968) and 400m drops about 13 seconds (Raines 1972).

The only major pitfall with sounding is that one can never be sure that the rock has actually hit bottom. The rock may have only bounced on a ledge and leapt into another void.

WALLS

The formula becomes almost useless for drops where the rock can be heard distinctly bouncing on ledges and against walls. The rock will be considerably slowed by the bouncing, and will often knock off other rocks as it falls, causing a continuous clatter. Experience is the only real guide in these common cases. Some idea is gained by considering how distant the noise sounds to be.

CHOOSING THE PRIMARY ANCHOR POINT

Having gained some idea of what the pitch is like, attention turns to constructing a single or multiple anchor for rigging the rope. The position of this primary anchor point is critical. Consideration must be given to the dangers of rope abrasion, waterfalls, loose rock and to the provision of safe access for getting on or off the pitch. These points are now treated in detail.

ROPE ABRASION

It must again be stressed that rope abrasion is the greatest single danger in SRT. If one is to safeguard ropes against abrasion, the causes of it must first be understood.

Abrasion results from rope bounce produced by the motions of prusiking and to a lesser extent, abseiling (page 2). Because of bounce, there is some likelihood of rope abrasion at every point where the abseil/prusik rope touches the rock. Whether or not this likelihood will amount to a danger at any particular point of rubbing (rub point) depends on a number of factors, which have already been presented by the author in an earlier paper (Montgomery 1976. Most of the subsequent discussion on abrasion and padding in this chapter also acknowledges this source):

Type of rock. To determine the abrasion risk at a rub point, it is important to examine the roughness of the rock surface, the grain of the rock, its hardness, and whether it contains chert or quartz mineral veins.

Rough, coarse grained, hard rock with mineral veins (eg, some marble) is the most abrasive type, while smooth, fine grained, soft rock with no veins (some chalk) is probably the least dangerous. Most rock types encountered in caves will lie between these extremes.

Shape of the Rubpoint. In general, a sharp lip poses more of a risk than a rounded bulge, but care is required if a rounded bulge has a small ir-

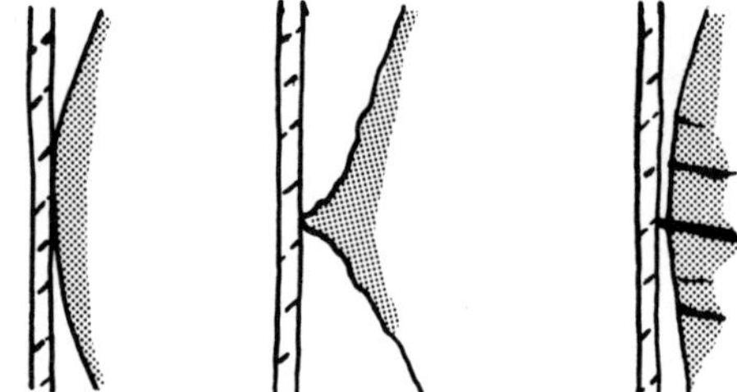

FIGURE 50: A rounded bulge (left), a sharp lip (centre), and a rounded bulge with a small irregularity — a mineral vein in this case (right).

regularity which is only obvious on close inspection (Figure 50).

The Bend in the Rope. The situation where the rope forms a sharp angle over a lip is more dangerous than that where it only touches (Figure 51). The abrupt edge at the top of many pitches is a very dangerous point. The smaller the radius of the bend, the greater will be the abrasion risk.

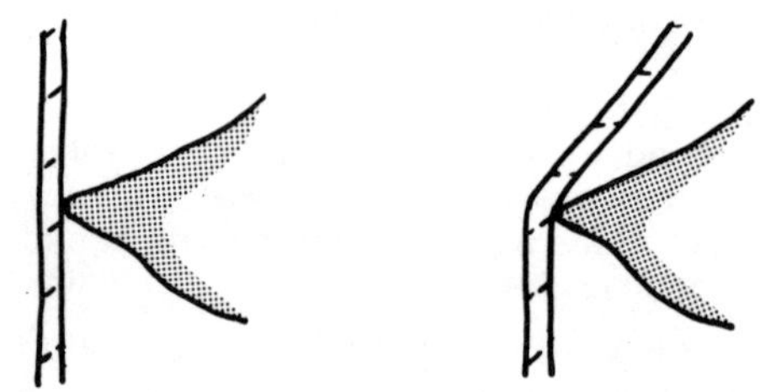

FIGURE 51: Glancing rub (left), and sharp angle bend (right).

Length of the Pitch. The amount of abrasion caused by any rub point will be greater on a long pitch simply because of the greater amount of abseiling and prusiking involved. On a short pitch (10m or under), the abrasion risk is rarely substantial, although care is still required. On pitches longer than about 25m, abrasion risk must be seriously considered.

The Position of the Rub Point on the Pitch. Eavis' (1974) tests on ropes strongly suggest that the amount of abrasion at any rub point depends on the length of each rope bounce at that point. The greater the bounce length, the greater the danger of abrasion. In turn, bounce length depends on the position of the rub point on the pitch. The further from the anchor a rub point is, the longer will be the bounce. The net effect is that (all else being equal), rub points become more serious further down, until they become so close to the pitch bottom that relatively little abseiling and prusiking is done below them. The general picture is shown in Figure 52.

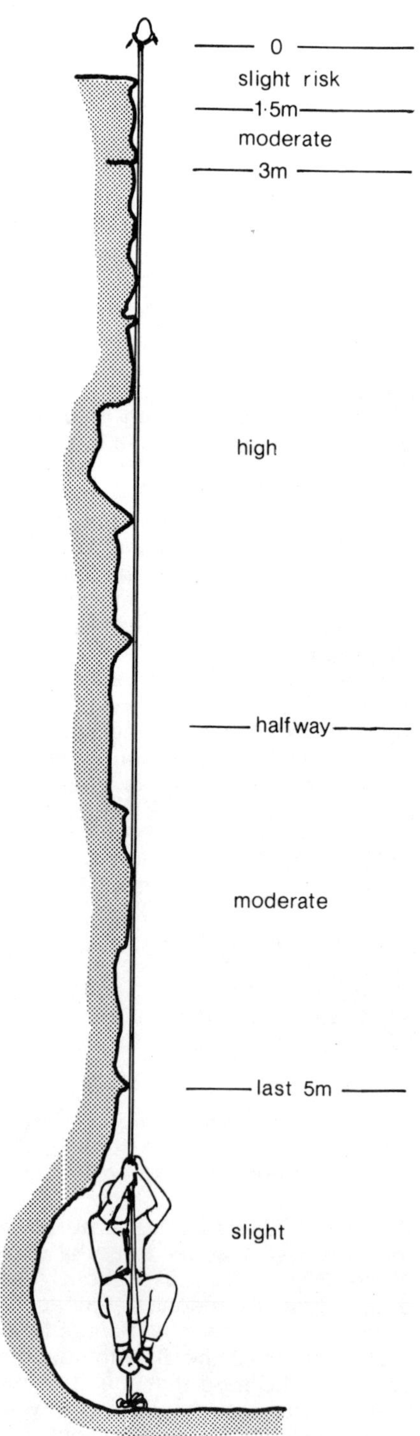

FIGURE 52: The way in which abrasion risk at a rubpoint depends on the position of the rub point on the pitch.

The Number of Rub Points on a Pitch. A rub point nearly always poses less risk if there are a number of other rub points below it. The reason is that friction at the lower rub points takes some of the bounce out of the rope. As a result, if the rope is rigged against a wall where there are many rub points, all but the worst can be ignored. The most dangerous situation arises where a rub point has a long free hang below it.

Rub Points on Wet Pitches. Where a rub point is actually in a stream, the action of the water alone can cause serious abrasion by swirling the rope back and forth across the rub point. For this reason, ropes should not be left rigged on wet pitches (Julia James, pers. comm.). Users of nylon ropes should take particular note, because nylon's abrasion resistance is much reduced by wetting (page 4).

Human Factors. Human factors also play a large part in determining the chances of serious abrasion at any rub point. The choice of rope used by a caving party, the number of people in the party, and their individual styles of abseiling and prusiking are all critical. In particular, the importance of abseiling and prusiking in a smooth, steady fashion cannot be overemphasized.

Having said all this, there is still no easy formula for recognizing rock lips or edges which could become significant rub points. The factors just presented should be borne in mind but there is still a large element of experience involved. Even very experienced vertical cavers have misjudged the effects of a rub point so that it is wise to err well on the side of safety. If this is done, a long life will be assured for both the rope and its user.

Consideration can now be given to the task of adequately protecting ropes from those lips and edges which are considered serious. The first line of protection is to choose a primary anchor point which hangs the rope in a safe looking position. Any significant rub points which still occur can then be padded with cloth mats or special rope protectors (page 39). One's judgment of a "safe looking position" may be later proven wrong when the pitch is descended and lower rub points encountered, but at least initially one should consider those rub points which can be seen from the top. Usually, natural anchors, chocks or pitons will provide a suitable anchor point, but sometimes the use of bolts will be justified to achieve a good hang.

The ideal anchor point will provide a free hang with convenient access for getting on or off the rope. Sometimes a little inventiveness is called for, as in the example shown in Figure 53. Here a free hang has been found by using two anchors on opposite sides of a shaft. Note that the angle between the legs is less than 120° (page 16).

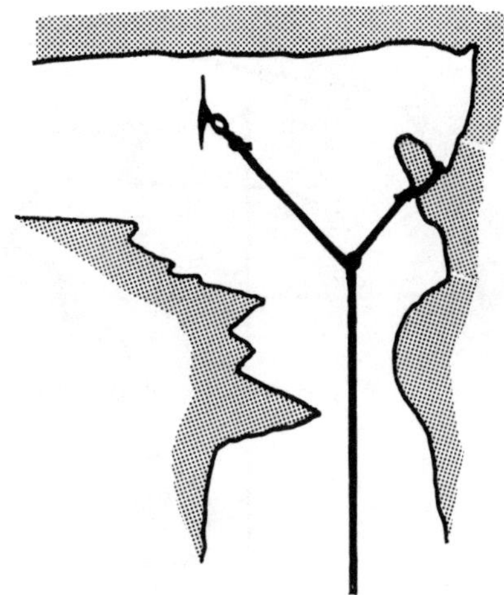

FIGURE 53: A free hang produced by two anchors. Neither anchor would have sufficed on its own.

If it is not possible to rig the pitch as a free hang then, as is clear from the earlier discussion of abrasion risk, the nearest to a free hang is not necessarily the best alternative. For example, two rub points close to the rope anchor would often pose less risk than one rub point 10m below it. If the shaft edge forms the rub point then it is best to anchor close to the edge to avoid a sharp bend in the rope and also reduce bounce length (Figure 54). If it is difficult to determine whether a lip well down the shaft is likely to become a rub point, one could try dropping a rock from the proposed anchor point to see if it hits the lip.

It may be thought worth the time and effort to traverse out above the pitch to get a free hang. If this is done, it is usually necessary to rig a

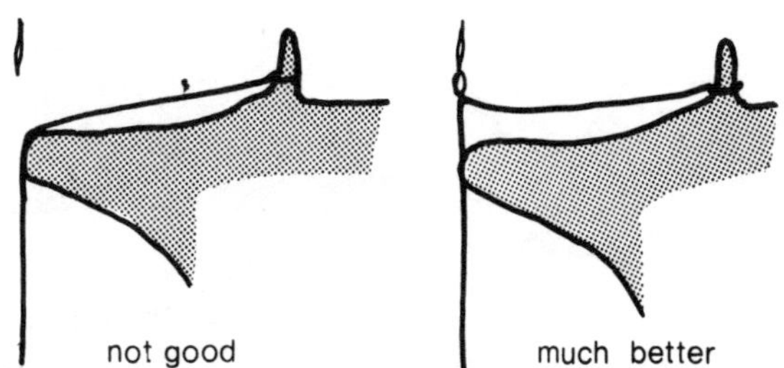

FIGURE 54: If the shaft edge forms a rub point, then it is best to anchor close to the edge to avoid a sharp bend in the rope and reduce the bounce length.

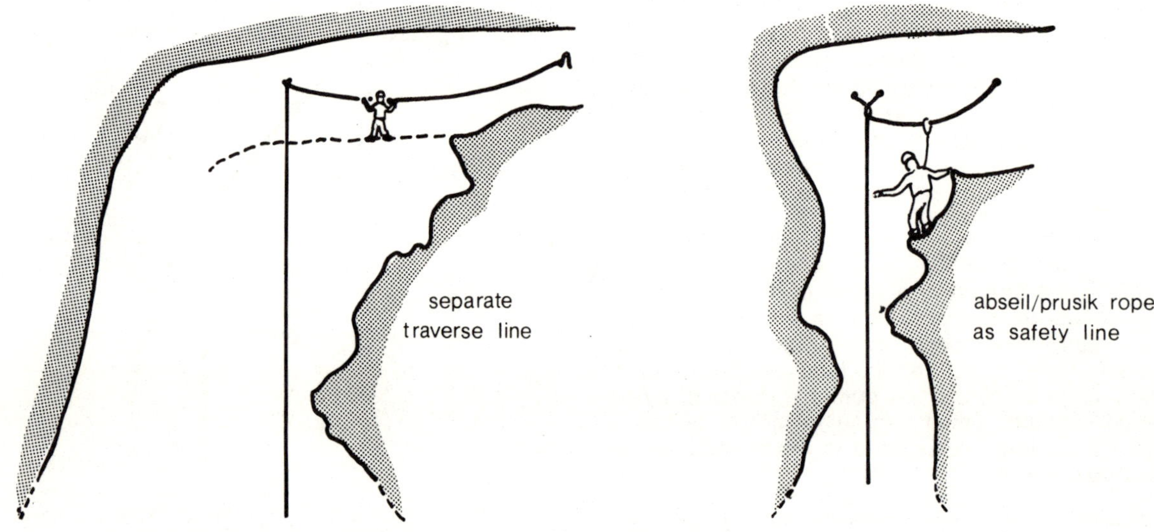

FIGURE 55: Traversing to rig the rope free.

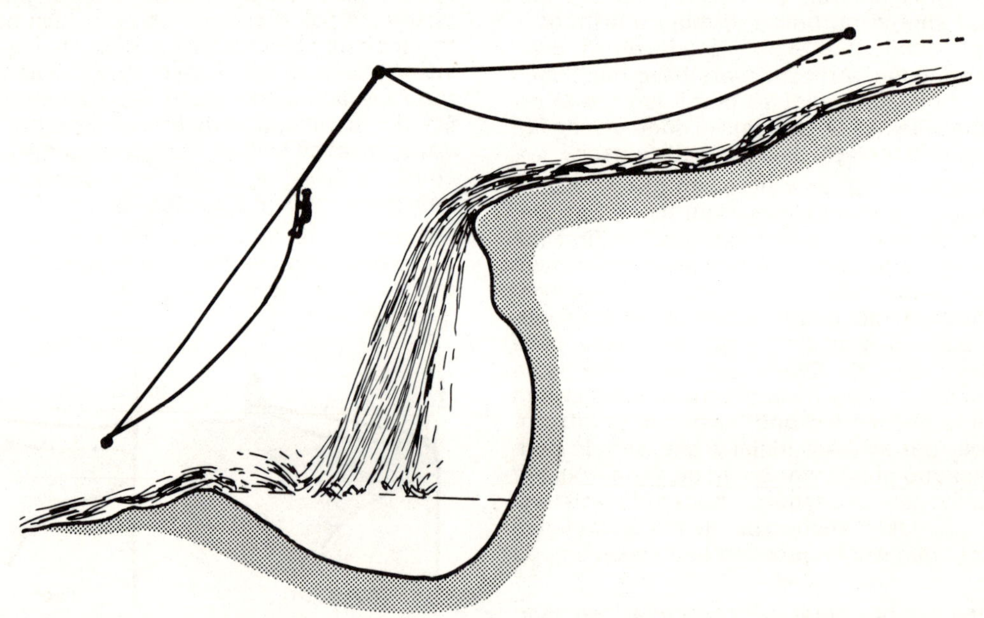

FIGURE 56: Rigging to avoid a waterfall. In this case two ropes have been rigged on each segment. This would not often be necessary.

separate traverse line. A traverse line should ideally be of dynamic rope tied slightly slack so that it does not impede traversing and will hold any fall which might occur. A fall onto a tight traverse rope could cause a tension in the rope greater than the applied force of the fall (page 16). If all that is required to reach the rope for clipping on is a long arm-stretch then the end of the abseil/prusik rope can be used as a safety line by anchoring it well away from the lip. These arrangements are illustrated in Figure 55.

WATERFALLS

Waterfalls are another major challenge to rigging technique. With judgment, ropes can be rigged directly through some waterfalls, but more often it is best to avoid them entirely. To cavers accustomed to climbing ladders under torrents of water, the idea of rigging a rope clear could seem rather unsporting. It must be realised, however, that waterfalls do create special dangers for the use of SRT. The main worry is that it is not easy to reverse an abseil or prusik if the going becomes difficult. Once committed to an abseil or prusik in a heavy waterfall, there may be little choice but to continue, knowing full well that to do so could prove fatal. In contrast, a ladder climber in trouble can back off without hesitation and even use the assistance of a lifeline. A second danger for SRT is that adequate rope padding is an almost impossible task on a waterfall pitch. A critical rub point may go unnoticed.

If waterfalls are to be avoided, then potential waterfalls should be also. Pitches in stream caves should be rigged with the possibilities of flooding kept firmly in mind.

After checking for any dry bypasses, the usual method of tackling waterfall drops is to traverse over the head of the waterfall and fix the primary anchor in a position which will hang the rope clear of the water, at least as far as can be seen. Similar traverses may be performed to protect a rope from abrasion, but seldom with the same sense of necessity. On an extremely wet pitch, there may be no choice. As a result, a traverse using advanced rock climbing techniques could be required. To attempt this one should have rock climbing experience and use a dynamic climbing rope. The actual techniques are beyond the scope of this book, but many beginner courses and books are available on rock climbing.

What does concern vertical cavers is the way in which such a traverse may be rigged for other members of the caving party (Figure 56). If it is not possible for them to follow with the aid of a handline, then one technique is to fix a rope on the traverse (with sufficient slack to avoid excessive rope tension, page 16), then rig another rope below this with about 4m or 5m more slack. An abseil/prusik system for crossing such an obstacle is presented in Chapter 7. It will also have use for traverses in general.

If spray from the waterfall is still a problem, or if the pitch lands in a deep pool, the first man down can draw the rope clear and anchor it (Figure 56). A diagonal pitch will result and, if necessary, this can also be ascended and descended by rigging a second slack rope and using the specialised abseil/prusik system.

LOOSE ROCKPILES

The only sane approach to loose rockpiles on pitches is to avoid them entirely. These can be treated in much the same way as just described for waterfalls.

SETTING UP THE ROPE

Having constructed a suitable anchor point with safe access and tied on the abseil/prusik rope (if it is not already part of the anchor) the stage is nearly set for throwing or lowering the rope down the drop. The last precautions are to clear the area around the edge of loose rock and tie a large stopper knot in the end of the rope. The rope can then be thrown or lowered down. Throwing is easier and reduces the chance that the rope will snag. The best approach is to pile the rope neatly and throw over a coil of 10m or so. The rest will rapidly follow. However, for pitches over about 100m, the shock loading produced as the last rope goes over could be quite substantial, and lowering would be preferred. One should be clipped into the anchor point during all these operations.

Throwing or lowering will be satisfactory for all pitches excepting those with scree piles or heavy bush on lower edges. If all the rope is sent down, it may need to be entirely taken up onto such a ledge to clear away scree or untangle the rope from branches or vines. (Rocks should never be thrown down a drop rigged with a rope.) A useful procedure is for the first man down to carry the rope in a pack below his waist and let it run out by itself as he descends. Any rock clearing can then be done with impunity and no tangles will occur.

RIGGING NEEDS BELOW THE PRIMARY ANCHOR

All of the above discussion has applied to the positioning of a primary anchor point to safely guide the rope past obstacles which can be seen from the pitch top. Rigging techniques do not end there. Often the obstacles cannot be entirely handled by primary anchor selection, or originally unseen difficulties with rope abrasion, waterfalls or loose rockpiles are met lower down. Any of these situations may require the use of lower anchor points. In such cases, the abseil/prusik rope itself acts as a safety backup for the lower anchor point. With this done, good single anchors may be used. Following are some specific rigging techniques.

STAIRCASE PITCHES

A frequent situation in caving is where drops occur one after the other with only short ledges in between. The whole series can be viewed as one big drop with a staircase profile. It is nearly always wise to rig such drops by anchoring on each ledge and connecting all the ropes, as in Figure 57. Just enough slack should be left between anchor points to make changeovers at them easy, keeping in mind that the rope is providing a safety backup for each anchor point below the first and that its effectiveness is reduced by slack. The exact amount of slack required will vary depending on the situation, but will usually be between 1 and 2m.

This method has two advantages over the alternative of rigging the series as one pitch. Firstly, each ledge is prevented from forming a serious rub point, and, secondly, the movement of the whole party is speeded up because several cavers can climb at once, one to each drop.

RUB POINTS ON A PITCHFACE

Even with the most careful attention to the placement of the primary anchor, it is still possible to come upon rub points on the rock face well down a pitch. Minor rub points can be padded with a rope protector (page 40), but serious ones require the security of a rigging technique. A rigging technique is more secure than padding in this situation because side-ways or vertical movements in the rope could move the pad away from its protective position. There are two techniques:

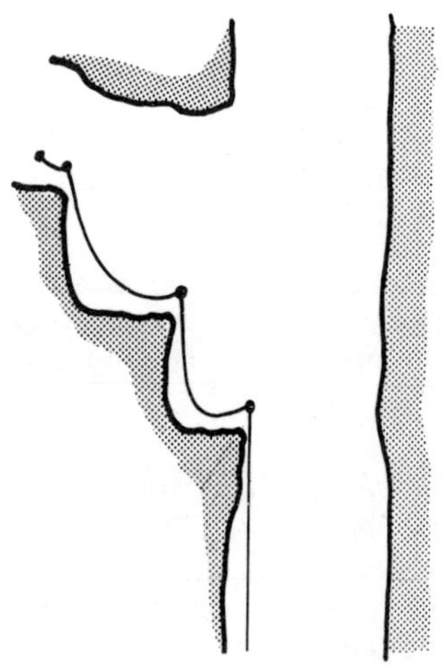

FIGURE 57: Rigging staircase pitches.

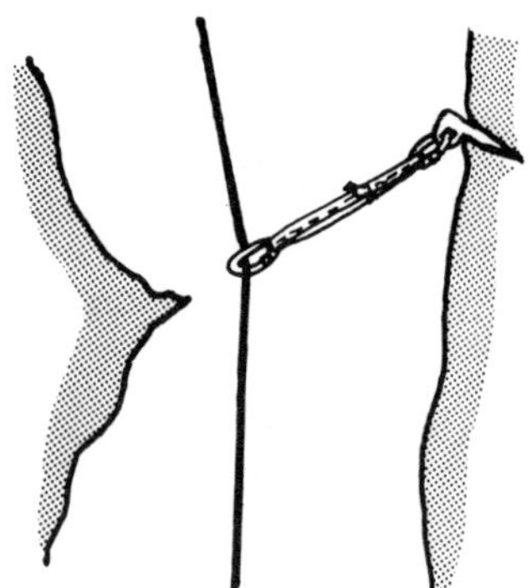

FIGURE 58: Redirecting the rope away from a rub point.

The first is to redirect the rope away from the rub point by constructing an anchor near the rub point and attaching a sling between the anchor and the rope (Figure 58). This is not often possible but it is a very effective technique where it can be used. The anchor can be positioned either on the opposite side of a narrow shaft or on a wall. To pass the redirecting sling and carabiner, it is necessary to release the tension on the sling, unclip the carabiner from the rope, then move down and reclip the carabiner. If the deflection is very large, it can involve some effort but for a small deflection it is an easy task.

The second approach is to reanchor the rope below the rub point, as in Figure 59. When reanchoring, a metre or so of slack should be allowed to enable easy passing of the anchor while abseiling or prusiking. Practice in passing these obstacles must be obtained before using the method underground. Reachoring has the added advantage of enabling two more people to climb the shaft simultaneously.

If there is more than one rub point at the problem spot, then the new anchor must be positioned below the lowest rub point. Otherwise, this rub point will still present a danger on the bottom pitch (Figure 59).

WATERFALLS

A waterfall which has been initially avoided by traversing will quite possibly flow back onto the

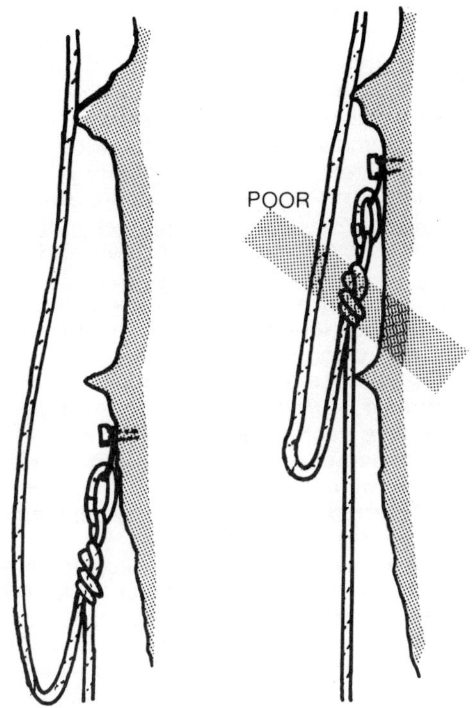

FIGURE 59: Reanchoring the rope. In this case there are two rub points and the anchor is sensibly chosen below the lowest one.

line of the pitch lower down. The problem must then be tackled anew, but it will be easier this time. The person rigging can now perform a pendulum and also possibly a tension traverse to reach another anchor point (Figure 60), but he must first ensure that the rope will not be rubbed against sharp edges by the swinging motion. The procedure is to stop above the water, lock the abseil device, pull up any rope hanging below, and then pendulum as far as is easily possible in the hope of reaching an anchor. (If the excess rope is not pulled up, it will damp the pendulum motion.) Should the distance gained be insufficient, further progress can sometimes be made by grabbing a handhold at the end of the pendulum and pulling across the wall on other handholds. Simultaneously, some rope can be slipped through the abseil device to control the direction of movement. This so called tension traverse requires considerable confidence and experience but can be very useful. Even further distance could be gained with artificial climbing techniques. The main point to watch is that if a fall occurs, one does not swing back under the waterfall, into an opposite wall, or into a deep pool.

LOOSE ROCKPILES

The approach taken with waterfalls may be also applied to loose rockpiles which are met below a pitch top.

PADDING

After rigging the rope, rope pads are used to prevent abrasion at those rub points which still do occur. There are two classes of pads; mats, which cover a rub point and leave the rope free, and protectors, which fit onto the rope on the endangered section.

MATS

Mats are strips of material which are tied in place with cords (Figure 61). The material should be about 0.5m wide to allow for sideways movement of the rope, and it is advisable to have a

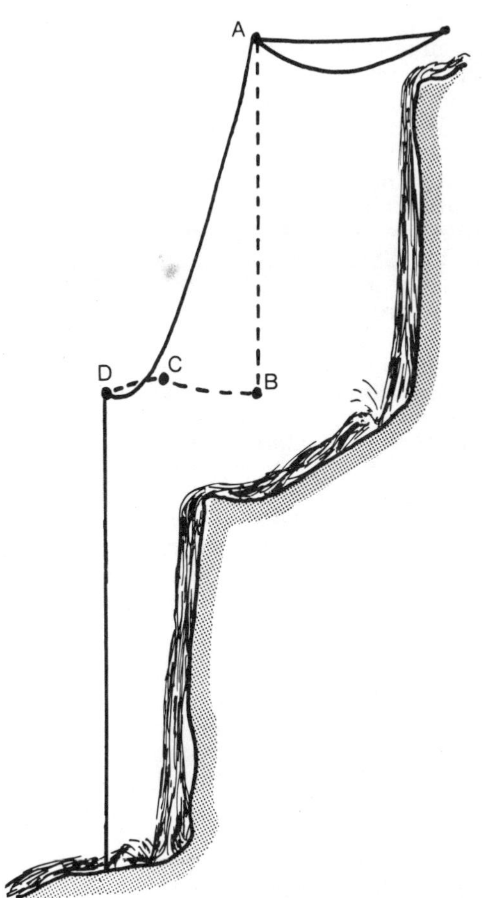

FIGURE 60: Rigging to avoid a second waterfall met below the pitch top. The rigging method was to abseil from A to B, pendulum from B to C, then tension traverse from C to D.

FIGURE 61: A mat.

range of lengths upwards of 0.5m. Mats are most useful for shaft lips where they can be easily attached to the rope anchor or even to the rope itself (Figure 61). Used in this position, they will cause no hinderance to the party. In contrast, protectors need to be removed and replaced each time a caver passes them.

If the rub point to be covered is some distance down the pitch, then the mat can be tied off to a suitable anchor or, failing that, onto the rope itself. A problem with this usage is that rope movements during an ascent or descent can either flip the rope off the mat so that the rope rubs elsewhere, or turn the mat over so that the rope runs underneath it, directly on the rock. Smith (1974b) recommends fixing extra cords to the sides of the mat so that it may be tied around the rope but this system suffers the disadvantage that each member of the party must untie and retie these cords as he passes. This is time consuming and often awkward. If there is a likelihood that the rope will work off the mat, it is better to consider a protector.

The mat itself rarely suffers much wear because it is stationary against the rock. Accordingly, light canvas should prove adequate for minor rub points, heavier canvas for serious rub points and occasionally carpet for critical cases such as the edge of a long free drop. The material should be heat resistant since heat is produced by the rubbing action. The actual amount of heat has never been measured, but nylon and Terylene seem to perform safely. Tackle bags used for transporting ropes in caves make quite effective mats for pitch lips and are in an appropriate position for their normal use when it comes to derigging the cave.

PROTECTORS

There are several types of protectors. Jerry protectors (developed by two Australian cavers) are generally the best pads for handling rub points below a pitch top. They are usually made from strips of tough canvas about 120mm wide and up to 600mm long fastened into a cylinder with heavy duty Velcro strip. Longer lengths are awkward to handle and rub points requiring such lengths can be covered by tying two or more protectors together. The construction and use of these pads is shown in Figure 62. It is important to have the Velcro the full length of the protector, and not skimp by using short Velcro tabs or by substituting press studs. The added security and ease of use is worth the small extra expense.

The Velcro fastening is durable and will not become muddied, provided that the pads are carried through the cave mated. The pads can easily be carried while on a pitch by clipping them to a carabiner on the waist harness.

To pass a Jerry protector, the Velcro is unmated by running a thumb up it. Usually the knot is untied as well but it can be passed when prusiking by removing the ascenders from the rope. This is useful if there is concern for retaining the protector's position accurately. However, the whole protector has to be removed when abseiling.

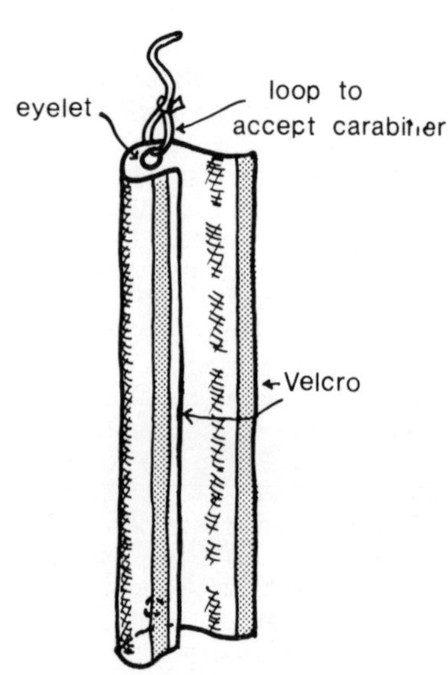

FIGURE 62: The Jerry protector. The protector is tied to the rope with two or three half hitches.

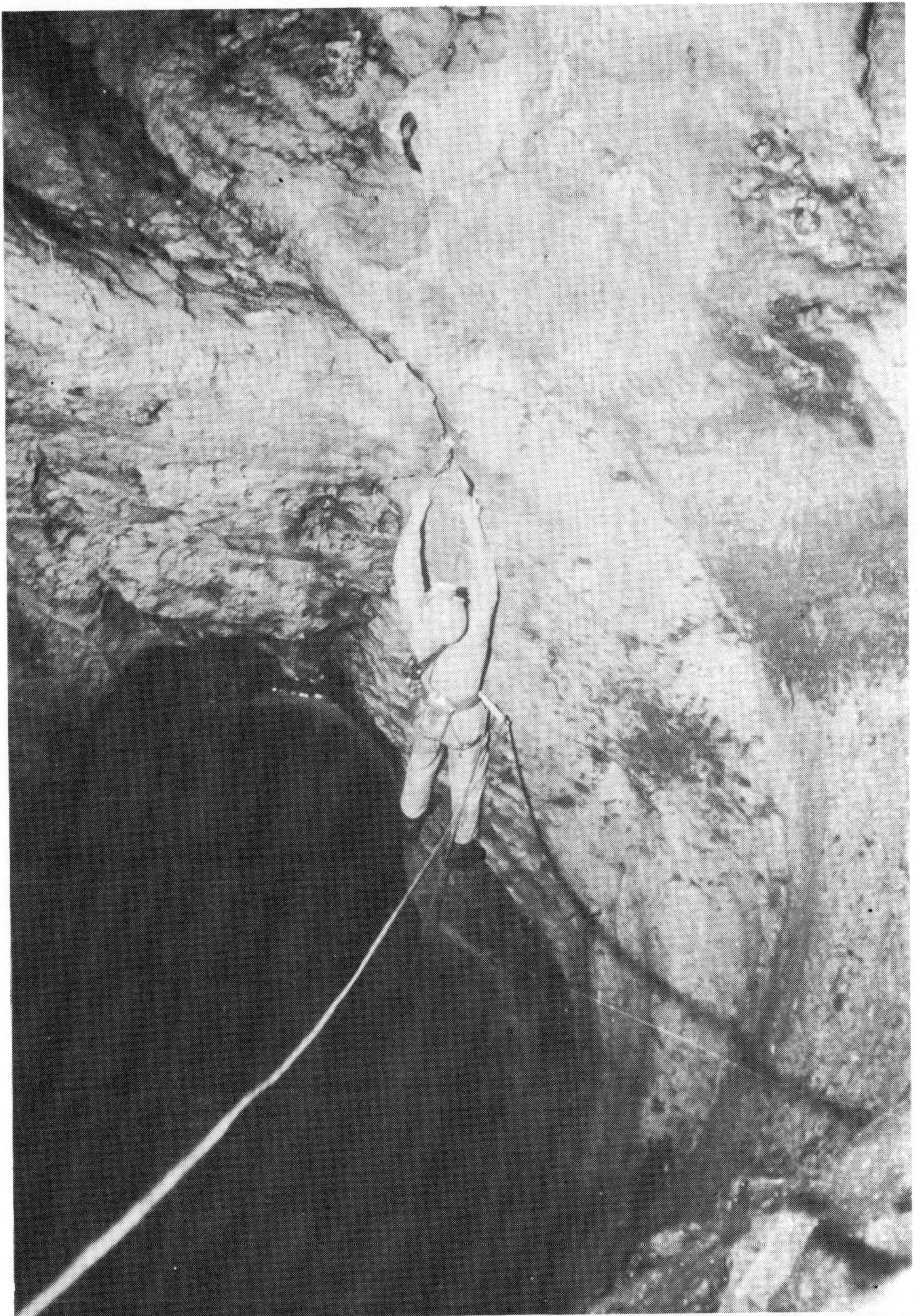

Julia James

A caver crosses a deep pothole in Kanada Atea, a vast river cave in Papua New Guinea. An abseil and a tension traverse took him to his present stance, from where a short climbing move enabled him to gain the passage at top left. A chock is being placed for aid.

Andrew Pavey.

A Jerry protector in use on a 30m pitch in Antro del Corchia, Apuanian Alps, Italy.

Hose protectors are lengths of plastic hose with a lengthwise slit. They are cheaper than Jerry protectors and can be as effective on mild rub points. Lengths of 400mm to 600mm are best, fitted with cords to tie them to the rope and enable them to be carried on a carabiner when not in use.

Various hose thicknesses can be used (Figure 63). The most popular has been thin wall (about 2mm) hose, of an internal diameter to fit snugly on the rope. The hose has a slit lengthwise with a half spiral at each end to stop the hose working off the rope. When fitting the hose to the rope, each end is twisted in the direction of the half spiral to secure the hose and the slit is positioned so that it faces away from the rub point.

Thicker hose (wall thickness of 4mm) is usually stiffer and harder to handle but can be more secure. The most flexible variety is chosen and even so it may be necessary to slit the hose in a spiral for its whole length to improve flexibility. The internal diameter can be chosen to give a snug fit or to be looser on the rope.

The major problem with hose protectors is that the rope can work its way out, especially on rub points where the rope is sharply bent (Figure 51). The hose flattens out at the bend and then flips over, forcing the rope out of the slit and onto the rock. Another problem is that hose also has an inherent curve from its initial storage on a reel and this increases the risk of rope loss. This problem is worse in long hose protectors and in stiffer thick walled types.

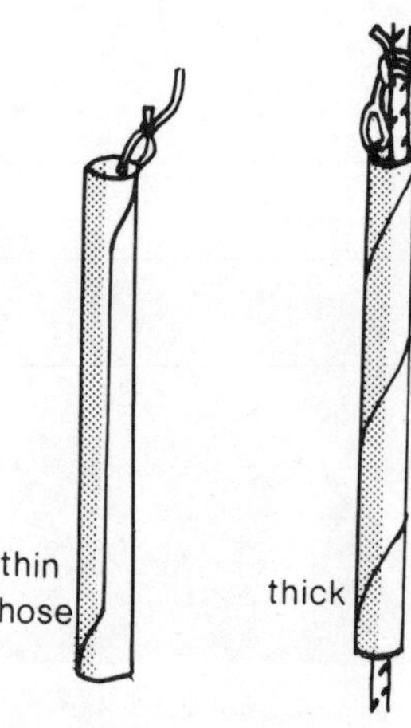

FIGURE 63: Hose protectors.

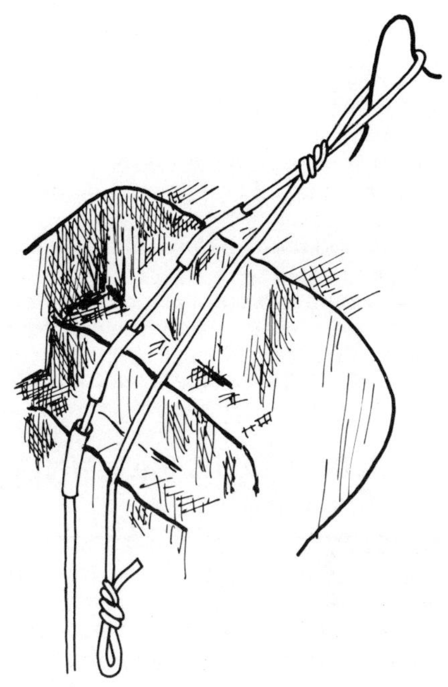

FIGURE 64: Use of a tail beside a heavily padded rope.

TOO MANY PADS?

The more pads that are fitted on each pitch the slower will be the party ascending or descending the pitch. The practical limit is three pads spaced fairly close together. Particularly on heavily used pitches, it is essential to find an alternative arrangement to save time and effort. It may be possible to use a long canvas or carpet mat but it would usually be better to rig for protection.

Another possibility if the rub points are near the top of a pitch is to rig a short rope alongside the heavily padded main rope (Figure 64). Cavers can then transfer between the tail (as the short rope is called) and the main rope, below the rub point.

The tail should have a knot in its end so that someone cannot inadvertently abseil off into space. The tail does not need padding itself due to its short length.

PLANNING PAD PLACEMENT

Planning pad placement by looking at the whole pitch can save effort. If the pitch is concave or vertical, then the caver's body will hold the rope away from the rock, and the only protector needed might be one on the top lip (Figure 65). If the pitch is convex, then a protector will almost always be necessary at the major rub points. If the pitch is too concave, then the rope may find a rub point on

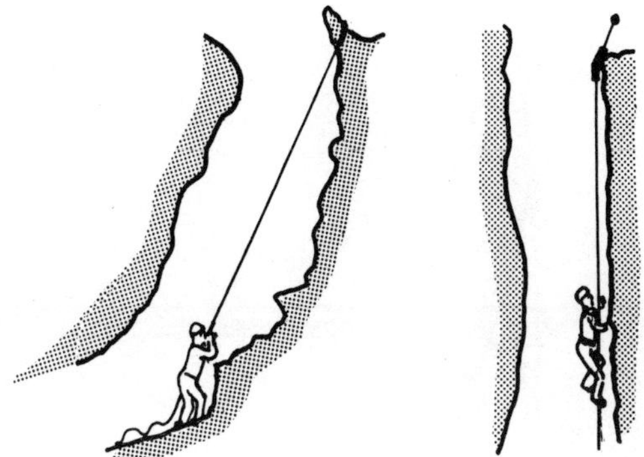

FIGURE 65: Concave and vertical pitches — few pads necessary.

the opposite side of the shaft (Figure 66). This type of rub point is often difficult to predict as it only becomes obvious after the caver has passed it on the descent. Cooperation between party members in watching for these rub points while others are on the pitch is essential.

It is possible that a rub point will be shielded by a larger, lower one (Figure 67). Here it is only necessary to protect against the lower rub point.

If it is uncertain whether a particular ledge or knob will become a rub point, it is advisable to flatten the body against the wall and watch where the rope lies. If a ledge can be seen to become a rub point when the caver is below it, then he should prusik back up and protect the rope.

SAFETY LIMITS TO THE USE OF PADS

A pad will be ineffective if it is placed or replaced at the incorrect position. The lower on a pitch that a rub point is encountered, the harder it is to judge the correct positioning of the pad, because of rope stretch and sideways rope movement. If the rub point is not severe, incorrect

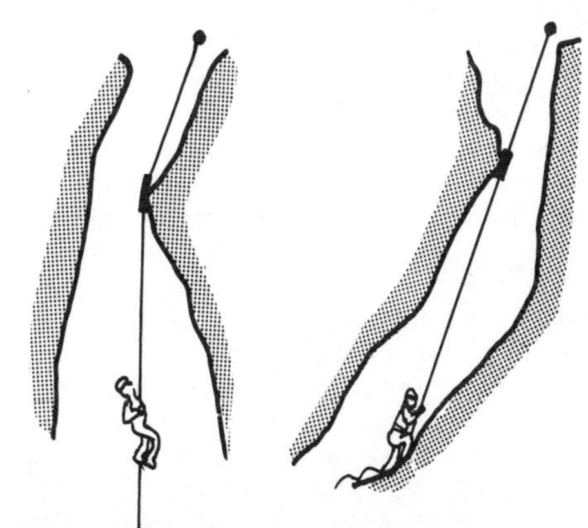

FIGURE 66: Pitches which are convex or too concave may need padding.

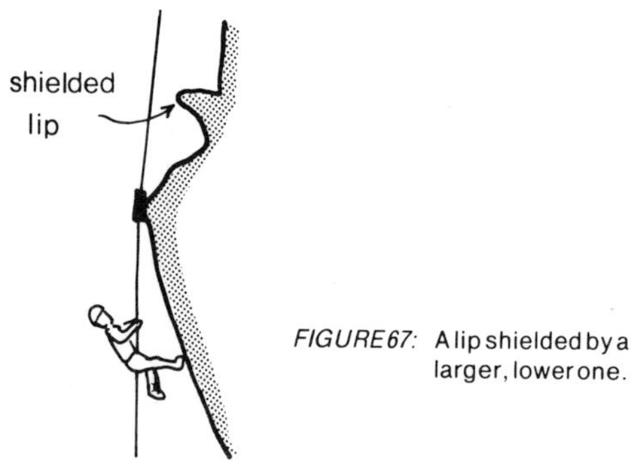

FIGURE 67: A lip shielded by a larger, lower one.

initial placement can be corrected by the next member of the party. However, in the case of a severe rub point, one descent or ascent could be sufficient to sever the rope, and rigging for protection is far safer than padding. Experience and common sense are the best guides. These situations generally only arise on pitches longer than 50m and here greater care is needed in all aspects of technique.

DIFFERENT PADDING NEEDS FOR ABSEILING AND PRUSIKING

Padding is more often necessary for prusiking than abseiling. With experience it is possible to abseil at a steady rate and cause virtually no bounce in the rope, but bounce is always present while prusiking.

Pads for abseiling should only be necessary when inexperienced cavers or large numbers of cavers are likely to use the rope, when sharp rub points are encountered, when there is grit or mud near the pitch top, or on long pitches. A pad at the top of the pitch is usually sufficient and it should be a canvas or carpet mat type for ease of passing.

Pads for prusiking are usually placed on the descent. The actual procedure depends on the pitch. The simple case is where it is possible to see the whole pitch from the top, or where the pitch is well known. The last man down fixes all the pads for prusiking.

The procedure is more complicated if it is not possible to see the whole length of the pitch and its nature or length is unknown. Here, the first caver to descend must place sufficient padding to enable a return should the rope not reach the bottom (or a convenient ledge) or, if some other hazard is encountered. If all is well, then the second caver to descend can remove any pads not needed for the descent and the last caver can fix all additional pads. The second last caver to descend should make note of all possible rub points and communicate with the last one down so that all points are covered.

When the time comes to ascend the pitch, the first one up should carry extra pads in case a significant rub point has been missed during the descent. If serious abrasion has already occurred at the rub point, it may be necessary to rig another rope or knot the one that is there. In less severe cases, the first man can raise or lower the rope so that the abraded section is higher or lower than the rub point, and then abseil back down to the rub point and place a pad.

If a troublesome rub point is located at or near a ledge, it can be a wise precaution for the first or second caver up the pitch to stop on the ledge and watch the pad whilst the rest of the party ascend the pitch.

MISCELLANEOUS RIGGING TECHNIQUES

WIRE LADDERS

The SRT caver should not consider wire ladders obsolete. In some situations they are far superior to ropes. Perhaps the main use is for short pitches which are so isolated from other pitches in the cave that it is hardly worthwhile for each caver to rig his abseil/prusik equipment. For essentially horizontal caves which only contain a few short pitches, the same applies.

Ladders may also be favoured for muddy pitches and short waterfall drops. Mud is damaging to SRT equipment and removes most of the pleasure from rope work. Short waterfalls for which a wet rigging is unavoidable may be easier and safer on ladders (if it is safe to descend them at all). A normal ladder lifeline can be used or a single rope can be rigged beside the ladder for abseiling, and used for self-lifelining on the climb

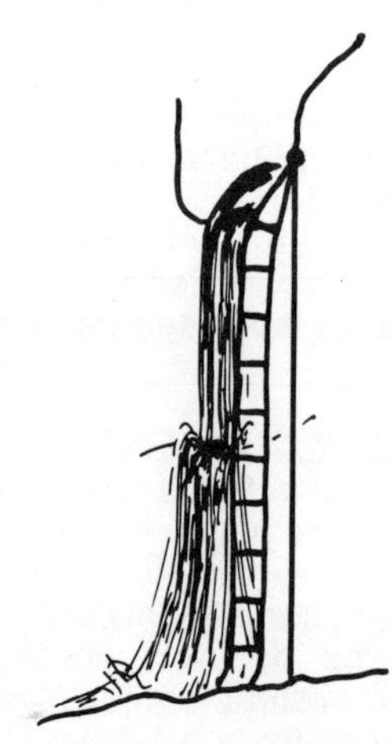

FIGURE 68: A ladder and single rope rigged on a short waterfall pitch.

FIGURE 69: Self-lifelining a ladder climb. (After Dobrilla and Marbach.)

(Figure 68). To self-lifeline, the rope is run through a ascender mounted on the chest (page 92) or an ascender on the hip in such a way that the ascender would not be shock loaded in the event of a fall (Figure 69).

For a complete treatment on wire ladders, see Baguley and Brandon (1969), Eyre (1969) and Dobrilla and Marbach (1973).

CLIMBING

Cavers are sometimes faced with the problem of climbing up a shaft, rift or wall in hope of finding high level passage. While general rock climbing techniques will not be treated in this book, a brief mention will be made of some climbing methods which may be found useful and were developed especially for caving.

The classic technique is to use a scaling pole, or maypole (Figure 70). Scaling poles have been in use since the 1930's and have led to some

FIGURE 70: A scaling pole erected against a cave wall and secured by guy lines.

spectacular discoveries. The fascinating explorations in the Trou de Glaz in France centred around their use. Pitch after pitch was forced upwards to find a high entrance to this systen and, in 1947, set a world record depth of 658m (Chevalier 1948).

In its basic form, a scaling pole is composed of about six pipe segments about 1.5m long which are carried underground and coupled together at the base of the climb. Aluminium scaffolding pipe with an outside diameter of about 50mm is suitable. A coupling method is shown in Figure 71, which has been used with good success by the Sydney Speleological Society. Others are discussed by Hensler (1969) and Haarr (1962 and 1968). A length of about 9m (6 x 1.5m) is the limit for a single pole. Longer ones require stays to lend rigidity (Hensler 1969). A bolt and hanger can be attached to the end of the pole for connecting the rope (or ladder and lifeline).

In use, the scaling pole is raised against the cave wall with the base firmly supported and the top secured by guylines (Figure 70). The top of the

FIGURE 71: A method of coupling scaling pole segments. Two angle brackets are clamped to the join with four bolts.

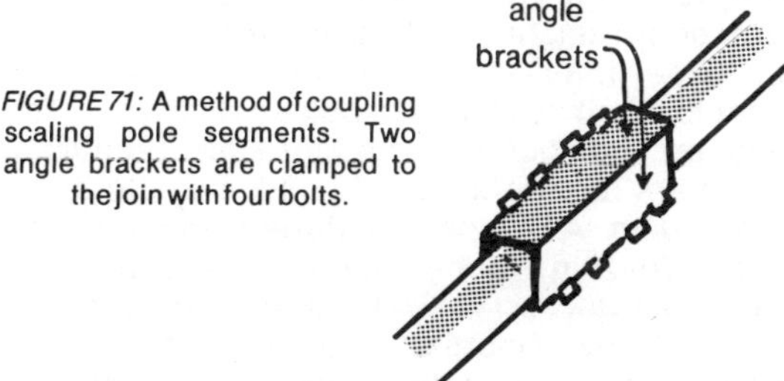

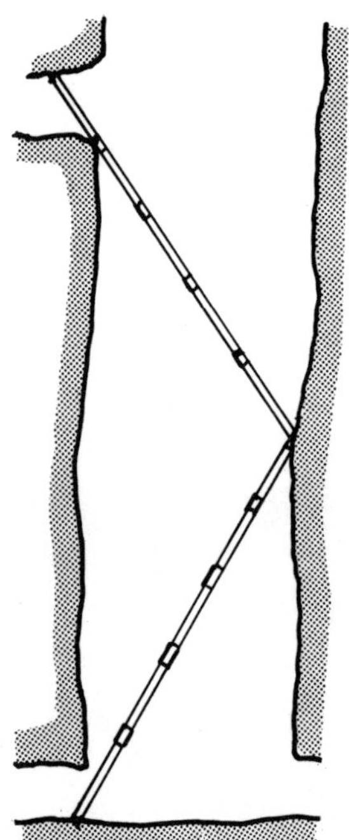

FIGURE 72: Climbing a shaft in successive steps.

pole should preferably protrude into the passage it is hoped to reach. A caver (preferably a light one) can then easily climb the rope to gain entry. If others are to follow, the rope should be anchored in the passage and the pole taken down.

A climb over 9m in height can also be scaled if it is in a narrow shaft or rift. Height is gained in successive steps by crossing back and forth between the walls (Figure 72). A very secure anchor must obviously be provided at each step, and a pulley system will probably be required for raising the pole each time.

The use of free or artificial climbing techniques is an alternative to erecting a scaling pole. It is a more widely applicable approach if one has the necessary skill and equipment (low stretch abseil/prusik ropes are certainly inadequate). French cavers seem to have been particularly involved in artificial climbing underground, and several special climbing platforms have been invented by them. Using one of these platforms, it is possible for a climber to comfortably place bolts about body height apart, and other anchors at even larger intervals. For example, a caver 1.8m tall could climb by placing a bolt about every 1.8m. Using the traditional mountaineering technique with etriers (eg, Robbins 1973), 1.3m would be an average gain. A compact platform is marketed by Fernand Petzl in France (Figure 73), based on the design of Rocourt (1974). Other designs are presented by Dobrilla and Marbach (1973), Dressler and Chazalet (1966), and Courbis (1976).

THROUGH TRIPS

Some of the most enjoyable vertical caving trips are "through trips" from one entrance to another. The usual approach is to start at the upper entrance and descend to the lower by abseiling each drop on a doubled rope and retrieving the rope each time by pulling one end. The length of the rope required for the whole trip will then only be equal to twice the length of the longest pitch, plus a little extra. The French word "rappel" meaning "retrieve" is given to this technique, although in English speaking countries the word has now almost lost its original meaning and has come to refer to abseiling in general.

Anchors for double roping need to be chosen and prepared in a way that allows the rope to pull freely. Sometimes a rounded natural anchor on the edge of a drop can be used directly, but more often a sling must be fixed to an anchor and left behind. Slings left by other parties can be included in the anchor as a safety backup, but should never be used alone. The main reason is that the previous party may have partially melted (weld abrasion, page 48) the rope sling during their own pull down (Smutek 1972). Even with a sling, the rope should not be sharply angled over the edge of the drop. If two ropes have been tied together to make the descent, then the knot

FIGURE 73: Climbing platform by Petzl. From Petzl brochure.

should be positioned so that it will pull down without jamming and the party must remember to pull the correct rope (ie, the one with the knot below the anchor). Twisting between the two ropes must also be avoided, particularly between the anchor point and the edge of the drop. The final test for the rigging is for someone at the bottom of the pitch to pull the rope and check that it runs before the last person descends. If the rope does not run, the rigging is then improved and retested. It is a bad mistake for all members of a party to abseil down without performing this test.

Despite all care, ropes do sometimes jam. An essential precaution is to carry prusik equipment. One half of the rope can then be anchored (perhaps to a caver) and someone can prusik up the other half and free the rope. That is, if both ends are still on the ground. Sometimes the rope will jam after some of it has already been pulled through. The group may then be left with one end on the ground and the other dangling some distance above. It will be risky to climb the rope, since it may suddenly give. In any particular instance, this risk will have to be weighed against the alternative of waiting for a rescue.

French cavers sometimes use a special device to release their ropes. The Shunt, described on page 69 in a different context, is one example. The method works by clipping one of these devices to the anchor point and hanging a single abseil rope and a trip cord from the device. After everyone has descended, a jerk on the trip cord causes the whole system, device included, to drop down the pitch. The method appears to have a good safety record in France, but it still seems risky. Two obvious drawbacks are that the trip cord could possibly be tripped accidently while someone is on the rope, and that the system could snag during its fall.

A scaling pole being manoeuvred into a high level lead in Odyssey Cave, Bungonia, NSW, Australia.

Harold Coleman

5: HARNESSES, CARABINERS AND HELMETS

Before one can learn to abseil or prusik, some basic items of personal equipment are needed. This chapter discusses harnesses, carabiners and helmets, while assuming a knowledge of clothing, footwear and lights.

HARNESSES

Seat and chest harnesses are worn to provide a safe, comfortable means of attachment for abseil and prusik equipment. Basic harness designs and construction method are presented here. Some specialised harnesses which have been developed to suit a particular prusik system are described in Chapter 7.

Tape

For harness construction, tape (also called webbing) is preferred over cord because of its comfort. Tape is made from nylon or Terylene and is available in a variety of types and widths from caving, climbing and army surplus shops. The Terylene tape is generally less stretchy than the nylon. If an acid or alkaline battery is worn on the waist, then the fibre with the appropriate chemical resistance should be chosen. Nylon harnesses run a risk of acid damage if a lead-acid battery is worn and Terylene harnesses may be damaged by the caustic soda in NiFe cells. The two basic types of tape are tubular tape and flat tape. Tubular tape is always flexible while flat tape is available in grades from flexible to stiff. A flat tape of medium flexibility is best for most harness purposes since it will be stiff enough not to twist or roll yet will be flexible enough to have good handling qualities. To ensure good comfort, 50mm is the best width for load bearing straps while connecting straps can be made from 12mm or 25mm tape.

Tape requires the same diligent care that is given to nylon or Terylene ropes. Harnesses should be carried in packs where possible and washed when dirty. They will need to be retired quite frequently since the large surface area of tape makes it particularly prone to abrasion and deterioration due to sunlight. There are two particular hazards for which to watch in the use of tape. One is any wear on the edge of the tape. Once this occurs, the harness should be immediately retired or repaired, since, otherwise, it will probably rip through after just a few more uses. Some cavers wear their harnesses under their overalls (coveralls) to give some protection from abrasion. This is a good idea for tight or dirty caves. The second hazard is weld abrasion caused by running a taut rope over part of the harness for a period of time, as may occur while abseiling. Weld abrasion is the name given to partial melting of the tape caused by frictional heat produced by the rubbing. In mild cases it appears as a brown discolouration. In severe cases the tape will partially or wholly wear through.

Harnesses can be bought or home-made. Commercial harnesses are normally sewn and buckled. They are very reliable when properly cared for. To construct a harness at home, joins must be made by sewing, knotting or buckling the tape. Most people use sewn joins where possible and have knots or buckles for adjustment. The sewing can be done on a home machine or by a bootmaker, etc. It is unsatisfactory to rely on hand stitching, especially in critical positions. Destruction testing by Brew (1976) shows hand stitching to be very unreliable.

Home Sewn Joins

Sewing is the neatest, strongest and most secure way of joining tapes. Properly sewn joins involve virtually no strength loss in the tape. However, there are drawbacks. Sewn joins are not adjustable and require the use of a sewing machine. Also, Knutson (1975c) observes that the sewing thread will protrude slightly above the surface of the tape and be prone to abrasion. There have been no tests done on thread abrasion, but the author knows of one caver whose commercially sewn Whillans Sit Harness (page 52) failed at a sewn join while abseiling. The harness had seen several years' hard use. This incident emphasizes the need for frequent inspection of sewn joins and for making the joins fail-safe. Fail-safe, in this context, means that if the join breaks, another part of the harness will take up the load.

Magnussen (1972) performed a series of tests to determine the best stitch pattern and the amount of stitching required to make a safe join. He only tested joins in tubular tapes, but it seems unlikely that flat tapes would produce significantly different results. The best pattern proved to be a series of parallel longitudinal runs (Figure 74). With a home sewing machine, using the thickest nylon or Terylene thread the machine can take, twelve runs with a stitch length of about 2mm and a tape overlap of about 75mm should be sufficient. Nylon thread should be used on nylon tape and Terylene

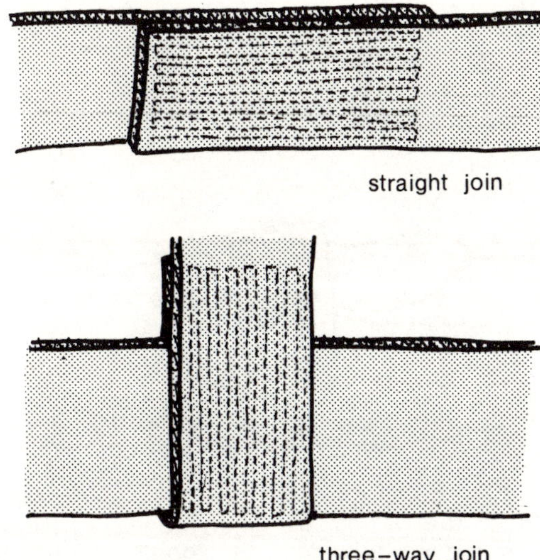

FIGURE 74: The best stitch pattern for joining tapes.

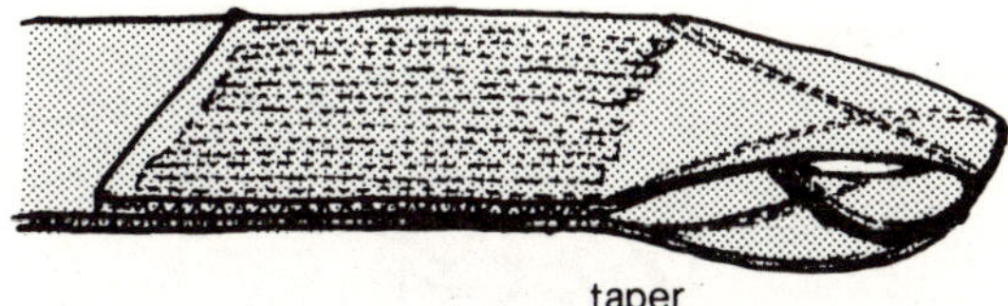

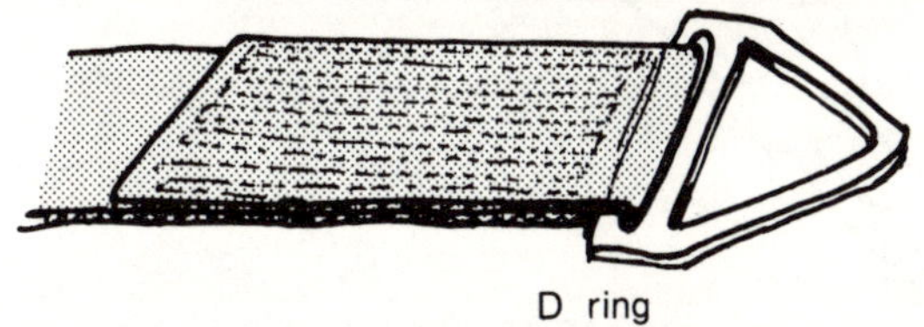

FIGURE 75: End loops for carabiner attachment.

thread on Terylene tape. It would be of little use to choose Terylene tape to resist acid attack and then sew it with nylon thread. Cotton thread is not strong enough; if the harness is professionally sewn be sure to specify the use of nylon or Terylene thread. If an industrial machine is available, the number of runs could be reduced to about eight by using a thicker thread.

Prior to sewing, the tape ends should be cut cleanly and melted to prevent unravelling (Figure 3). During sewing, efforts should be made to have all the runs the same length and not sew over the ends of the tape because this exposes a set of stitches to easy abrasion. For end loops, it is useful to sew in a taper or a D-ring for easy carabiner attachment (Figure 75).

KNOTS

Knots are very commonly used in harness construction because they can be tied easily and quickly. Provided they are not allowed to tighten excessively, they also offer a chance of adjustment underground. Drawbacks are found in their bulk and their tendency to work undone if not regularly checked. All knots in tape should have tail ends about 50mm long.

The tape knot (water knot, overhand bend, ring bend) is the best knot for a join in a critical load bearing portion of a harness. Once tied, it should be set with a hard pull and then checked periodically to ensure its tightness. For end loops the overhand loop is suitable (Figure 76).

A problem with the tape knot is that it cannot be tied in tape under tension. A knot which is suitable

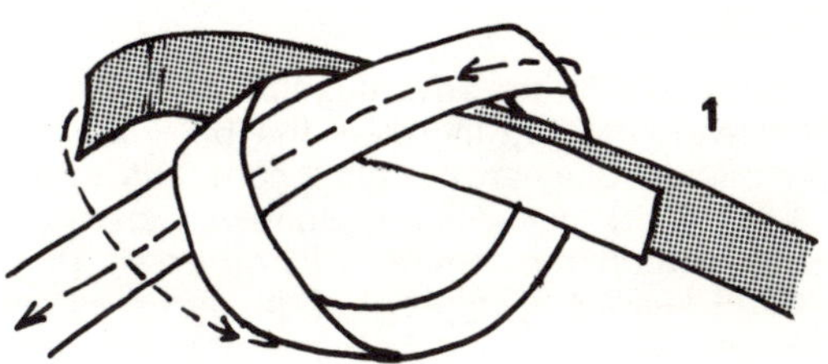

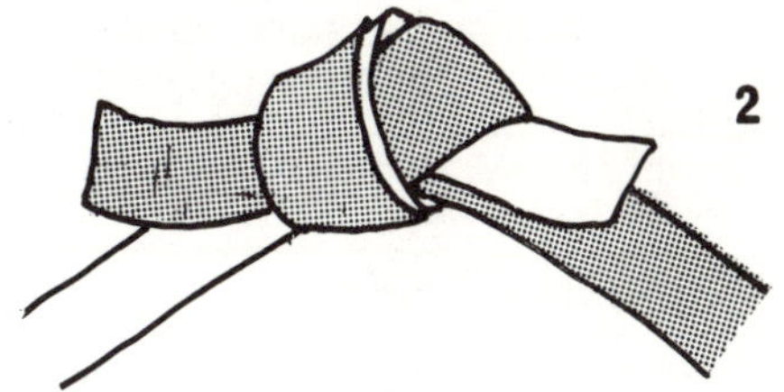

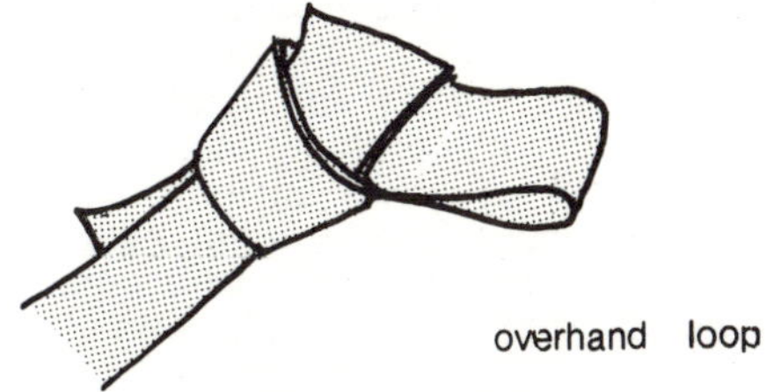

FIGURE 76: The tape knot and overhand loop.

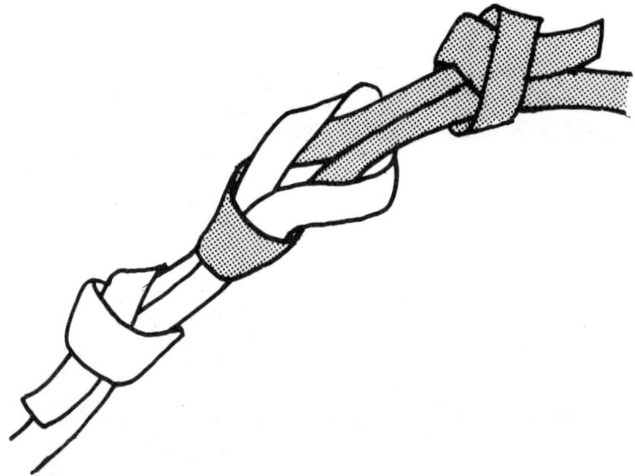

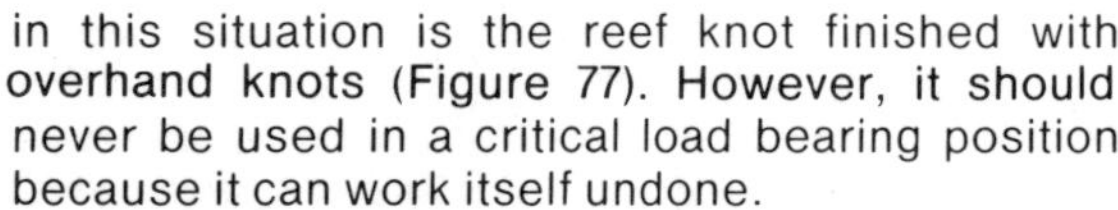

FIGURE 77: The reef knot finished with overhand knots.

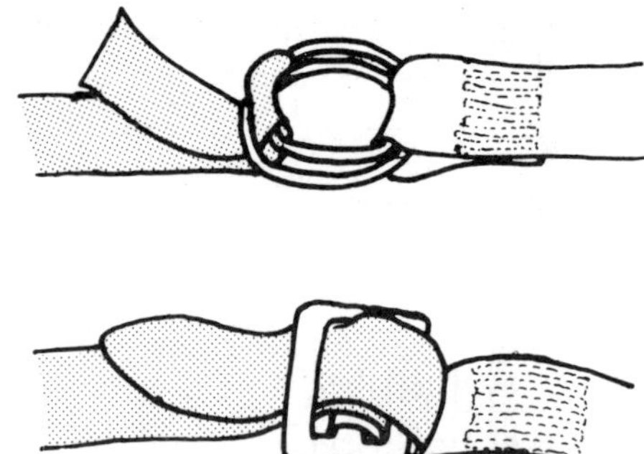

FIGURE 78: Examples of harness buckles — double harness rings (top) and the Troll climbing harness buckle (bottom).

in this situation is the reef knot finished with overhand knots (Figure 77). However, it should never be used in a critical load bearing position because it can work itself undone.

BUCKLES

Buckles offer the advantage of easy adjustment. However, they do increase the bulk, weight and complexity of a harness and should, therefore, be used with discretion. Buckles are usually incorporated into commercial harnesses and, with a little searching, high strength varieties can be bought for use in home manufacture. Double harness rings, and buckles from seat belts, climbing harnesses and parachute harnesses are suitable (Figure 78).

When using a buckle in a critical position, it is an essential security measure to thread the loose tape end back through the buckle or tie it down with an overhand knot, or both.

SEAT HARNESSES

Seat harnesses generally provide a caver's main means of support while abseiling and prusiking. Because of this, they must be fail-safe. This is usually achieved by having independent tapes around the legs and waist. Sometimes this feature is built into a one piece harness and sometimes two pieces are used. Most people use a large locking carabiner to clip the harness together and support prusik and abseil attachments. Occasionally, equipment loops are added. These are useful for carrying packs, rope pads, etc.

Harnesses should be snug and neat. It is important to ensure that the leg loops cannot slide down around the knees. For this purpose, tie up cords or thin tapes are often added. On long abseils, the leg loops may cut blood circulation to the legs. If one is prone to this, extra wide tape or a Whillans Sit Harness can be used (page 52).

There is a great deal of scope for individual modelling in seat harnesses. Only a few of the more popular types are described here. Dimensions should be chosen to suit the individual.

FIGURE EIGHT SEAT AND WAIST TAPE

A simple harness can be constructed from a sewn figure eight seat and a rock climbing waist tape (Figure 79). The waist tape is a 3m to 5m length of 50mm tape which is wrapped around the waist three or four times and tied with a tape knot. To make the tape snug, the first wraps should be drawn overly tight, and then when the tape knot is tied, the inevitable looseness in the last wrap can be evened out through the tight earlier ones. The figure eight seat requires about 2m to 2.5m of tape. It should be made large enough to accommodate the heaviest clothing one will wear. A thin tie-up tape is needed at the back to prevent the leg loops sliding down.

An attractive feature of this harness is that the waist tape can double as a hand line for short drops or traverses. On many occasions this usage has enabled an exploration party to penetrate further into a cave than would otherwise have been possible. The waist tape can also be utilised in an emergency situation. Troll Products in Britain market a waist belt in nylon or Terylene tape which can replace the waist tape. It fits around the body once and is fastened with a high strength buckle. The Troll belt doubles as a battery belt, but otherwise lacks the versatility of the waist tape.

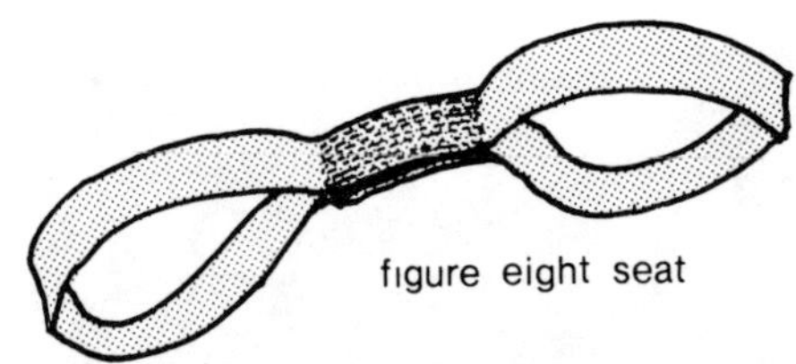

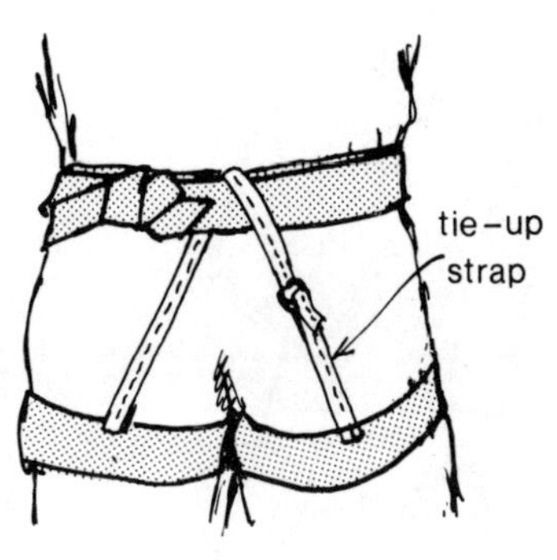

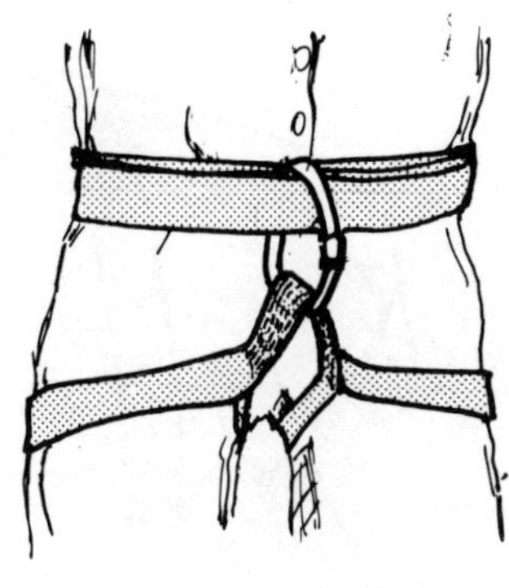

FIGURE 79: Figure eight seat and waist tape, showing front and back views.

SWAMI SEAT

The swami seat is made from 3m to 4m of 50mm tape. The tape is sewn, tied or preferably buckled to form a loop, which is fitted around the waist and legs as shown in Figure 80. The sewn or tied varieties require a tie-up strap at the back (as in Figure 79), but the buckled ones can be pulled tight enough to obviate this. The buckle is worn on the groin for ease of use and should be finished with an overhand knot (as in Figure 77) to prevent slippage (Howie 1975).

In its basic form, the swami seat is not fail-safe. To this end, a waist tape can be worn or the seat can be split into two buckled pieces, as is commonly done in France (Dobrilla & Marbach 1973) (Figure 81). The end loops in the French version are best made as in Figure 75 to allow easy clipping into the harness carabiner.

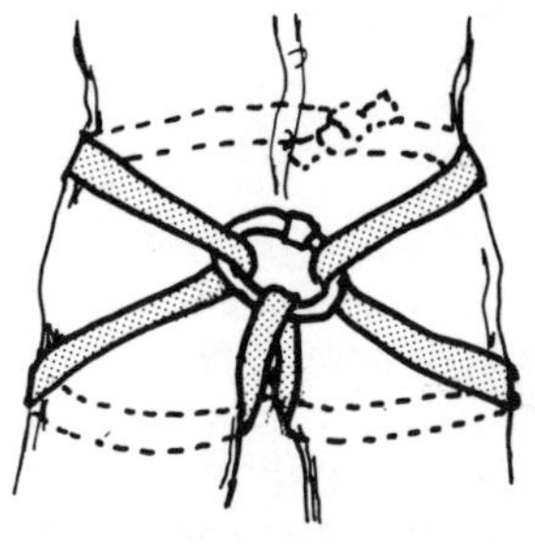

FIGURE 80: The Swami seat — knotted and buckled varieties (after Howie). A waist tape must be added to make the harness fail-safe.

GIBBS HARNESS

While originally designed for the floating cam system of prusiking (page 87), the Gibbs harness is suitable for use with any prusiking or abseiling rig (Figure 82). It is sewn from one length of tape (3m to 4m) and is neat and light. As for the figure eight seat, there is little scope for adding adjustment buckles. It should therefore be made large enough to accommodate heavy clothing. Tie-up straps may be needed for the leg loops.

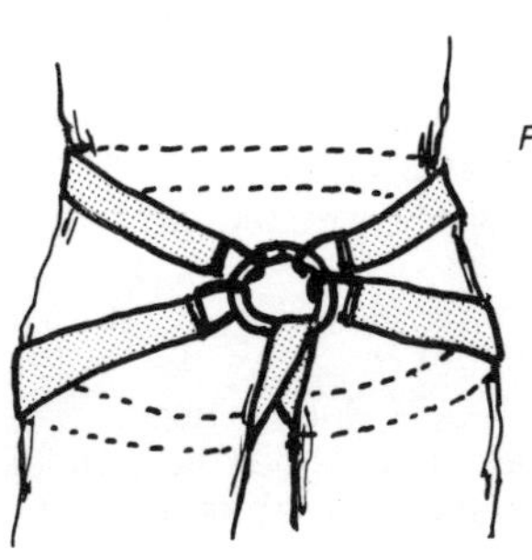

FIGURE 81: French version of the Swami seat.

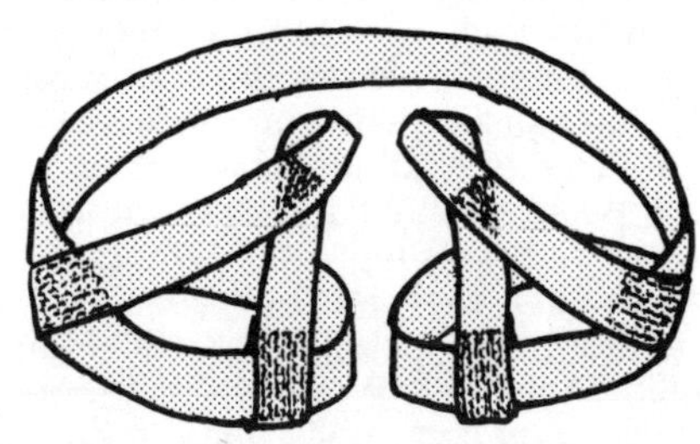

FIGURE 82: Gibbs Harness (after Smith).

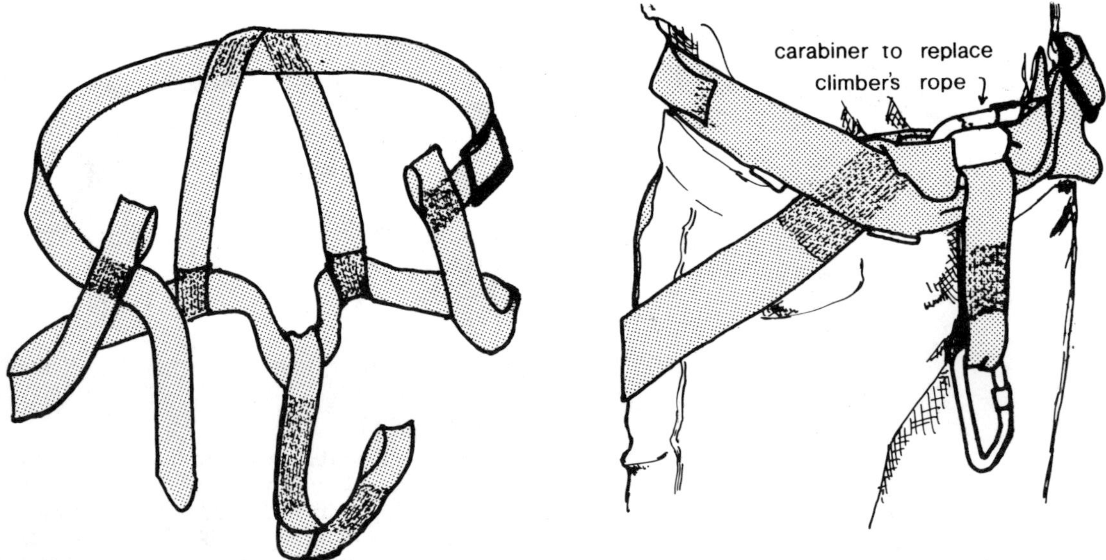

FIGURE 83: The Whillans sit harness (climbing version).

THE WHILLANS SIT HARNESS

In response to the varied and rigorous demands of mountaineering, the British climber, Don Whillans, developed a versatile harness which has become known the world over in climbing circles, and is capturing an increasing share of the caving market as well (Figure 83). The Whillans Sit Harness has copious strength, is easy to put on, and fits in a manner which allows complete freedom of movement. If one is prepared to outlay the price, it will be found excellent for caving with the following notes.

The harness is available in a climbers' model made from nylon tape and a cavers' model made from Terylene tape. The cavers' model has none of the specialised climbing accessories incorporated in the climbers' model and is reinforced at points of probable wear. Mention of the climbers' model is necessary because cavers using NiFe cells may prefer the nylon construction. Also, at the time of writing, it is still the model most frequently used, the cavers' model having been developed only recently. When the climbers' harness is used in mountain climbing, the climbing rope is attached in such a way as to ensure that the harness is fail-safe. Since a rope is not tied into the harness when abseiling or prusiking, the climber's rope attachment must, therefore, be simulated with a short rope loop or locking carabiner (Figure 83). The caver should also remove the equipment loops, since they can easily snag in constricted cave passages. Using either model, muddy conditions make the buckling system hard to use, but this has no easy solution (Standing 1972).

The harness is unsuitable for some prusik systems because it supports the body in a reclining position. In those systems where the caver sits in his harness between each step (page 91), too much weight will need to be taken with the arms to stay upright. Enthusiasts of these methods will find any of the previously described harnesses more suitable.

The Whillans Sit Harness is made by Troll Products, who supply full instructions for use with every sale.

CLAUDE LOOPS

The Claude loop is a useful safety accessory for technical caving. It is a length of 7mm to 8mm dynamic mountaineering rope which is tied with a loop at each end or made into a sling (Figure 84). The Claude loop is primarily used as a safety tie-on when traversing on a fixed line or when doing exposed climbing moves at pitch tops. One end is clipped into the harness carabiner and the other allows a carabiner attachment to the traverse rope or pitch anchor point. Being of dynamic rope, the Claude loop is a much better alternative to clipping on an ascender from one's prusik rig since ascender cords are generally of low stretch rope having poor energy absorption (page 82). In addition, it is risky to shock load an ascender, particularly if a Jumar (page 78) is used. The Claude loop can also be used to dangle a pack below the body while prusiking or abseiling. The

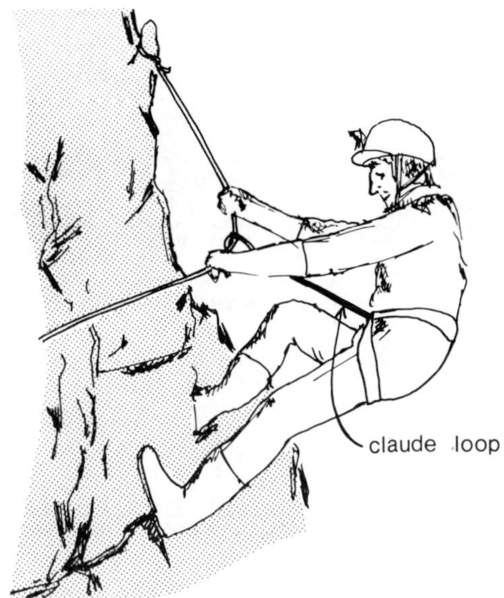

FIGURE 84: Claude loop in use and a roped traverse (after Dobrilla and Marbach).

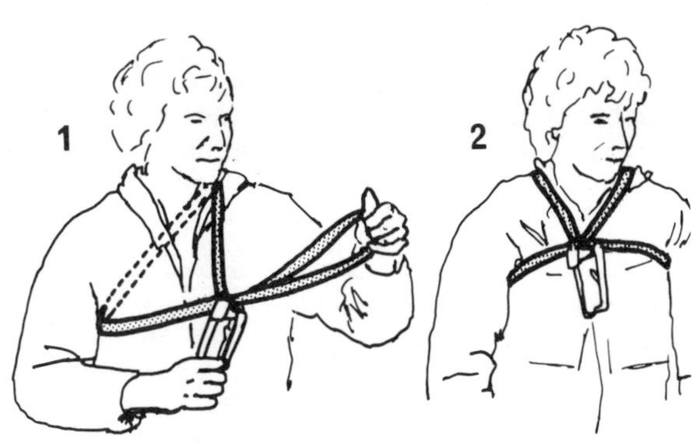

FIGURE 85: Figure eight chest harness to accept an ascender (above) and figure eight chest harness to accept a carabiner (below).

optimum length for the loop (excluding the carabiner) will vary from one person to another but should be in the range of 400mm to 500mm (Steve Perry, pers. comm.).

CHEST HARNESSES

Most prusik systems use a chest harness to hold the body close to the rope. This ensures an upright stance which aids efficiency while climbing. Attachment to the rope is made with an ascender, a chest box (page 91) or a carabiner. Several harness designs are in use, commercial or home-made. The simplest ones are fashioned from tape slings, while more complex (and comfortable) types utilise sewn and buckled straps. There is considerable scope for individual modelling, as long as the design has sufficient strength to hold full body weight if required, and that it is tight without restricting breathing. This latter condition is best met by mounting the harness as high as possible on the chest.

FIGURE EIGHT CHEST HARNESS

To be a proficient vertical caver, one should have a working knowledge of simple harness rigs. While not as comfortable as a sewn harness, a tape sling can form a safe and easily assembled chest harness. Twenty-five mm. tape is preferred. Worn in one way, the harness can accommodate an ascender (Figure 85). A second arrangement accepts a carabiner (Figure 85).

A SEWN HARNESS

A basic sewn harness is illustrated in Figure 86. Many minor modifications are possible to suit individual needs.

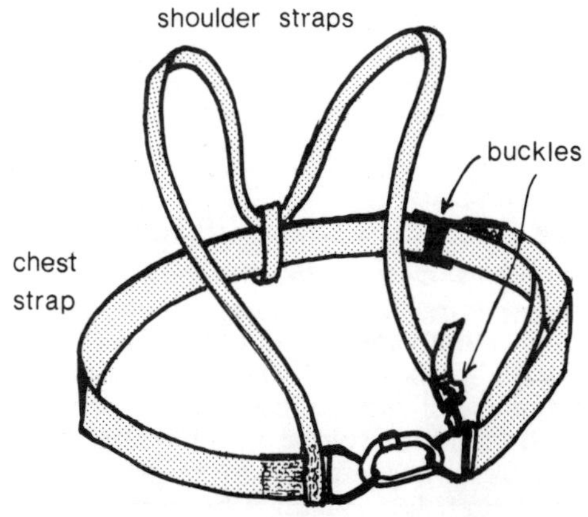

FIGURE 86. A sewn harness with adjustable chest and shoulder straps.

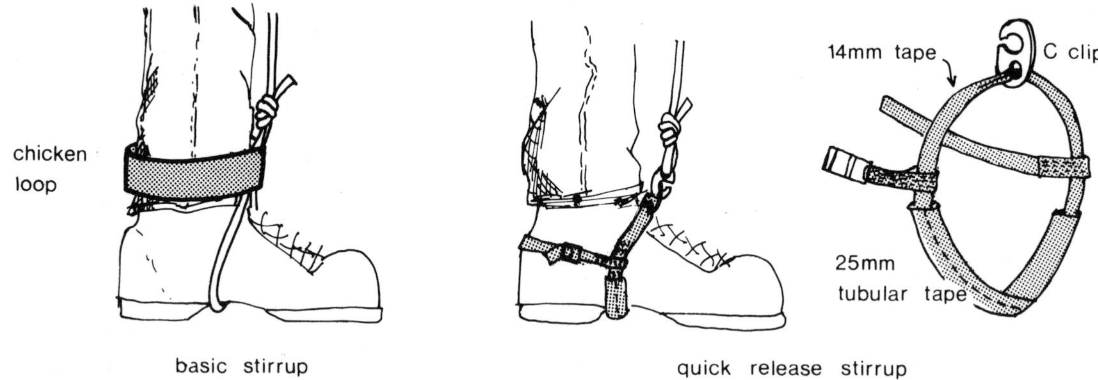

FIGURE 87: Foot stirrups.

FOOT STIRRUPS

In all prusik systems, ascenders will need to be attached to the feet in some way. Except in the case of direct strapping, foot stirrups are used.

BASIC STIRRUP WITH CHICKEN LOOPS

To form a basic stirrup, a figure eight or overhand loop is made in a length of 25mm tape or 7mm to 8mm cord (Figure 87). A sewn join is not recommended for tape as it will tend to rip apart. Cord should be used if found comfortable because of its greater neatness and durability (page 82). The loop should fit easily over the boot, yet still be snug. To prevent the stirrup from slipping off, chicken loops should be added. These are sewn bands of 25mm or 50mm tape which are fitted onto the ankle before putting on caving boots. They are then worn throughout the cave. During prusiking, each foot stirrup is passed through its chicken loop. The stirrup is then totally secure, provided that the chicken loop is made small enough to resist falling off over the boot, and strong enough to sustain a backwards flip onto the feet in the unlikely event of all waist and chest attachments failing. (Warren 1969, Smith 1974g).

QUICK RELEASE FOOT STIRRUP

Australian cavers developed a special foot stirrup (Figure 87) to allow a foot to be freed quickly (Montgomery 1977b). It makes use of strong stainless steel C clips which are available from boating shops. The stirrups are secured with a buckled strap which, like the chicken loop, should be strong enough to sustain a back flip onto the feet. The stirrup is generally attached at the first prusik in a cave and left on throughout the trip. It is unlikely to be abraded because the tape passes through the boot instep and is given extra protection by encasing it in 25mm tubular tape.

CARABINERS

Carabiners are metal links which are commonly made in D or Oval shapes (Figure 88). They have an opening gate for attachment purposes, which may be locking or non-locking. The usual locking mechanism is a screw sleeve. Locking carabiners are more secure than their non-locking counterparts. Non-locking carabiners (also called snaplinks) were developed to enable speedy attachments in rock climbing, but this is generally of small importance to cavers. Security is much more critical and, accordingly, locking carabiners are preferred for use in all key positions in harnesses and pitch anchors. Shape is of little importance. At the time of its introduction, the D shape was a design improvement on the oval shape because the D shape caused a preferential loading of the stronger, ungated side of the carabiner. However, modern production methods now ensure copious strength in either shape.

A decade ago there were some lethal brands of carabiners on the market (Smith 1974a), but today's methods of manufacturing and testing now give cavers a wide selection of products with adequate and reliable strength. The biggest boon has been the refinement of aluminium alloy carabiners to the point where they have almost entirely superseded the heavier steel varieties. Any modern alloy carabiners with screw gates can be used for all normal caving purposes, except for the seat harness carabiner. This carabiner must be large enough to accommodate three or more attachments, and strong enough to sustain any stresses these attachments can impose, for example, a three way pull (Figure 80). Most people favour an extra large locking carabiner for this crucial position.

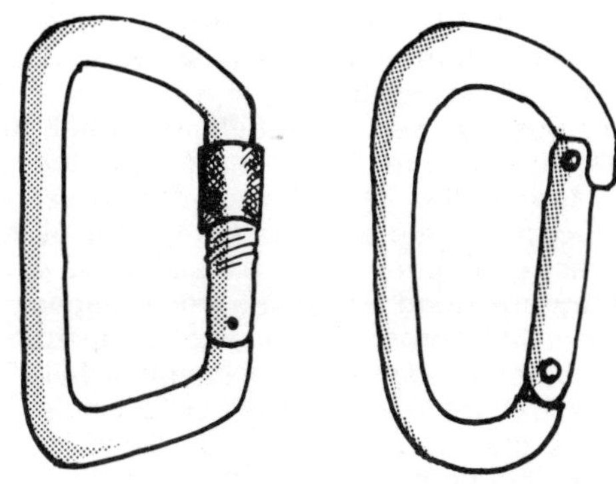

FIGURE 88: Lock D carabiner (left) and non-locking oval carabiner (right).

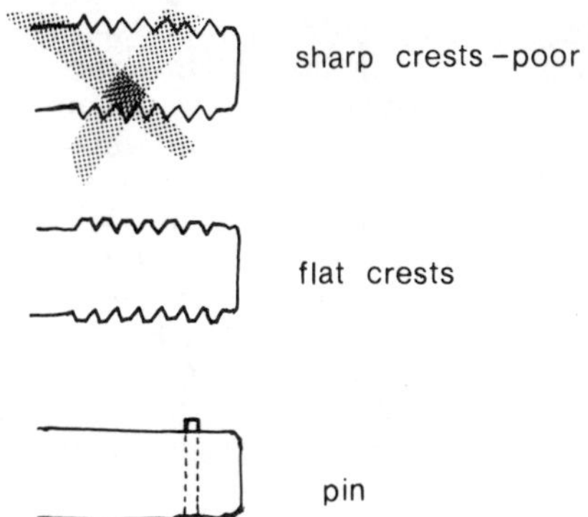

FIGURE 89: Screw mechanisms of locking carabiners.

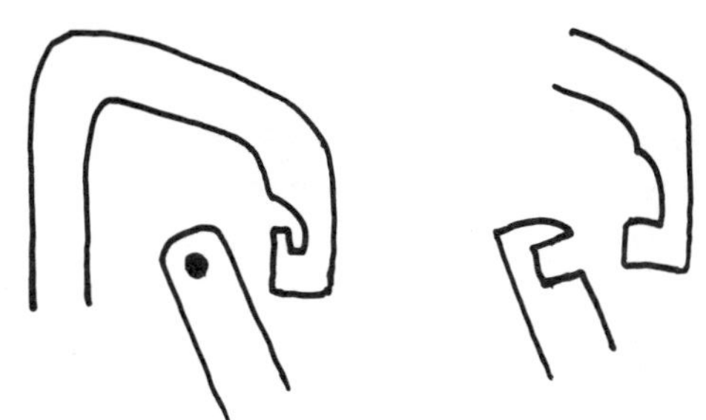

FIGURE 90: Pin and slot latch carabiner (left) and slot latch carabiner (right).

Before buying a locking carabiner, the screw mechanism should be examined. Figure 89 shows the two screw mechanisms in common use, one a regular screw thread, the other based on a pin design. Threaded models with sharp crests should be avoided; they have been known to cut harness tape (Smith 1974a). A failing with pinned models is that they sometimes lose their pins after a period of use. Whichever is chosen, it should be ascertained that the gate sleeve screws up firmly. It is an added advantage if the sleeve can be screwed right off for easy cleaning.

Gate latch designs should also be checked at the time of purchase. Dunster (1976) has shown that locking carabiners of a pin and slot design offer higher security than those with a slot only (Figure 90). While the designs are equally strong with the sleeve locked up, if the sleeve should come undone for any reason the slotted type of carabiner loses roughly half its strength (under a long axis loading) while the pin and slot type is relatively unaffected.

Non-locking carabiners usually have a pin and slot latch.

MARKING CARABINERS

Most people like to mark their carabiners in some way. Painting is the safest method, though paint wears off quickly. Initialling is more durable, but should be restricted to the carabiner gate, particularly if letter punches are used. This avoids any weakening of the carabiner body.

CARING FOR CARABINERS

Some cavers treat the carabiner as an indestructible piece of equipment simply because of its sturdy appearance. In reality, the carabiner and all other metal equipment require thoughtful inspection at time of purchase and diligent care during use. A mistreated carabiner may appear to be in perfect condition right up to its time of abrupt failure. A chief safety precaution for carabiners is to avoid dropping them. A carabiner which has fallen more than a few metres could contain hairline fractures which are invisible under ordinary inspection. They will show up under X-ray but it would be cheaper to replace the carabiner. The risk of fracture is, of course, extremely slight, but it is hardly worth the price of a carabiner to go caving with an element of doubt such as this.

Of equal concern is the weakness of the gate on most carabiners. Any direct loading of the gate should be avoided where possible. If a gate must be loaded, as in the brake bar abseil rig (page 59), it is essential that the gate is not allowed to open under the load, since it may snap off sideways.

Routine carabiner maintenance consists of scrubbing off mud and, with steel carabiners, cleaning off rust. Often in dirty caves, the gate hinge can become clogged with dirt causing gate stiffness. A toothbrush is handy here, followed by light lubrication. The spray lubricants (e.g. WD40, RP7) are especially good. Heavy oil should be avoided since it can easily pick up grit.

RETIRING CARABINERS

Treated properly, carabiners have an indefinite life. However, carabiners which have suffered a severe impact or heavy rusting should be retired. The safest approach is to throw them away, and not merely relegate them to such duties as pack hauling. Otherwise, someone may pick one up and use it in a moment of inattention.

HELMETS

In view of the severe forces that can be generated by falling rocks or falling bodies, the human head is very fragile indeed. In vertical caves, the head needs as much protection as possible.

The basic function of a helmet is to reduce the severity of any impact to the head by deflecting the blow as much as possible and then by spreading the remaining force. To do this, a helmet must have a dome shape, it must be rigid enough to spread the area of impact, and it must contain a crushable liner and a suspension system to reduce the peak force of the impact by absorbing some of the shock (Figure 91). Since the impact may come from any direction, the helmet must offer all-round protection and be completely secure. A helmet is useless if it comes off the head in an accident.

Unfortunately, very few helmets meet these criteria. Motor-cycle helmets do, but they are much too bulky and heavy for cave use. Construction helmets of the type worn by most cavers are quite poor. Industrial standards ensure that they are good under a vertical impact, but they offer little protection against a hit from the side, a common danger in a tumbling fall. Even worse, most are only attached by a single strap under the chin and can easily come off in a fall. Climbing helmets are generally much better, having a crushable liner, padding against a sideward impact and a secure fastening system (Figure 91). However, one still needs to be discriminating. Many brands have weak shells, poor side to side rigidity and contain rivets and buttons in exposed positions. Nevertheless, fitted with a lamp bracket in a safe way (i.e. no exposed bolts), climbing helmets are our best option. The safest one on the market at present seems to be the Mountain Safety Research (MSR) helmet (Penberthy 1972b). The popular Joe Brown and Ultimate helmets are reasonable, but still not as safe as the MSR model. Any helmet should be retired after sustaining a heavy blow.

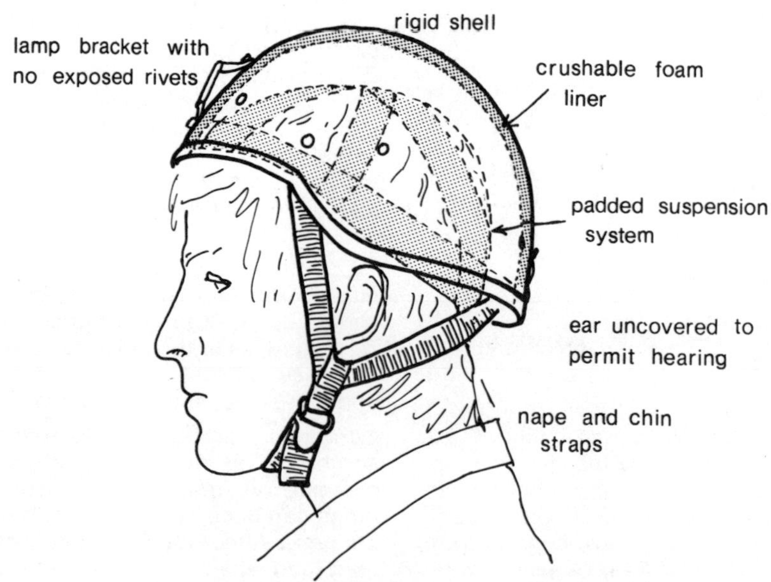

FIGURE 91: Features of a good caving helmet.

6: ABSEILING

Over the years, many methods have evolved for descending a fixed rope. These so-called abseiling or rappelling techniques involve threading the rope through a friction device (either an arrangement of carabiners or a specialised descender) which is securely attached to a seat harness. During the descent one hand is held above the device and one hand is held below it. The hands give balance and regulate friction. There is, however, one useful technique known as the classic or dulfer abseil, which requires no harness or descending device.

THE CLASSIC ABSEIL

The classic abseil involves the use of one's body to provide friction. The method is to straddle the rope facing away from the drop, draw the rope over the left shoulder and then hold it in the right hand (left handed people use the right shoulder and left hand). The right hand controls the descent while the left hand is used to maintain a suitable posture (Figure 92). The technique functions best with a doubled rope, though a single rope is adequate.

The classic abseil is uncomfortable and slow, but it should be learnt because of its usefulness in an emergency situation where no other abseiling equipment may be available. It is also handy for those short isolated pitches where it is a nuisance to rig up one's normal abseil gear.

While classic abseiling, it is advisable to wear thick clothing and have a shirt collar. Under no circumstances should the rope be released with either hand since total loss of control will probably result.

The classic abseil can be made more comfortable and controllable by using a seat harness with a single locking carabiner as depicted in Figure 93. This method obviously has less emergency value than the regular classic.

Beginning the 167m abseil into Aven Jean Nouveau, Vaucluse, France. *Andrew Pavey*

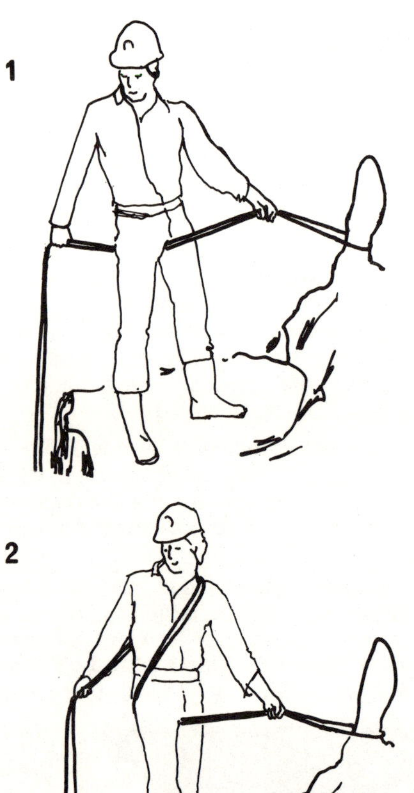

FIGURE 92: The classic abseil.

FIGURE 93: Classic abseil with a carabiner — also called the over-the-shoulder abseil.

ABSEIL DEVICES: SOME GENERAL COMMENTS

Abseiling is one area of technique in which cavers have had to develop their own equipment to meet the unique demands of caving. Over the years, there has been a steady flow of gadgets of all shapes and sizes, and some guidelines are needed to assist the selection and use of a good device.

STRENGTH

Abseil devices should be capable of holding a load of at least 500kg applied in the same way as in actual use. This should give a safety factor of at least five over body weight. All devices described in this chapter meet this standard.

SECURITY

If the rope is threaded into the device incorrectly, the fault should be readily apparent, even to a bleary-eyed caver on a twenty hour trip. When correctly threaded, the rope should be unable to pop out unexpectedly.

CONTROL

It should be easy to regulate the rate of descent and stop when desired.

VERSATILITY

For general caving purposes, abseil devices should be capable of controlled descents on ropes of different types and thicknesses in a variety of conditions (wet or gritty ropes give more friction than dry or clean ones). If the device can take a doubled rope, this will prove useful on through trips where a doubled rope is pulled down behind the party (page 46).

SPIN

The device should not cause the caver to spin during the descent. None of the devices described in this chapter generally cause spin.

HEAT

Unless the rope is wet, abseil devices become heated during use. Heating can become serious on drops over approximately 50m. On such drops, one should use a device which will not become too hot to hold since then a degree of control is lost and there is a risk of burns to the body and in extreme cases, rope damage. In general, the mass and type of metal in a device are the most reliable guides to its thermal properties. Large aluminium devices seem to perform best.

ON-OFF TIME

Speed in getting on and off ropes increases general efficiency of underground movement, and is useful in emergencies. Practice time spent attaching and detaching your abseil devices from the rope would not be wasted effort.

DURABILITY

Abseil devices wear out due to the abrasive effect of grit on ropes. High abrasion resistance is desirable and the parts affected (i.e., the surfaces the rope touches) should preferably be replaceable.

WEIGHT, SIZE AND COST

These three should be minimized, but not to the detriment of safety. The best all-round devices happen to be among the heaviest, largest and most costly.

VARIABLE OR NON-VARIABLE FRICTION

Practically all of the above factors are affected by a basic choice one needs to make between variable and non-variable friction devices. Rappel racks and whaletails are examples of variable friction devices while brake bar rigs, figure eight descenders and bobbins are of the non-variable friction type. Variable friction devices allow one to alter the rope position in the device so as to increase or decrease the amount of friction between the device and the rope. Such control is expedient on long pitches (over about 50m) or in caves where ropes of different types, diameters and conditions have been rigged. The advantage on long pitches arises from the fact that as one descends, the weight of rope steadily decreases, causing less friction in the device and a consequent tendency to speed up. Using a non-variable device, one may find it necessary to vigorously feed the rope into the device to generate any movement at the pitch top, while, near the bottom, much hand pressure may be needed to avoid excessive speed. The user of a variable friction device would simply increase the friction in the device as he descends and enjoy a controlled abseil all the way.

Variable friction devices are larger than the non-variable ones, usually causing them to dissipate heat better, and so gain an extra advantage for use on long drops. They are also heavier and more costly so that in choosing between the two types cavers should consider the style of caving they are doing. Deep pits and vertical caves with numerous pitches favour the variable friction devices, while caves with just a few short pitches favour the non-variable friction devices simply on the grounds of size, weight and cost.

For detailed technical treatments of frictional properties, readers are referred to Wefer (1968a and 1968b) and Hoffman (1975). The most popular devices of each type will now be described.

NON-VARIABLE FRICTION ABSEIL DEVICES

There are four widely used non-variable friction abseil devices, two of which are carabiner arrangements and two are descenders. Provided they are restricted to short drops, the choice between them is largely a personal one. On long drops factors such as heating would come into play. Whichever method is used, it is wise to have a knowledge of the simple carabiner systems in case one needs to abseil without specialised descenders.

THE BRAKE BAR RIG

The brake bar rig is popular in Australia and North America. It requires two or three carabiners together with one or more brake bars to fit across the carabiners. The brake bars may be themselves carabiners, angle pitons, or short lengths of metal rod.

Metal rod brake bars are readily available commercially and also can be easily made in a small workshop (Figure 94). Lengths of rod (about 18mm diameter bar) are cut to fit across a carabiner, a hole is drilled in one end and a diagonal or square slot made in the other (Figure 94). Diagonal slots offer more security than square ones when properly engaged since it is necessary to slightly open the carabiner gate to clip them in. Once the gate is shut, the bar will not normally flip open, as it may do if the slot is square cut. However, care needs to be taken in threading

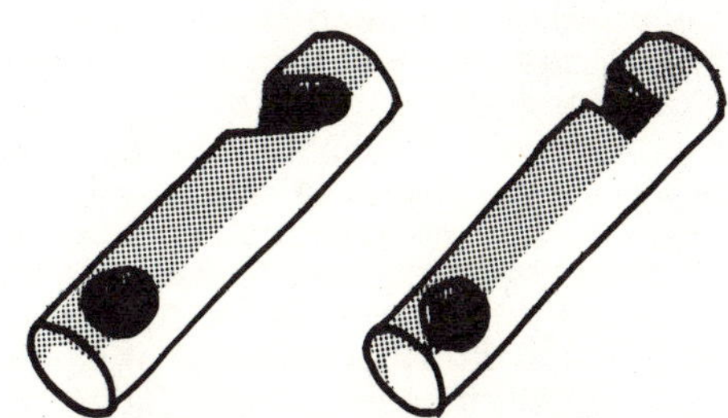

FIGURE 94: Brake bars — diagonal slot (left), and square slot (right).

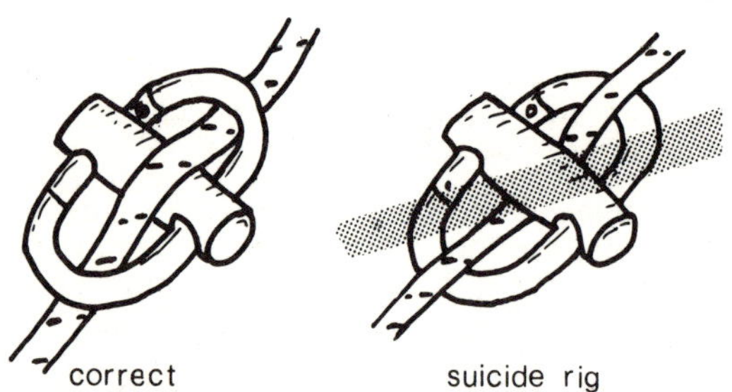

FIGURE 95: Threading the rope.

the rope. If the rope was carelessly placed in back to front (Figure 95) one might begin an abseil seemingly in control, only to have the rope pop out while perched perilously on the brink of a drop. It has happened. The same fault in rope placement with a square cut bar will be immediately obvious.

The rods are made of solid aluminium or tubular stainless steel. The steel must be hollow to give it extra surface area for heat loss. Even so, it does not dissipate heat as well as solid aluminium, since aluminium is a far more thermally conductive metal (Hoffmann 1975). This difference in thermal properties becomes important later when rappel racks are considered (page 62) but it is hardly significant here because we are only concerned with short drops. The critical factor for the present is abrasion resistance, and on this score stainless steel is many times tougher than aluminium. For this reason, tubular stainless steel bars are recommended. Likewise, the carabiners used in the rig can be of steel or aluminium. Steel ones are a must if gritty ropes are to be used, since just one or two abseils on a gritty rope can cause severe wear to the aluminium varieties. Normally, a single carabiner rig will give insufficient friction for abseiling on a single rope, though it should be suitable for a doubled rope (page 46). **The solution is to add an extra bar to the single rig or use two single rigs in tandem (Figure 96).**

A potential hazard in brake bar abseils stems from the weakness of the carabiner gate. The gate takes a considerable force during an abseil and has always been the first part of the rig to fail in test situations. Tests reported by Boyd and Frater (1968) and Smutek (1973a) produced gate snapping at 500kg or more with a variety of popular carabiners and commercial brake bars. Stainless steel carabiners were found to have the highest strengths. While gate strength is adequate if the gate remains shut, it certainly is not should the gate open slightly for some reason during the descent. There have been several incidents involving gates snapping off under these conditions (Cuddington 1966). Trouble will most likely occur with

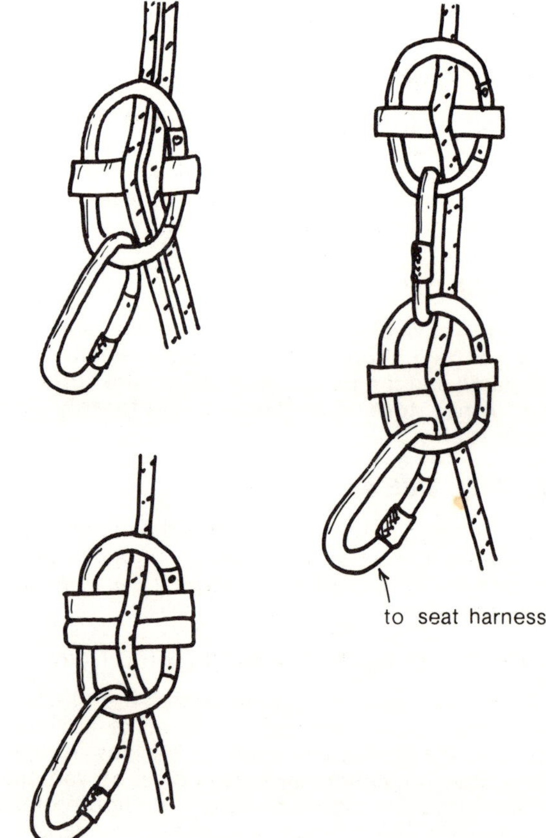

FIGURE 96: Carabiner brake bar rigs for single and double ropes.

diagonally slotted bars, since when sliding over a pit edge on one's belly, the bar could be pushed outwards against the rock, forcing the carabiner gate open (Sproull 1973). Square cut bars are more secure in the same situation and are generally recommended, though they still require care. A good precaution is to rig the carabiners with the gate openings upward. It will then often be found that the bars slide upwards during the abseil to cover the gate openings and avert any problems.

Angle piton and carabiner brakes work in the same way as rod bars, but must be used either with locking carabiners or a set of two non-locking carabiners with their gates opposed. These are essential safety precautions, since there is always the possibility of an unlocking carabiner opening and the gate snapping off. Some safe piton and carabiner rigs are illustrated in Figure 97. Suitable sizes for angle pitons are 15mm and 20mm (Royce 1977).

Angle piton and carabiner brakes have an attraction in requiring no specialised equipment. They could be of particular use in an emergency.

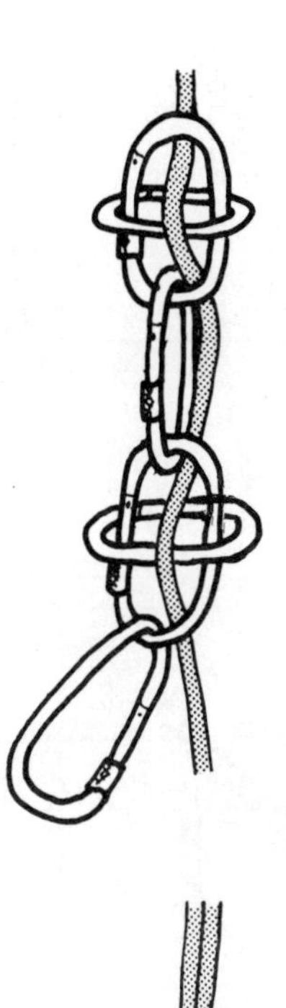

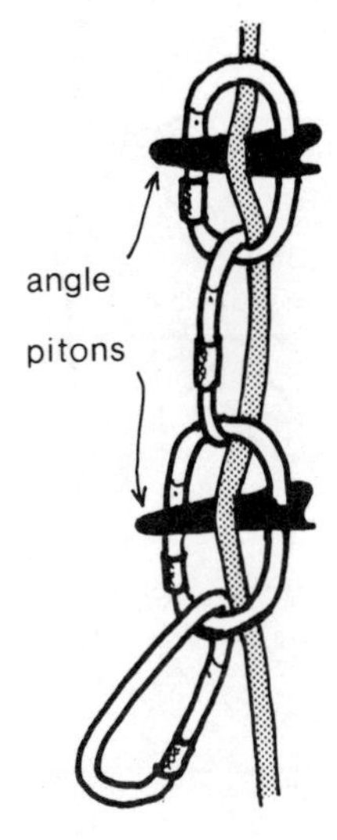

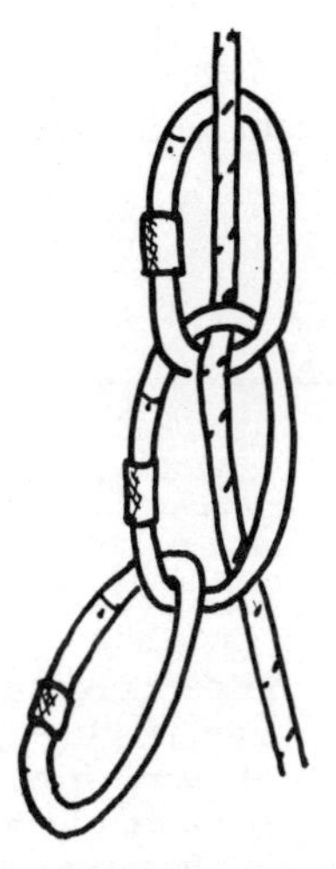

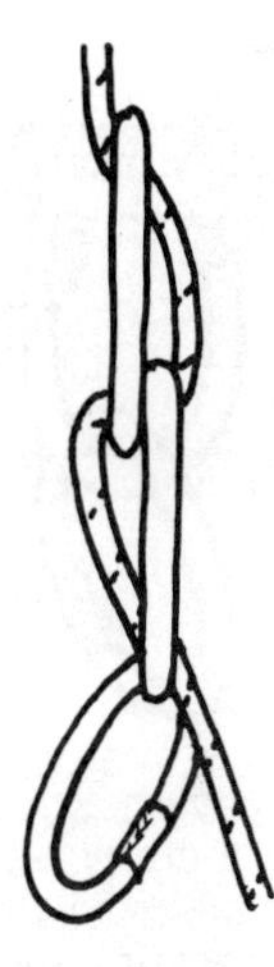

FIGURE 98: French crossed carabiners.

FRENCH CROSSED CARABINERS

Some French cavers use a technique which requires only two locking carabiners, preferably of steel (Figure 98). If desired, friction could be increased by using a third carabiner. Any fault in rope placement will be immediately obvious, and, provided the carabiners are locking ones, the rope cannot pop out.

FIGURE EIGHT DESCENDER

The figure eight descender offers exceptional strength and security (Figure 99). It has achieved widespread use among British cavers, who find its light, compact build ideal for the tight caves with short to medium length pitches which are common in Britain.

Several different brands of aluminium descender are on the market and are widely sold by climbing

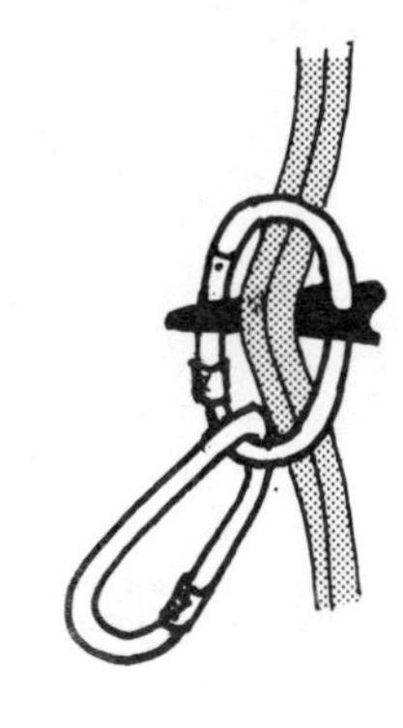

FIGURE 97: Angle piton and carabiner brakes for single and double ropes.

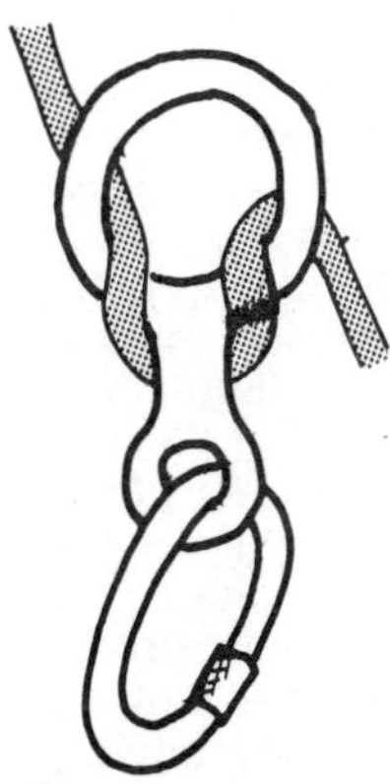

FIGURE 99: Figure eight descender.

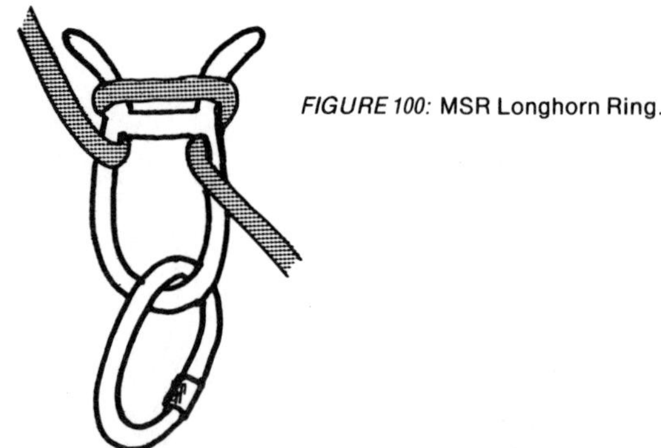

FIGURE 100: MSR Longhorn Ring.

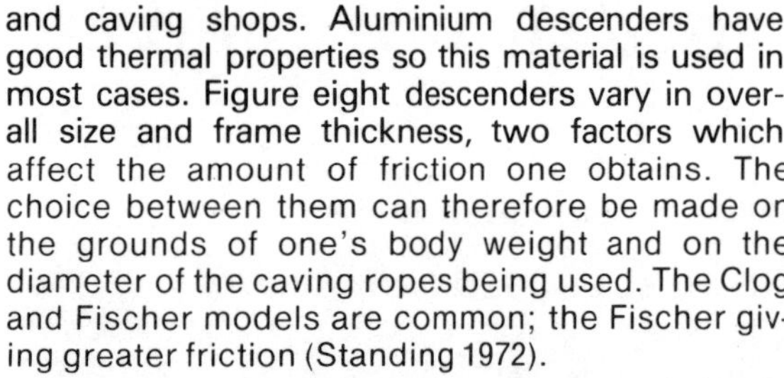

and caving shops. Aluminium descenders have good thermal properties so this material is used in most cases. Figure eight descenders vary in overall size and frame thickness, two factors which affect the amount of friction one obtains. The choice between them can therefore be made on the grounds of one's body weight and on the diameter of the caving ropes being used. The Clog and Fischer models are common; the Fischer giving greater friction (Standing 1972).

Compared to the carabiner systems, the figure eight descender suffers one disadvantage in that it is necessary to detach it from the seat harness to thread the rope in and out. The figure eight is also occasionally criticised for causing slight spin.

The problem of detaching the figure eight descender from the seat harness to insert the rope has been solved by MSR with the marketing of a device called a Longhorn Ring (Figure 100). At the time of writing, it has only recently appeared and has not had the same extensive use as the figure eight descender, but it seems to be a superior device. It even offers the possibility of increasing friction by wrapping the rope once around the horns.

THE BOBBIN

The bobbin is the leading abseil device in France and probably Continental Europe (Paul Courbon, pers. comm.). It is made by F. Petzl in France in two models, one for single ropes and one for double ropes, though the double rope model takes single ropes as well (Figure 101). Both models are light and compact. Sizes are available for 9mm and 12mm ropes.

The bobbin consists of fixed pulley wheels inside an aluminium frame. The rope is inserted by swinging open one side of the frame and is locked in by clipping the seat harness carabiner.

Control is good and can be made even better by passing the rope through a carabiner separately attached to the seat harness (Figure 102).

Manufacture details are given by Torode (1974).

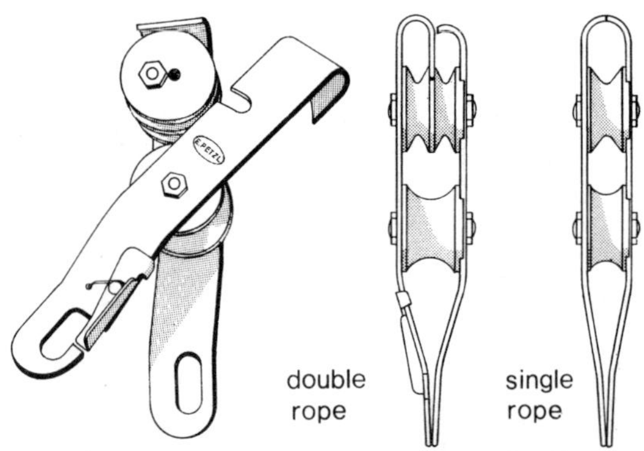

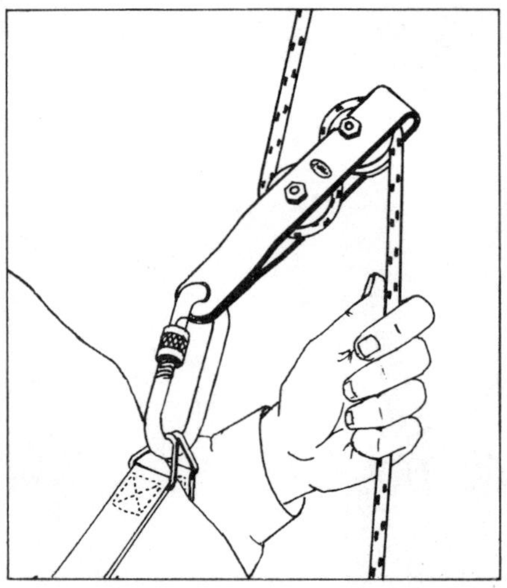

FIGURE 101: F. Petzl's bobbin — from the Petzl Brochure.

VARIABLE FRICTION DEVICES

THE RAPPEL RACK

The rappel rack is the original variable friction device and by far the most popular. It was developed in the United States by John Cole as a logical extension of the brake bar rig (Cole 1966). His original design is still the one most frequently used, though since 1973, a variation called the Super Rack has been gaining popularity (Isenhart 1974a).

THE STANDARD RACK

Racks made approximately to Cole's design (Figure 103) are commercially available (see Appendix 1) and, in addition, many people make their own. The rack consists of a steel bar frame to which metal rod brake bars (usually 18mm

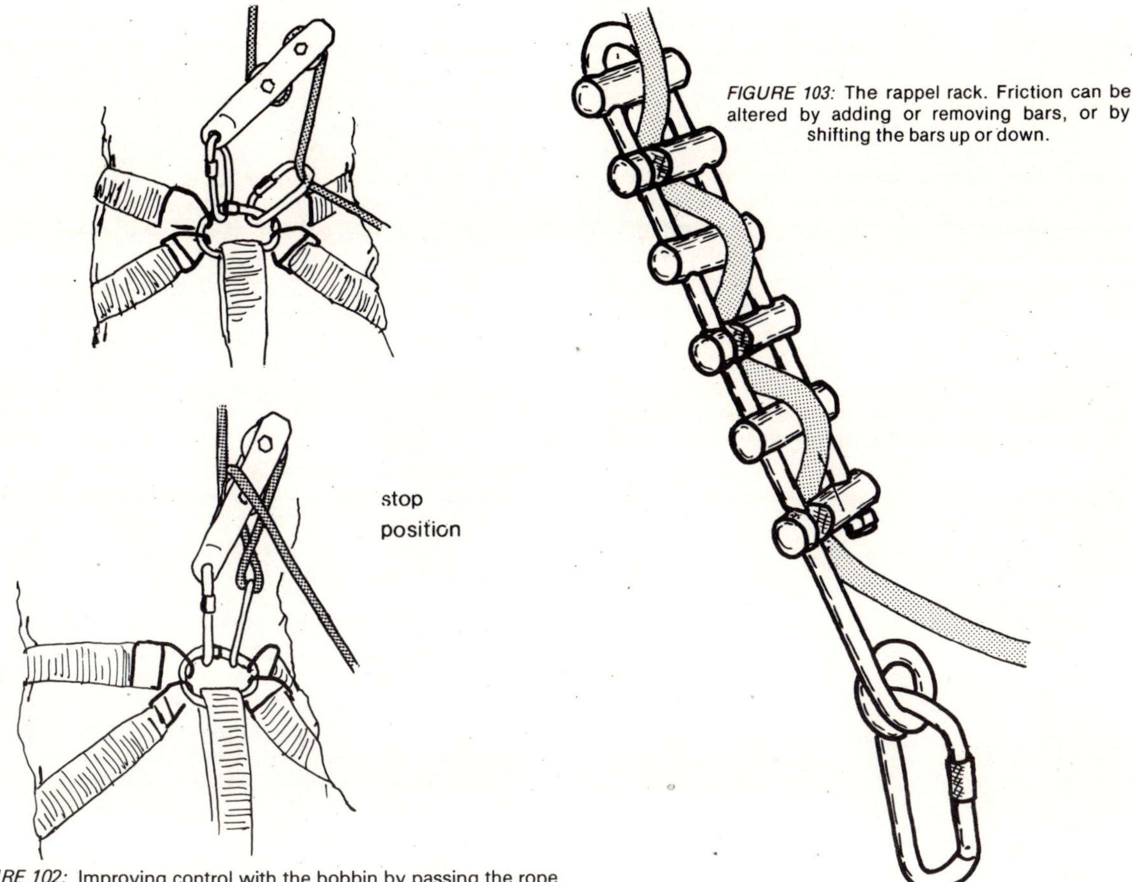

FIGURE 103: The rappel rack. Friction can be altered by adding or removing bars, or by shifting the bars up or down.

FIGURE 102: Improving control with the bobbin by passing the rope through an extra carabiner (after Dobrilla and Marbach).

diameter) are added, of the same design used in the brake bar rig (page **59**). The bars should fit snugly on the frame. Bars from brake bar rigs will usually have holes that are too large. Most people use six bars, although light people should be able to manage with five. Diagonally slotted bars are preferred, though as for the brake bar rig, one must ensure that the rope is threaded correctly (page **60**).

There is some contention among cavers as to what material is best for the brake bars. Tubular stainless steel or solid aluminium are the two options, as for brake bar rigs, but the choice is now complicated by the issue of heat dissipation. While the stainless steel undoubtedly wears better, it was thought by some people that it did not dissipate heat nearly as well as the aluminium and was inadequate for long drops (Isenhart 1974a). Research by Hoffmann (1975) confirmed that it was inferior to aluminium, but he found that the difference was only small if 25mm tubular stainless steel rod was matched against the usual 18mm aluminium rod. Even so, the extra bulk, weight and cost of the stainless steel bars favours the aluminium ones, unless an exceptionally muddy cave is being explored.

The rack has adequate strength, though it is weak relative to most other devices. Some models begin to bend under loads as low as 250kg (Stiles 1971). Final failure occurs at two or four times this value by unrolling of the carabiner connecting eye. At the time of purchase, the eye construction should be examined. A single loop is inadequate (Figure **104**). The rack's tendency to bend is caused by its open end at the bottom, a feature which

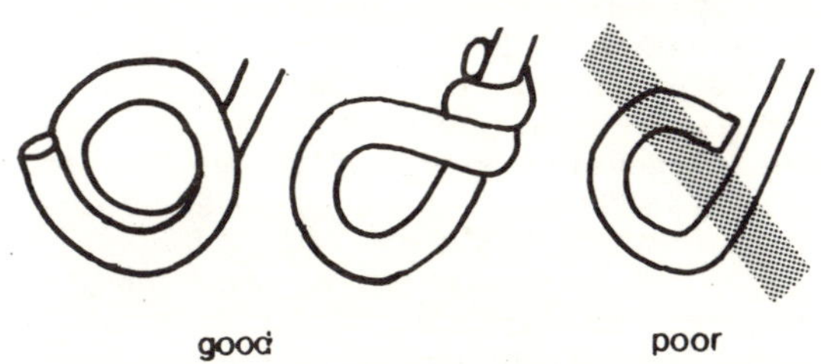

FIGURE 104: Eye designs of rappel racks (after Davison).

is necessary to allow extra bars to be added during a descent. Special caution must be exercised when sliding over a pit edge or else the rack may pivot on the edge and bend.

Friction can be altered in two ways. One is to change the number of bars in use and the other is to shift the bars up or down. Bar shift works by changing the angle of bending of the rope. It is the more useful one since it is much easier to perform and offers a continuous adjustment. Normally, sufficient control is obtained by shifting the bottom two bars. This is usually done by continuously cradling the bars in the upper hand and moving the hand up or down. Bar shift also allows a stop to be made by forcefully jamming the bars upwards. In addition, one can stop more securely by wrapping the rope over the top of the rack (Figure 105).

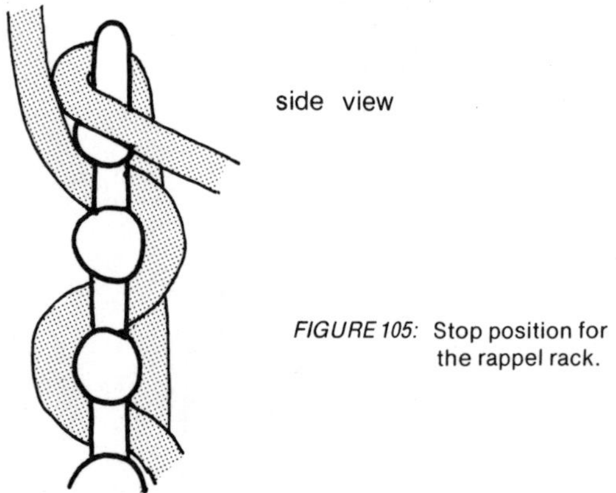

FIGURE 105: Stop position for the rappel rack.

On shorter pitches bar shift can be used exclusively by starting the drop with all bars engaged and spread out, then simply shifting them upwards during the descent. The maximum length of pitch which still allows this method is determined by the length of the rack, since the longer the rack is, the further the bars can be shifted. Two hundred metres is a rough ceiling for the standard rack of 350mm. On longer drops, one or two bars will have to be removed at the pitch top and then added some distance down when extra friction is necessary. Some people have made 450mm racks which function by bar shift alone on drops of up to 400m or so. They would never be used for normal caving because of their ungainly size.

The bars on a rack quickly develop grooves from rope wear, especially if the bars are made of aluminium. The first and second bars are most susceptible and it is wise to exchange them for the fifth and sixth ones when the grooves become deep enough to substantially reduce friction by not bending the rope sufficiently. When the bars are so deeply worn as to be of little use, they can be easily and cheaply exchanged for new ones. The steel frame has an indefinite life.

It is advisable to always run the rope straight down the centre of the rack and not let it slip off to one side. If the rope does slip, off-centre grooves are worn on the bars and the rope may sit in these grooves permanently. With the rope in an off-centre position, Padgett and Padgett (1975) warn that it becomes harder to shift the bars, which reduces control. They recommend filing shallow grooves in the centre of the first three bars to guide the rope from the start.

Even though the standard rack with 18mm bars has quite a large mass of metal, each of its bars is somewhat thermally isolated and it controls heating no better than a double brake bar rig (Isenhart 1975). The first two bars can become especially hot on long drops and for this usage are best replaced; either by 25mm square aluminium bars of the Super Rack design (page 65) or four regular bars stacked in two pairs (Figure 106). Only two or three extra single bars would be needed.

Another problem on long drops is that the first two bars can be pinched tightly together by the rope weight, thus causing excessive friction and heating. The two bars may become so hot that they cannot be handled and separated (even with gloves), leaving the caver little choice but to continue down by feeding the rope into the rack, until rope weight reduces sufficiently to allow normal control to be regained. The best solution is to fit 20mm long spacers of brass tubing (good conductivity) onto the frame between the first and second bars (Figure 106).

Construction details for the rack are given by Baz-Dresch (1974), Cole (1966), Eavis (1976) and Goulbourne (1974). Goulbourne's rack is only 225mm long. It is more compact than the other designs at the sacrifice of performance on long drops.

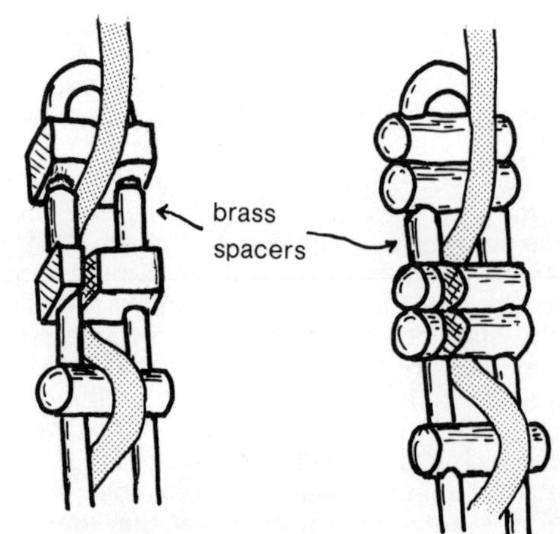

FIGURE 106: Modifying the rappel rack for long drops.

THE SUPER RACK

Problems of heating and the inconvenience of adding bars onto the standard rack during long abseils prompted the development of the Super Rack, depicted in Figure 107 (Isenhart 1974a). Only four bars are normally fitted on the Super Rack and they are always all used. They are made of 25mm square aluminium bars which are notched in their centres to save the rope from the sharp corners. The large size of the bars makes control possible purely by bar shift and allows very effective heat dissipation. Brass spacers 20mm in length are added between the first two bars to avoid pinching.

As a result of its different frame design, the Super Rack is far stronger than the standard rack, though it is also a little harder to thread. Its length of 300mm makes it more easily transported.

While, by its name, the Super Rack sounds to be the answer to all abseil needs, its performance is only exceptionally good with the large rope weight found on long abseils. Control problems have been experienced by some people on short drops and near the bottoms of long drops, particularly with new smooth ropes. Apparently, the four bars do not give sufficient friction at these times, especially for heavy people (Davison 1977a). A solution is to add a fifth bar and have the frame 50mm longer. However, the resulting rack will then be heavier and bulkier than the standard rack. Any caver who experiences control problems with a Super Rack should probably use the standard rack instead.

Test results and construction details for the Super Rack are given by Isenhart (1974a and 1977) and Ellis (1977). They are sold by The Speleoshoppe in the USA under the name SupeRack (see Appendix 1).

FIGURE 107: The Super Rack, (after Speleo shoppe advertisement).

THE WHALETAIL DESCENDER

The whaletail (Figure 108) was invented in America by G. A. Wood (1967). It did not achieve popularity there due to competition from the better established rack, and because the American design did not include a safety gate across the first two slots. The lack of a gate caused several serious incidents where the rope popped right out of the device (eg, Baz-Dresch 1974). A safety gate was added in Australia (Montgomery and Montgomery 1972) and there the whaletail has become the popular device for vertical caving.

Like the Super Rack, the hefty aluminium construction of the whaletail produces strength far in excess of minimum requirements and ensures good heat dissipation. With its length of 280mm, the whaletail is shorter than the rack.

Friction is controlled by winding the rope through an appropriate number of slots. Security against the rope popping out is normally provided by the fact that the rope runs at right angles to the slot direction (Figure 108). However, it is possible to carelessly flick the rope out of the slots, especially on long drops when there is a considerable weight of rope involved. This has happened a few times in the history of usage of the whaletail. In such cases, the safety gate holds the rope in the top two slots and sufficient control will remain to descend safely.

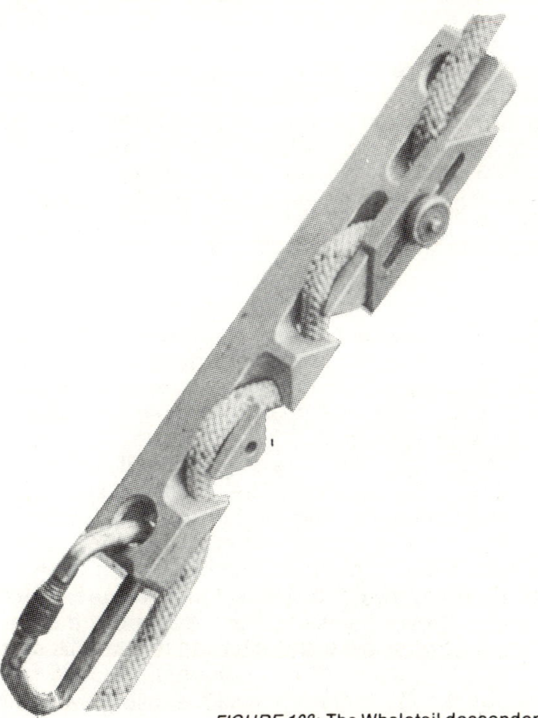

FIGURE 108: The Whaletail descender.

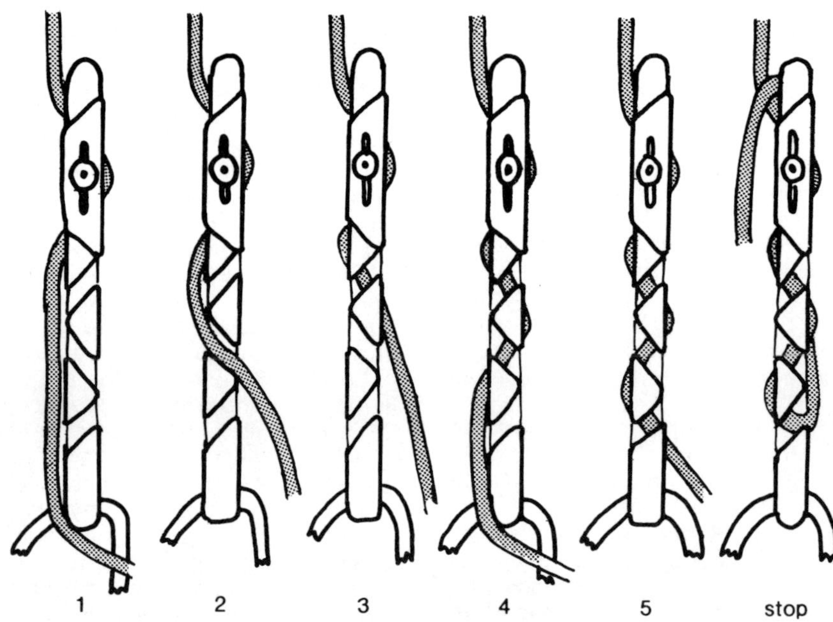

FIGURE 109: Friction positions of the Whaletail descender.

The whaletail has five friction positions and a stop position (Figure 109). In positions 1 and 4, the rope is guided under the base of the whaletail by a shallow notch. With a little practice, it will be found fairly easy to vary friction except on drops over about 200m where there is a large weight of rope. Some people find they have insufficient strength to lift this weight. A solution from them is to start the abseil with more friction than is required (say position 3 in Figure 109) and feed the rope for a time. The extra friction allows them to descend much further without having to lift the rope through another slot.

The whaletail has no fine control mechanism corresponding to bar shift on the rack. It is inferior to the rack on drops of over about 200m because of this. On shorter drops it gives ample control. It excels in caves with many drops where its compact size and rapid on-off time on pitches give it superiority to the rack.

On current pricings the whaletail is 35-40% more expensive than the rack. The rack is also easier to maintain because worn bars can be easily removed and replaced. The whaletail's knobs can be built by welding on fresh aluminium, but this is a far more awkward process (Julia James, pers. comm.). Nevertheless, several years of hard use should be possible without having to take this step (except in very muddy conditions), since, when the top knob on the whaletail is badly worn (it wears faster than the others), the whaletail can be reversed by shifting the gate along and using the carabiner hole in the other end. The top knob then becomes the bottom one, and vice versa.

The whaletail should not be used on ropes with very loose sheaths since it can cause sheath bunching (Quigg 1976).

Cast whaletails are on sale in Australia (see Appendix 1) or else they can be machined from aluminium plate or bar at the cost of four to five hours work in a well-equipped machine shop. Manufacturing details and test data are given by Montgomery (1977a).

SAFETY AND TECHNIQUES

KNOTTING THE ABSEIL ROPE

During pitch rigging if it cannot be clearly seen that the abseil rope reaches the foot of the pitch, a large knot should be tied in the rope end before the first man descends. A figure eight loop is suitable (Figure 7).

STARTING AN ABSEIL

At the start of every abseil, one should ensure that the rope is securely anchored and that the abseil device is properly secured.

STYLE

Abseiling is undoubtedly one of the most thrilling aspects of vertical caving. It can also be one of the most dangerous. The sensation of gliding down a rope sometimes blinds people to danger and causes them to descend at exhilarating speeds or leap out against shaft walls. Less cautious beginners are especially subject to such behaviour. It should be discouraged since it causes unnecessary stresses and wear on personal equipment and ropes, and vastly increases the risk of an accident.

It is good style to move at a *slow, steady* speed without straining the arms, and with enough control to be able to stop easily at any time should the need arise. Where possible, one should avoid using an abseil device with so much friction that constant feeding of the rope is necessary, since this causes arm tiring and a jerky motion which provokes rope abrasion. Equally well, one should not use so little friction that excessive body friction is required. Of course, some control of friction must be achieved with the body. As far as possible, friction should be taken with parts of the body other than the arm, because the arm tires easily. Good methods are to run the rope across the thigh, behind the back, or to wrap it around one or both feet (Figure 110). These procedures also have value in emergencies. When using thigh friction, care must be taken not to run the rope heavily across the seat harness since it may melt (page 48). Davison (1976a) records two cases where harnesses melted completely through.

LEARNING TO ABSEIL

Novices should learn to abseil on short cliffs on the surface before using the technique underground. It is prudent to use a separate lifeline of the kind practised in ladder work or rock climbing (see any basic climbing book, eg, Robbins 1971).

LIFELINES FOR UNDERGROUND USE

Abseiling is potentially dangerous because the abseil device offers only one point of contact with the rope. If the device breaks or control is lost, then a serious accident could result. While feasible, lifelines are almost never used in SRT because of the possibility of tangling with the main line, the danger of rockfall due to a moving line and the general awkwardness of organising extra people and equipment. Part of the appeal of SRT is that while on the rope one travels as a self-contained unit. A lifeline would only be warranted for a caver who is injured. For most purposes, a bottom belay or a trailing ascender belay (page 68) is perfectly adequate.

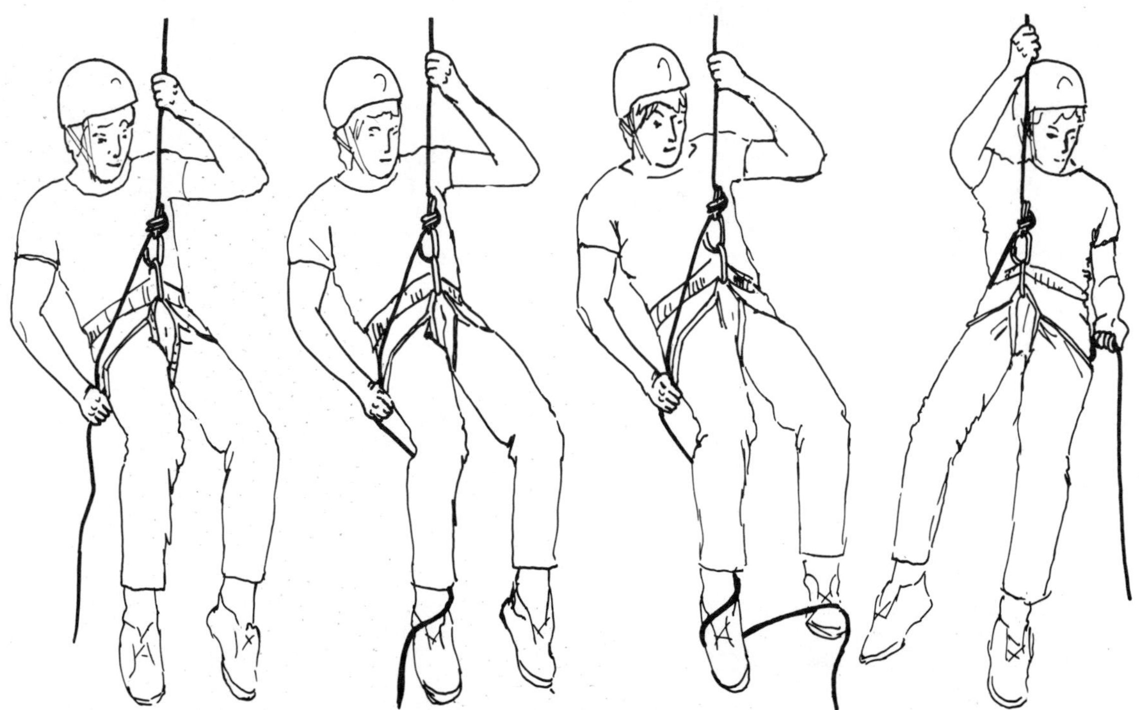

FIGURE 110: Methods of controlling abseils with the body.

THE BOTTOM BELAY

A bottom belay is simply effected by having an attentive person hold the rope at the bottom of the pitch in a stance sheltered from rockfall. If the caver making the descent has trouble, he can shout "help" (preferably before control is actually lost) and the belayer will heave the rope taut with both hands. This technique will usually bring the one in danger to an abrupt stop. The abseiler could then even release the rope and be brought down to safety by the belayer, who can easily adjust rope tension to control the descent.

Special measures may be necessary on a long pitch where a considerable amount of rope stretch would need to be taken up before the belay takes effect. Where possible, the belayer should select a position where he can run, holding the rope, down a steep incline. If the shaft floor is flat, a carabiner or pulley can be fixed by a sling to the floor and the rope passed through it (Figure 111). The belayer then exerts force by running across the floor (Pete Strickland, pers. comm.).

It is up to the individual to decide whether a bottom belay should be used. Normally, inexperienced cavers would be given one on nearly every pitch, while experienced cavers would require one only on drops of around 30m or more.

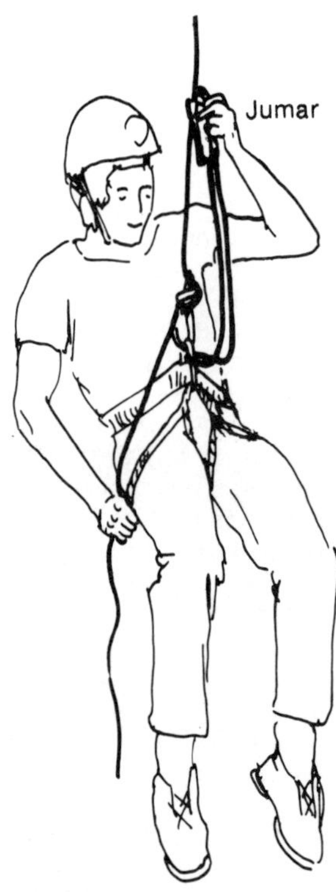

FIGURE 112: Trailing ascender belay.

THE TRAILING ASCENDER BELAY

Though very safe, the trailing ascender belay (Figure 112) is seldom used because it requires the management of an extra piece of equipment. However, it is more widely applicable than the bottom belay. The bottom belay is obviously impossible if there are no people at the bottom of the pitch or the ones that are there are out of voice or whistle contact. It is impractical if there is no shelter from rockfall. A trailing ascender belay can be used in any situation. It even covers the unlikely possibility of the abseiler becoming unconscious, or of the abseil device breaking or becoming detached from the rope.

FIGURE 111: Bottom belay for a deep shaft.

Several different belay rigs are in use, but they all work by attaching an ascender (or climbing knot) to the rope and trailing it along, so that if control is lost, the ascender immediately stops the descent. The most basic technique is to attach an ascender or climbing knot above the abseil device and run a sling down to the seat harness. The ascender is held open with the upper hand and if trouble appears, one has only to release the rope and the ascender will grip. If a climbing knot is being used for this purpose, it should be held just loose enought to slide, or it may not grip. In fact, the value of a climbing knot is questionable since in a panic it is likely that one will keep a tight hold on the knot and prevent its gripping (Smutek 1976c). An ascender is better. Whichever is used, a precaution is to carry prusik gear so that if the device is activated, it can be removed afterwards.

FIGURE 113: Removing the trailing ascender after use.

Alternatively, the rope can be wrapped around one foot, allowing one to stand up and remove the device (Figure 113). F. Petzl in France makes a device called a Shunt especially for safeguarding abseils (Figure 114). It works in the same way as an ascender, but has a lever permitting it to be released by hand after use. This is an attractive feature. Unfortunately, the Shunt was developed for use on double ropes. Using a Shunt on a single rope, any shock loading may distort the cam (Bedford 1977).

A problem with holding an ascender above the head is that it does not leave the upper hand free for adjusting abseil friction. Users of rappel racks will notice this especially. To overcome the problem, several American cavers have experimented with the idea of building a trigger mechanism into a Gibbs ascender (Davison 1976c and Moss 1977). A trigger cord is attached to a chest harness and in the event of a mishap, the Gibbs will automatically be activated by the natural reaction of leaning backwards. The chest harness should be tightly connected to the seat for safety and comfort. However, the system will not operate if the trigger cord is attached directly to the seat, since then leaning backwards will have no effect. While the rigs work well, they are rather complicated. Also, the Gibbs has no hand release mechanism similar to the one on the Shunt. Maskasky (1977) developed a modification enabling hand release, but did not combine it with a trigger.

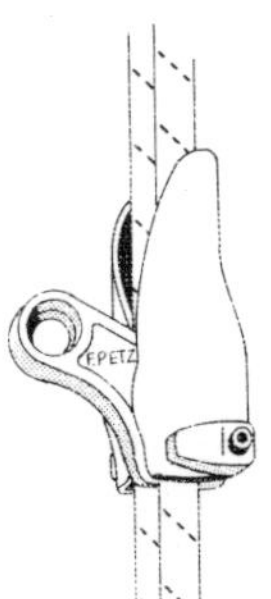

FIGURE 114: Petzl's Shunt — from Petzl Brochure.

Inspired by these designs, two Australian cavers appear to have solved the entire problem in a highly satisfactory manner (Toomer and Welch 1977). Their Gibb's modification, called the Spelean Shunt, requires only a chest sling and a locking D carabiner in addition to a standard quick release Gibbs (Figure 115). The carabiner is attached to the Gibbs with its longer (ungated) side resting on the head of the quick release pin. During a normal abseil, the carabiner weights the Gibbs cam, stopping it from gripping and obviating the need to continuously hold the Gibbs open by hand. In the event of a mishap, the Gibbs is activated by leaning backwards. To release the Gibbs, moderate hand pressure is applied to the carabiner using it as a lever. Upon release, the abseil control hand should hold the rope below the abseil device ready to resume the descent.

The Spelean Shunt is so simple that it could be used to make routine stops on any abseil, rather than being reserved only for emergencies. This would be most useful when using an abseil device such as a brake bar rig which does not have a ready stop position.

GLOVES

Beginners are normally taught to always wear heavy gloves while abseiling. This is certainly a sensible practice any time a non-variable friction device is in use, but on shorter drops is not usually necessary with a variable friction device since control is possible without much hand pressure. Only on pitches greater than about 60m do gloves become worthwhile, and even then, one on the controlling hand will suffice. On the shorter drops, their omission saves time and leaves and hands unhindered to work the device, fix rope pads, etc.

One might argue that on any pitch gloves are an essential precaution in case control is lost. However, it is a sure result of human nature that if they are not worn, loss of control is less likely because, for the sake of hand comfort, one will make greater efforts to adjust friction properly.

HAIR AND CLOTHING PROBLEMS

Through carelessness, cavers occasionally find that hair or loose clothing is drawn into their abseil device, producing a troublesome tangle (and possible a bald patch). If it happens, the first approach is to stop and try to calmly rip out the offending material, perhaps with the aid of a pocket knife. If this fails, one should attach an ascender above the abseil device, stand in a foot stirrup, and remove the tangle.

ABSEILING OVER ROPE KNOTS

Occasionally, two ropes are joined to descend a pitch or a rope is reanchored below the pitch top (page 39). The resulting knot will have to be crossed while abseiling. Since the procedure uses prusik techniques, it is treated in the next Chapter (page 98).

ABSEILING ON DIAGONAL ROPES

Ropes are occasionally rigged horizontally or diagonally to avoid water or some other hazard (page 36). Such ropes require a special abseil-prusik technique also covered in the next Chapter (page 99).

DEEP PITS

Deep pits present one of the most exciting challenges in vertical caving. One has to often overcome immense feelings of isolation and exposure in abseiling sometimes hundreds of metres in a single drop. To do this, rope and abseil equipment have to be managed calmly and expertly and, to this end, some special techniques and precautions will prove helpful. It is assumed that a variable friction descender is being used.

NEGOTIATING THE EDGE

Rope weight can sometimes create difficulties in negotiating the edge of a deep pit. This usually only happens if the drop is over 200m, and even then, it can often be eliminated by judicious rope rigging (Chapter 4).

Left to one's own devices, strenuous rope feeding may be necessary to get to the edge, followed by a real struggle on the edge itself. Depending on the nature of the edge, one of two techniques will help.

If the edge is fairly gradual and has minor ledges, one can clip an ascender on the rope and, holding it open, walk backwards to the edge. The descender is then threaded, the ascender removed, and the abseil can begin.

Sharp lips require a different tactic. A short length of rope with an ascender at its end is anchored well away from the edge, and the ascender is clipped into the abseil rope a few metres below the lip. As each person starts over, someone on top can take the whole weight of the rope by pulling on the ascender line (Figure 116) and the lip becomes easy. Once over, the rope weight is released and the ascender is passed by detaching it. It is reattached above the head for the next person (Pete Lord, pers. comm.). The last man down

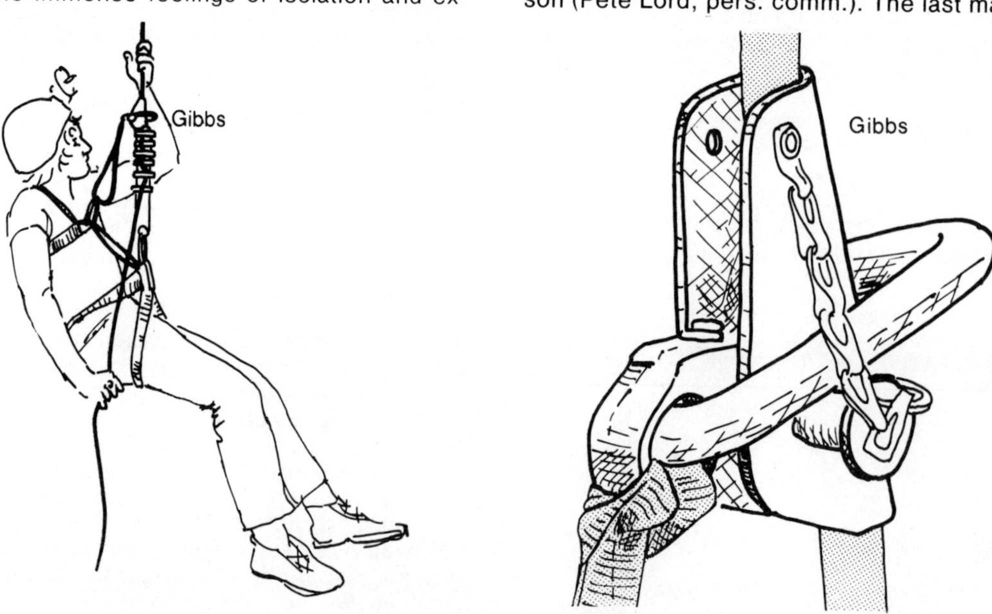

FIGURE 115: The Spelean Shunt.

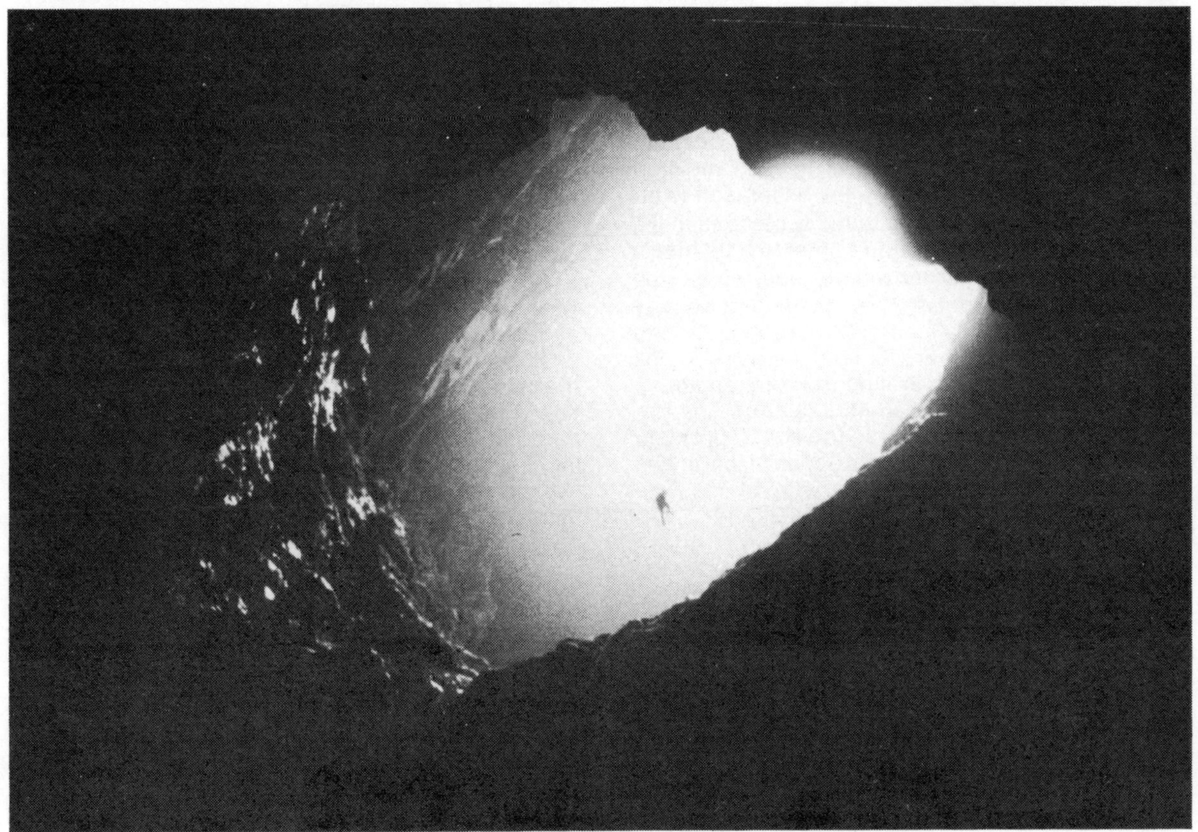

Author

Nearing the bottom of the 176m drop into Harwood Hole, South Island, New Zealand.

will need to use a rope tail (page **43**) or muscle over as best he can.

ABSEIL SPEED

Once on the pitch, to avoid heating problems and ensure that control is not lost, it is wise to descend at a steady speed of around 15m to 20m per minute. There are twc crucial elements of speed control. The first is to start at the top with adequate friction. This may be hard to judge, since full body weight is not applied to the rope until one is over the edge. A good practice is to start with too much friction and, once over the edge, remove some.

Second, if an extra bar on the rack or knob on the whaletail needs to be added on the way down, this should be done **before** control is at all jeopardised. A common mistake is to abseil at one friction setting until speed is too great, and then decide to add the extra bar or knob. At this point, however, it may be impossible to stop and actually make the addition. Several severe accidents have resulted from errors of judgment of this kind (eg,

FIGURE 116: Assistance at the edge of a deep pit.

Mitchell 1968). People have found that once control was lost, it was very difficult to regain without the aid of a belay. There is an inconspicuous reason for this. Suppose that a caver is 200m from the ground in a deep pit and has adjusted friction so that the rope weight of 15kg is just adequate to keep him motionless. He starts himself moving, and after 20m has carelessly allowed himself to go too fast (say 2m/sec). It is intuitively obvious that if a force of about 15kg is required just to hold him, a force several times larger will be required to stop him from his high speed. This means that he may have to bodily apply a load of 30kg or more to the rope, an extremely hard task if he isn't quick enough to wrap one leg around the rope or jam up the bars on his rack (should he use one). The further down he slides, the worse the contol problem will become. The same loss of control on a 30m pitch would require only about 5kg of loading, which is applied quite simply with one hand.

HEATING PROBLEMS

If an abseil device overheats, then abseil speed is too high and must be reduced. It is advisable not to stop, as this subjects one short section of the rope to heating.

CIRCULATION PROBLEMS

Sometimes blood circulation can be cut off from the legs due to pressure from the seat harness. Certain people seem to be more prone to this than others, and those affected should take special care in choosing a harness of good design with wide tape and perhaps with extra padding. Often circulation problems are only discovered at the pitch bottom when the legs feel dead on touching the ground. To avoid this, it pays to check circulation now and then by moving around in the seat harness and wriggling the toes. If the legs are going dead, vigorous movement of them will help, as will clipping an ascender onto the rope and standing in a foot stirrup until circulation returns.

7: PRUSIKING

Prusiking, the companion technique to abseiling, entails climbing up a fixed rope. Modern prusiking techniques make use of mechanical climbing devices called ascenders, or prusikers. These have the property of being easy to slide up a rope, while holding secure against the downward load of a climber. Ascenders evolved from the discovery in 1931 of a simple climbing knot called the Prusik knot. Relegated to second place, the Prusik knot and other similar knots gradually assumed the function of safety backups to the ascenders. Currently even this usage is being threatened by the practice of carrying a spare ascender as a backup. However, it is still felt that climbing knots have value in emergencies because of their simplicity and, consequently, a brief account of them is given here. For an in-depth treatment, readers are referred to Thrun (1973) and Smith (1964).

Climbing knots and ascenders are both used in a similar way to support the body on a single rope. There are many methods of arranging the knots or ascenders giving rise to different motions in making upward progress. These range from a sit-stand motion to a walking technique similar to that used in ladder climbing. Each of the different climbing arrangements is called a prusik system. After examining the component climbing knots, ascenders and ascender cords, this Chapter devotes considerable attention to the better prusik systems that have been devised. They all make use of harnesses of the kinds described in Chapter 5.

CLIMBING KNOTS

In the heyday of knot prusiking, over a dozen different knots were invented, but only a few have withstood the test of time. The two outstanding ones are the prusik knot and the helical knot. Both are known for their holding power, ease of tying and untying, security and versatility.

The type of cord used for the knot will obviously have important effects on the knot's performance. As a general recommendation, the cord should be 2mm to 3mm thinner than the climbing rope and of tight construction. Cord thinner than this will tend to jam (becoming immovable) and thicker cord will tend to slip under load. A tight construction enables the cord to retain its roundness, and so improves holding power. It also produces stiffness which is an aid to loosening the knot. Any of the synthetic fibres should have adequate holding power, though polypropylene is generally the best and it is also light and cheap (Thrun 1973, Knutson 1973a, Graham 1969).

THE PRUSIK KNOT

The Prusik knot still maintains an important place in prusiking, even though many other knots were invented after it, and tested against it. It is tied in a sling as shown in Figure 117. If laid climbing rope is used, the bottom half of the knot should be spiralled in the direction of the lay (as in Figure 117), rather than in the opposite sense (Figure 118) (Smith 1964).

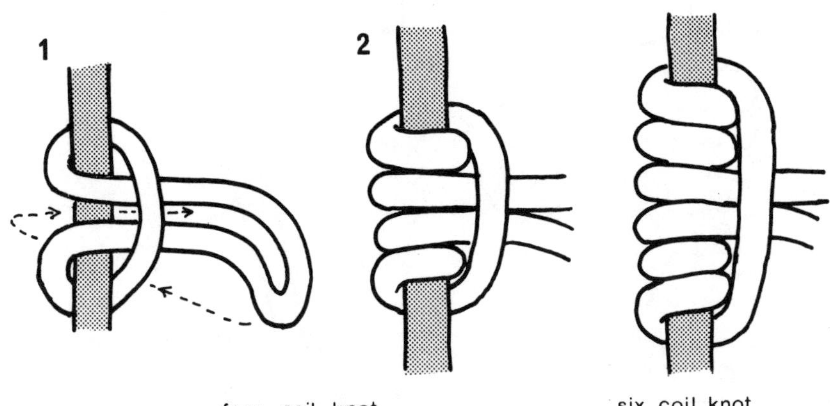

FIGURE 117: The Prusik knot.

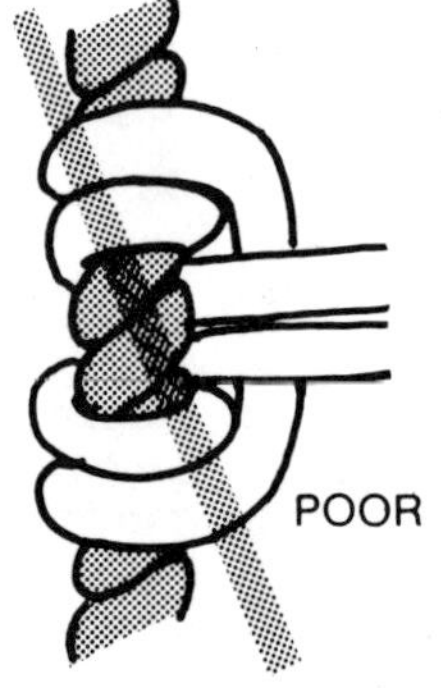

FIGURE 118: Poor version of the Prusik knot, for a laid rope. The bottom half of the knot should spiral in the direction of the lay.

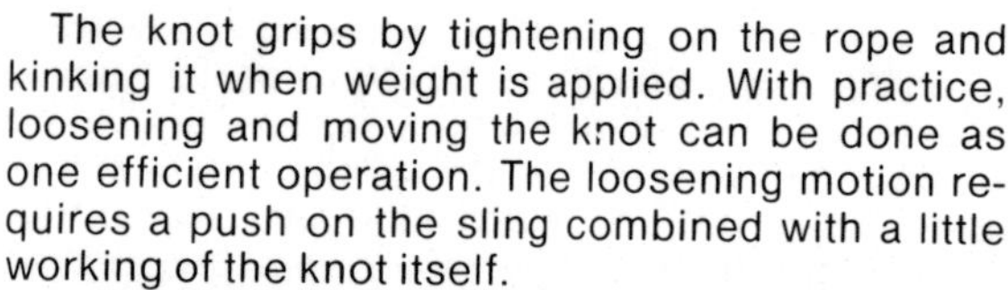

The knot grips by tightening on the rope and kinking it when weight is applied. With practice, loosening and moving the knot can be done as one efficient operation. The loosening motion requires a push on the sling combined with a little working of the knot itself.

A good feature of the Prusik knot is that it can be made larger to increase hold power simply by tucking the sling one more time through the loop. The four coil Prusik knot is adequate for most purposes, but in muddy conditions the six coil knot is generally preferred.

THE HELICAL KNOT

While the Prusik knot is quite safe and adequate, it is surpassed by the helical knot (also called the Path, Penberthy or Ascender knot), which has about 50% greater holding power and is considerably easier to loosen at each upward step (Knutson 1973b). There are two versions of the helical knot (Figure 119 and 120) (Knutson 1973b, Pierson 1975). Whenever possible, the carabiner version is preferred since it is much simpler to tie and the carabiner can act as a handle. It could be particularly useful as a direct substitute for a failed ascender, where the ascender itself is simply removed and the knot clipped into its place in the prusik system. Whichever version is used, it is important to keep slack in the knot to a minimum. In the case of the carabiner version, this involves choosing the cord length in advance to give the desired number of coils.

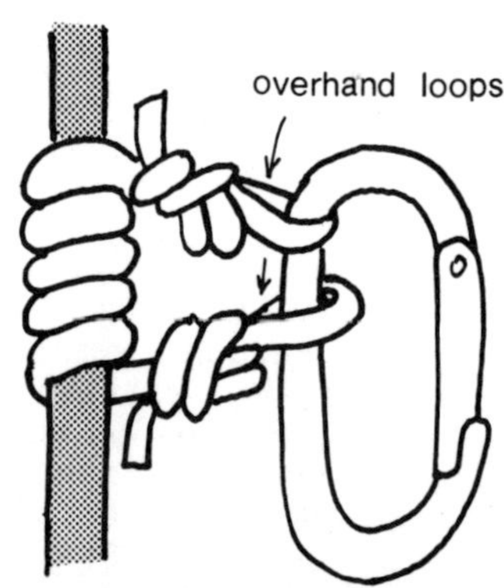

FIGURE 120: The carabiner version of the helical knot.

As for the Prusik knot, holding power is dependent on the number of coils in the knot. The optimum number for any particular application is best determined in a practice session, but at least four will normally be needed (Graham 1969). If a laid climbing rope is in use, greater holding power is given by spiralling the knot in the direction of the lay (Knutson 1973b).

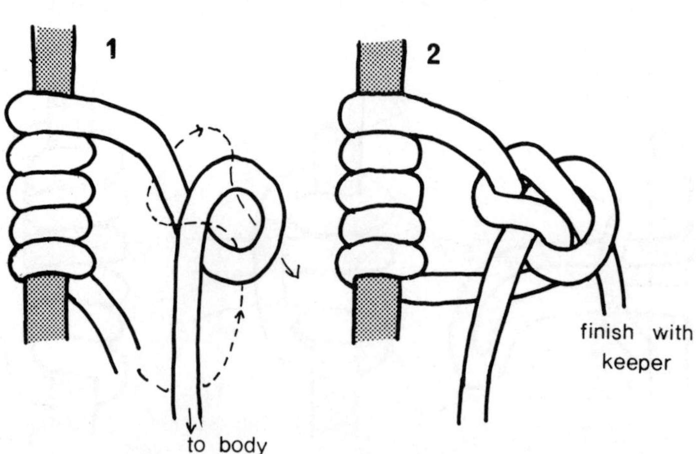

FIGURE 119: The helical knot tied in the end of a single cord. After finishing the knot all slack is taken out and the loose end secured with an overhand knot as a keeper.

Paul Caffyn

Prusiking out of Uli Oogua, a 60m shaft in Papua New Guinea.

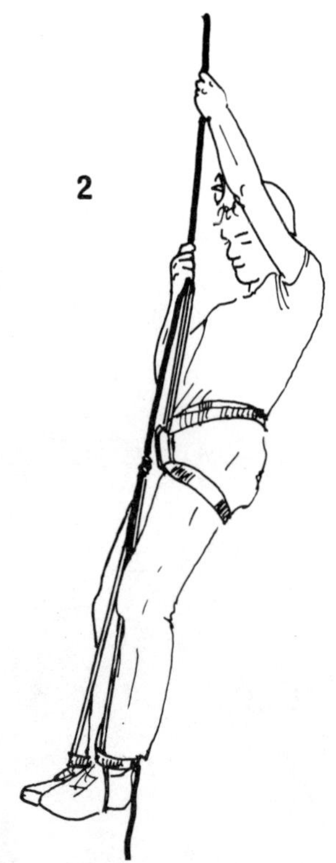

FIGURE 121: The Texas prusik system with two knots. One is connected to the seat knot and the other to both feet. The climbing motion is to sit in the seat harness and raise the knot connected to feet (1), then stand on the feet and raise the knot connected to the seat (2).

CONSTRUCTING AN EMERGENCY PRUSIK SYSTEM

There are several different ways in which climbing knots can be built into an emergency prusik system. The simplest approach is to carry no extra equipment and rely on constructing something with gear on hand, possibly using a length of climbing rope. The author once got himself out of a tight spot by forming prusik slings from a spare 25m climbing rope. It worked but was not very efficient. A much safer approach is to carry short cords to form carabiner versions of the helical knot. These will substitute for ascenders which have broken or else cannot operate because the climbing rope is muddy or icy. The number of cords carried will vary from situation to situation. One cord would suffice to cater for the unlikely event of an ascender failure, but replacement cords for all ascenders may be required in exceptionally muddy or icy conditions. Some improvisation may be needed to get the knots to work in a particular prusik system. This is best done in a practice session on the surface.

Ultimate security is given by carrying cords to rig a completely separate prusik system based on climbing knots. The Texas prusik system described by Thrun (1973) is very suitable, since it requires only two knots and is operated with an easy and comfortable sit-stand motion (Figure 121 and page 94). One can choose to have cords to both feet or only one. Use of only one foot requires less cord but is more strenuous, even though it is possible to change legs upon tiring. Since injury or shock may be inflicted in an emergency situation, it is prudent to provide for the two-feet method.

ASCENDERS: SOME GENERAL COMMENTS

Ascenders nearly always operate on a camming principle. They consist basically of a cam and a U-shaped housing to accommodate the rope. When weight is applied to the ascender, the cam grips the rope, usually with teeth, and pushes it tightly into the housing. The cam action is so effective that ascenders usually fail in destruction testing by cutting the rope or by breaking themselves, rather than by slippage. While climbing knots are similarly effective, ascenders are undeniably superior because of their speed, versatility and ease of handling.

It is hardly surprising that the ingenuity of climbers and cavers has provided a wide range of ascenders from which to choose. There are about ten ascender models currently on the market. Probably ten more have been invented and described in caving journals, but never achieved sufficient popularity to merit commercial production. Many were basic forerunners of the modern designs. A number of them are covered by Thrun (1973), but they will not be treated here.

A checklist of questions concerning ascenders will once again aid in the detailed examination of popular models.

STRENGTH

A breaking strain (with the load applied as in use) similar to the one recommended for abseil devices is desirable, that is, about 500kg.

BRITTLENESS

Commercial ascenders are nearly always partially or wholly cast from hard, wear-resistant alloys. These may be prone to brittle fracture if the ascender is shock loaded in a fall or dropped. All ascenders require special care because of this, but some require more care than others (page 78).

SECURITY

There should be a mechanism to securely hold the rope in the ascender.

EASE OF HANDLING

It should be possible to quickly clip the ascender on or off the rope, preferably with one hand. During each prusik step it must be easy to unload the ascender and move it upwards with one simple hand or foot motion. In the case of hand movement, it helps if the ascender has a handle.

VERSATILITY

It is important that an ascender can accommodate a range of rope sizes without jamming or slipping. It should also be possible to use the ascender for descending, both as an emergency resource and as an aid to crossing knots while abseiling (page 98).

DURABILITY

Ascender cams are prone to wear, particularly under muddy conditions. They should be durable and yet easily replaced when they do wear out.

WEIGHT, BULK AND COST

Light, compact equipment has always been demanded by cavers and climbers and, consequently, most ascenders are about as light and compact as safety requirements allow so weight and bulk are not generally important deciding criteria when choosing an ascender. Neither do prices vary greatly enough to make cost a deciding factor. It is strongly recommended that cavers buy the ascender they feel to be the best, and ignore the small differences in price.

POPULAR ASCENDERS

JUMAR ASCENDERS

On a world basis the Swiss Jumar is probably the most popular ascender. Its name derives from Jusy and Marti, the surnames of the two men who developed it in the late 1950's. As a game warden Jusy had often to make steep mountain ascents in order to band young eagles for nature research. For this special job, Marti constructed the Jumar (Walter Marti, pers. comm.) (Figure 122).

Jumars have a high quality cast aluminium alloy frame and a replaceable spring loaded cast alloy steel cam. Each ascender weighs 210g. The Jumar frame features top and bottom attachment points for slings; the top one for hauling purposes and the bottom one for body loading. The top hole should not be body loaded. The cam is plated to prevent rust, though the spikes will rust after their tips become worn. There is a plastic safety catch to prevent the rope from coming out unintentionally. Every time a Jumar is clipped on a rope the catch should be checked to see that it is in the lock position. Sometimes mud or rusting of the catch spring will prevent it from closing properly. Attaching the Jumar to a diagonally fixed rope may also prevent the catch from closing (Figure 123). Jumars have a handle, which will avoid knuckle grinding when prusiking against walls and which provides a ready grip when the Jumar is used for gear hauling (page 104). When climbing free drops, the handle is not very useful since better balance is obtained by gripping the top of the Jumar.

Jumars are generally sold in pairs consisting of a left and right handed ascender. This design feature seems to have been introduced to suit a

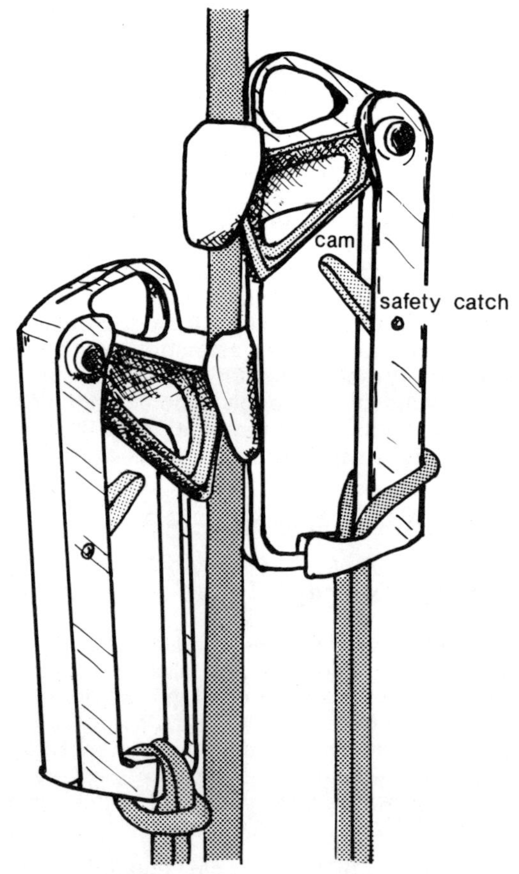

FIGURE 122: A pair of Jumar ascenders. The attachment cord may be tied in to the slot in the base of the handle (left), or through the hole in the handle (right). The hole attachment is stronger (after Jumar Brochure).

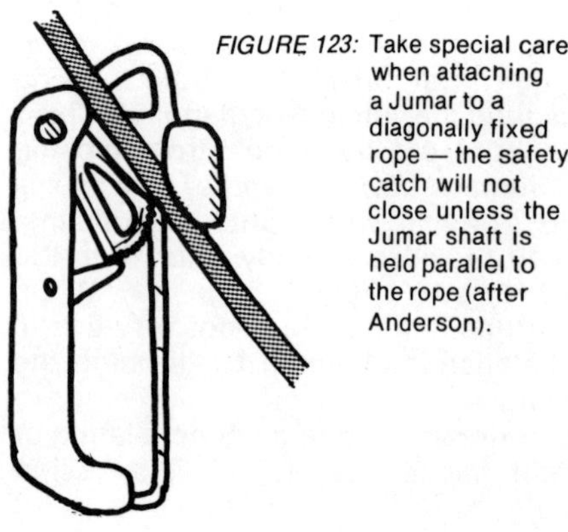

FIGURE 123: Take special care when attaching a Jumar to a diagonally fixed rope — the safety catch will not close unless the Jumar shaft is held parallel to the rope (after Anderson).

simple prusik system described in the leaflet provided with each purchase of Jumars. In this system, a Jumar is held in each hand, using the left and right handed ascenders appropriately. However, it is a poor prusik system for general cave usage. Most systems do not involve such an obvious left-right positioning, but generally it will be found best to use left handed Jumars for any positions on the left side of the body, and right handed ones for the right side.

Jumars are advertised for use on 7mm to 14mm ropes, though in practice they accept 13mm and 14mm ropes only with difficulty and may jam. The outstanding feature of the Jumar is the ease with which it can be clipped on and off a rope. With a little practice, it can be done one handed in just a few seconds. This ease gives the Jumar matchless speed for getting on and off pitches and crossing rope knots and other obstacles. Descending is also simply done by fingering open the cam while leaving the safety catch in position.

Jumars are strong enough for prusiking purposes, having withstood loads of over 500kg in several different tests (Smutek 1973b, Thrun 1973, Wade 1973). They failed by buckling of the cam or by cutting the sheath of the rope to which they were attached. These tests, however, only apply to a loading placed on the Jumar in the same way as in normal prusiking. Ullin (1973) points out that a Jumar is much weaker when used on a horizontal or diagonal traverse rope since it twists under loading and easily cuts the rope's sheath (Figure 124). The problem is accentuated with 7mm or 8mm ropes, since they were found to be thin enough to squeeze and cut their way right out of the Jumar at very low loads. Ullin found that an extra carabiner could be used to solve the problem.

The tests described by Wade examined the strength of the Jumar frame as well as the Jumar's holding power. When loaded between the top eye and the bottom notch, one Jumar frame broke at just under 1200kg. Each frame is tested in the factory to 300kg.

The brittleness of Jumars is their most worrying feature. There are many instances of Jumar frames breaking when shock loaded, typically through the handle. Sometimes a fracture would lie concealed until a slight bounce during prusiking caused the actual cleavage (Davison 1976b, Davison 1977b, Wade 1972). Care should be taken never to drop a Jumar or use one in any belay situation when even a small shock load might occur. After a severe impact a Jumar should be thrown away or X-rayed. Should fracture occur, it is most likely in the thin part of the handle underneath the rope housing, rather than through the entire handle. To take account of this, it is best to tie in through the hole rather than the notch in the Jumar's base since, preferentially, this loads the strongest part of the handle (Figure 122). Users of Jumars will be pleased to know that Walter Marti plans to release a new model in 1978 which will sustain a shock load and have an improved facility for gear hauling. It will be called the Jumar-Combi (Walter Marti, pers comm).

It has been an early criticism of Jumars (and other ascenders) that the spikes on their cams might cause serious rope damage, but experience has since shown that the effect is small. Still, it does exist and Planina (1975) has shown experimentally that Jumars wear out ropes marginally faster than their main rival, the Gibbs ascender.

Jumars can perform disappointingly in very muddy or icy conditions. The mud or ice packs solidly in between the spikes on the cam and can cause a sudden slippage of the Jumars. In one muddy cave in Australia, a caver slid 10m to the floor after both his Jumars slipped (Mike Martin, pers comm). Usual remedies are to push the cam hard with the thumb each time the Jumar bites or to use a toothbrush to clear away the mud before it consolidates. However, in bad conditions neither approach may work and a Gibbs ascender would be preferred. Gibbs have a reputation for holding under almost any conditions. After a muddy trip, Jumars should be cleaned (a toothbrush works well), paying particular attention to the cam, and the moving parts should be lightly lubricated.

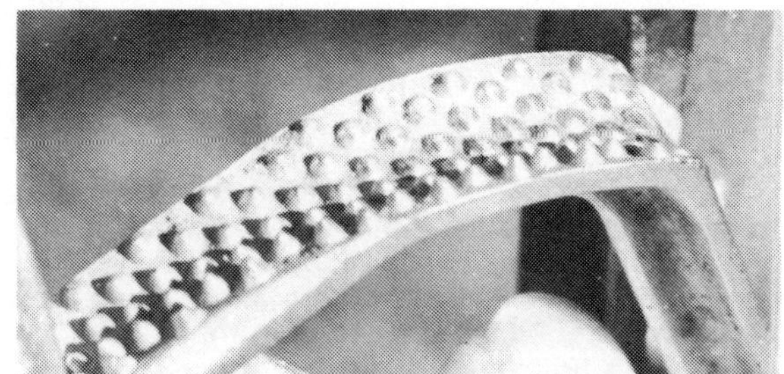

FIGURE 125: Enlargement of a worn Jumar cam. The Jumar has just started to slip on a clean rope.

Jumars wear out by abrasion of the cam spikes, as do all other toothed ascenders (Figure 125). They should withstand several years of hard underground use before replacement becomes necessary. It is cheapest to only replace the cams, but new cams can be difficult to acquire in some countries. The lead Jumar in a system tends to wear worst, because it always grips a rope under the tension of body weight applied to a lower Jumar (Richards and Hosely 1965). If wear goes unchecked, the lead Jumar may begin to slip on clean ropes; a sure sign that retirement is necessary. As a stopgap measure until the cam is replaced, the lead Jumar can be exchanged for the bottom Jumar. It will probably grip in the bottom position because of the lower rope tension there.

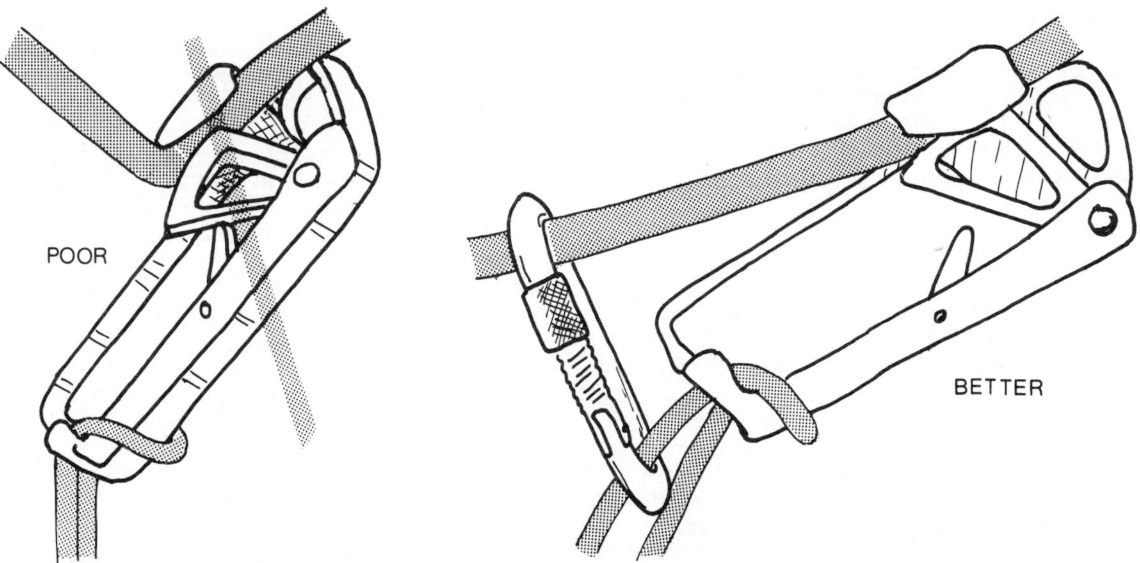

FIGURE 124: Using a Jumar on a diagonal traverse rope. At left the Jumar is poorly attached since loading will twist the Jumar and possibly cut the rope. A much better arrangement is shown at right. Ullin recommended clipping the carabiner into the Jumar handle, but the method shown is felt to be better. A Claude loop alone can often be used as an alternative to a Jumar on a short or horizontal traverse (page 52).

GIBBS ASCENDERS

Gibbs Ascenders are manufactured in the USA and retail at a lower price than Jumars. In addition to being smaller and slightly lighter (200g), the Gibbs is quite different in appearance and concept to the Jumar (Figure 126). It consists of a cast aluminium alloy cam, a U-shaped rope housing bent from aluminium alloy plate and a steel lock pin, available either as a wire pin or a quick release pin (Pinchak and Gibbs, 1972). The quick release pin is more expensive, but its greater speed of attachment and durability make it the better option (Davison 1976a). The lock pin and the cam are both connected to the housing to prevent loss. To engage the ascender on a rope the cam is inserted into the housing, centred on the pinhole, and then the pin is pushed through. Provided the pin is properly locked, the rope cannot come out.

The most striking difference between the Jumar and the Gibbs is that, while the user of a Jumar attaches his slings to the Jumar frame and relies on spring loading to cause the cam closure, the Gibbs user attaches **himself** to the cam and uses his own body weight to make the cam close. The cam is the Gibb's only attachment point, a fact which has important implications later for the way in which a Gibbs can be built into a prusik system (page 82). For the moment, this interesting difference affords the Gibbs two advantages over the Jumar. The most important one results from the fact that body weight gives more positive cam closure than a spring. The Jumar's spring may not have sufficient force to cause the cam to catch onto a muddy or icy rope, with consequent slippage. In contrast, the Gibbs cam will almost always grip. This even holds true for ropes with cut sheaths. The Jumar is far more likley to pull the sheath down the core than the Gibbs (Eavis 1976). The second advantage is that when a Gibbs is moved up a rope, its cam hangs loose and does not drag against the rope. This minimises wear, and also reduces the annoying tendency of an unweighted rope to ride up with the lower ascender on starting a pitch. Being spring loaded, Jumars cause more wear, both to themselves and the rope (Planina 1975) and induce more rope hitching.

Since the first appearance of the Gibbs about nine years ago, the manufacturers have made a number of design improvements. Modern Gibbs Ascenders are effective and strong on ropes from 5mm to 14mm in diameter. In strength testing by Pinchak and Gibbs (1972) on a variety of popular caving ropes, failure usually occurred by cutting of the rope at loads of about one-third of the rope's rated strength. An exception was provided by Blue Water II rope with a rated strength of

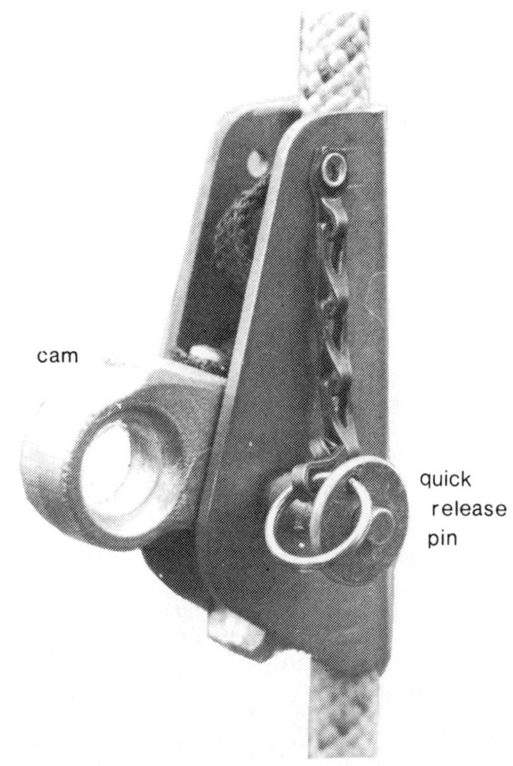

FIGURE 126: The Gibbs Ascender.

3175kg. It caused a Gibbs failure at about 1000kg, a higher figure than any obtained for Jumars. Separate tests were performed by Cal Magnussen to see if the Gibbs caused significant rope damage well before actual failure (Smutek 1973b). Using braided mountaineering ropes, little damage was apparent at loads of 550kg. In the same tests, Jumars frequently caused visible damage at loads of under 450kg. Good quality control is an attractive feature of the Gibbs with the manufacturers testing each one to 454kg before sale.

As well as being stronger than Jumars, Gibbs do not appear to seriously suffer from brittle fracture. Indeed, some rock climbers use them to belay solo climbs, a practice which would be suicidal with Jumars because of the likelihood of a shock loading. Humphrey (1973) applauds the Gibbs in this usage, having seen them hold several leader falls.

In view of the Gibbs superiority to Jumars in so many ways, the Jumar's greater popularity may seem mystifying. The reason is to be found almost solely in the Jumar's better handling qualities and versatility. The worst feature of the Gibbs

Ascender is its awkward three-piece construction. Compared to the Jumar, it requires a slow and fiddly process to get the rope in or out. This is a particular problem in cold conditions, in caves with many short pitches, or on technical pitches which have rope knots, sharp overhangs, or traverses at the top or bottom. It is also very difficult to use a Gibbs to descend a rope. These differences are certainly significant enough for most people to prefer Jumars over the Gibbs for nearly all technical caving purposes. However, Gibbs do have superiority in small caves or deep pits where on-off time is not significant. For interested readers, Delbert Province in the USA has developed a one-piece ascender similar to a Gibbs but with better handling qualities. It is complex and difficult to manufacture, however, and is not available commercially (Smith 1974c).

Gibbs give good trouble-free service, except that occasionally the quick release pins malfunction in muddy caves. Mud can work its way inside the pin's locking mechanism and cause it to jam in the open position leaving the pin free to fall out. Fortunately, it is possible to pick an insecure pin by simply looking at its release button, which will be fully out in the lock position. A jammed pin can be freed by working it a couple of times, if possible, under running water or in the worst cases by prodding it into the lock position with a sharp instrument such as a marlin spike on a pocket knife. After a muddy trip, a Gibbs should be cleaned under a running tap and then lubricated with light oil or powdered graphite. Use of heavy oil or grease is inadvised since they can pick up grit (MacGregor 1975, Davison 1976b).

Gibbs cams are easily replaceable. Davison (1975) recommends retiring them when polishing first becomes apparent on the seventh tooth (Figure 127). By this stage, the high teeth will show marked grooves. Davison's experience is that cams which become too worn are subject to sudden, repeated failure to grip under load.

An ascender similar to the Gibbs is marketed in Britain under the name Lewis Ropewalker though it is not as well finished as the Gibbs.

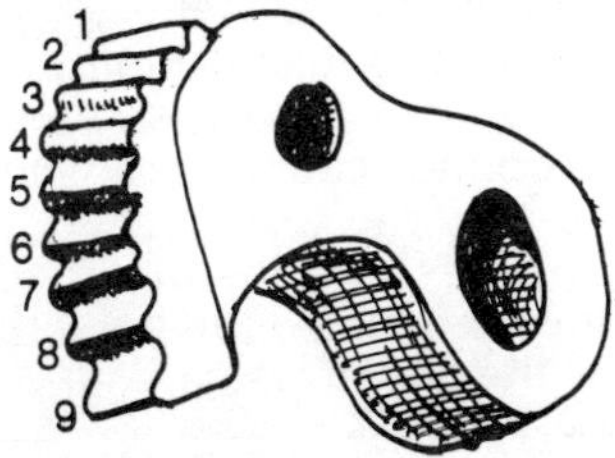

FIGURE 127: A Gibbs cam should be replaced when wear first becomes apparent on the seventh tooth.

CLOG AND PETZL ASCENDERS

Clog Climbing Gear in Wales and F. Petzl in France have been producing quite similar ascenders for many years. Similar developments in design have even occurred. Petzl set an original trend by fitting a spring loaded toothed cam inside a frame bent from plate aluminium. The basic Petzl Ascender is a lightweight (125g), one-piece device with carabiner attachment holes at top and bottom (Figure 128). There is no handle. Like the Jumar, the rope can be inserted from the side, though unfortunately not with a carabiner clipped into the top attachment hole. (Any carabiner here has to be removed to get the rope in or out.) Rope insertion requires the use of both hands. The Petzl has a unique safety catch, which allows the catch to be fixed in an open position, possibly a useful feature for crossing knots. The catch gives good security when in the lock position. In his brochure, Fernand Petzl rates the breaking strength of his ascender at 400kg, a figure which was closely confirmed in a test by Thrun (1973). The ascender failed by bending of the frame to the point where the cam swung through. The Petzl's strength is only just adequate for prusik use and would not be sufficient for situations where a shock load might occur. The plate aluminium frame would give good resistance to brittle fracture if the ascender were dropped.

Some years later, Clog Climbing Gear produced a similar ascender, the only major difference being that Clog used the lower carabiner attachment to hold in the rope instead of a separate safety catch. This is absolutely secure, but requires the user to detach from the ascender to get the rope in or out, a relatively lengthy procedure.

Since 1974, both companies have produced an ascender with a handle. The Petzl model has the same locking mechanism and strength as the original. It is about 50% larger than the Jumar while of similar weight (200g). The Petzl brochure advertises the new device as being easy to open one handed, but the author tried one and does not agree. The safety catch is certainly much harder to operate than the one on the Jumar.

The Clog Expedition Ascender is of similar size to the Petzl model having a large enough handle to accept a heavy mountaineering mitt. This gives it needless bulk for caving. There is no lower carabiner hole but instead a rope is tied through the handle. One should resist the temptation to drill a carabiner hole; it has been purposefully omitted to avoid the demonstrated possibility of carabiner failure (Moorehouse 1976). The carabiner locking mechanism has been replaced by a safety catch somewhat like the Jumar's. However, while the catch is easily operated with one hand to take an ascender off a rope, it is difficult to use to put the ascender back on (Smutek 1976b).

Even with the addition of a handle, the Clog and Petzl Ascenders do not have the handling qualities of a Jumar, nor its strength. They are easier to use than the Gibbs but, again, are not as strong.

HIEBLER ASCENDERS

Hiebler Ascenders are made by Salewa in Germany. They are light, compact and inexpensive ascenders which, like the Gibbs, work well under almost any conditions because attachment is made to them at the cam (Figure 129). However, these are their only strong points. Hieblers have long held a reputation for popping off the rope while they are being moved up or when loaded in unusual directions. They are inefficient because the cam uses a lever action which causes a height loss of about 80mm each time a step is made (Thrun 1973). Finally, Hieblers would be difficult to incorporate into almost any of the popular prusik systems used in caves. They are best left to the mountaineer as a lightweight piece of equipment to be used only occasionally.

ATTACHING ASCENDERS TO THE BODY

Cords and tapes are used to attach ascenders to the body. They can be fashioned into slings or provided with loops at each end (Figure 130). Wherever possible, cord should be used in preference to tape because cord is neater, better wearing and can be used to tie climbing knots in an emergency. Tape should only be used in positions where cord is found uncomfortable. Foot stirrups (page 54) are the most common application.

The criteria for choosing cord type are much the same as those for choosing the prusik rope (Chapter 1). High strength, high abrasion resistance and low stretch are all desirable. Eight millimeters is about the optimum diameter for providing these features without incurring excessive bulk. The low stretch is important because as weight is transferred to an ascender after each prusik step, the ascender cord stretches and causes some height loss. The cumulative effect of this stretch over an entire pitch may be quite large. There is, however, one precaution with low stretch cord. The problem arises at pitch tops where a short exposed move is often required to get off the rope. It is a common practice to leave an ascender on the rope to safety this move. Should a fall occur onto the ascender, the stretch in the ascender cord will be needed to reduce potentially harmful stresses on the body and the ascender. A low stretch cord may cause injury or ascender breakage. If one intends using an ascender for safety purposes, then it should be provided with a dynamic mountaineering rope designed especially for catching falls and, preferably, a Gibbs ascender should be used. However, a safer and better alternative is to retain low stretch cord for all ascenders and use a Claude loop as a safety.

In most positions requiring tape, 25mm tubular tape is a suitable choice because of its good handling qualities. Tape requires very diligent care and inspection because it is prone to rapid wear when used for ascenders. The author has knowledge of several instances of tapes snapping or abrading through during cave use. Tapes should be retired when their condition is at all doubtful.

PRUSIK SYSTEMS: SOME GENERAL COMMENTS

Attention will now be focused on the many ways in which ascenders, ascender cords and harnesses can be built into prusik systems. Similar to the treatment given to abseil devices, only the six or seven most effective or popular systems will be presented. As a general safety measure, it is recommended that cavers have a knowledge of several of these. For the experimenter, Robert Thrun records nineteen systems in his book on prusiking (Thrun 1973).

Even though there is a wide variety of prusik systems, it is possible to recognize major similarities between them. For the purposes of this book, systems are placed into one of two groups, namely, ropewalking systems and sit-stand systems. Ropewalking systems use a ladder climbing motion and sit-stand systems a motion similar to that used for knee bends. In addition, there is an emergency one ascender system which is not readily categorized (page 94).

While prusik systems can generally make use of any type of ascender, it will often be found that those with two attachment points (Jumars, Clogs and Petzls) are more easily accommodated than those with only one (Gibbs), or vice versa. Throughout the descriptions of prusik systems, one type or the other has often been recommended, using only the names Jumar and Gibbs for the sake of brevity.

Individual prusik systems have their good and bad points and it will not be possible to recom-

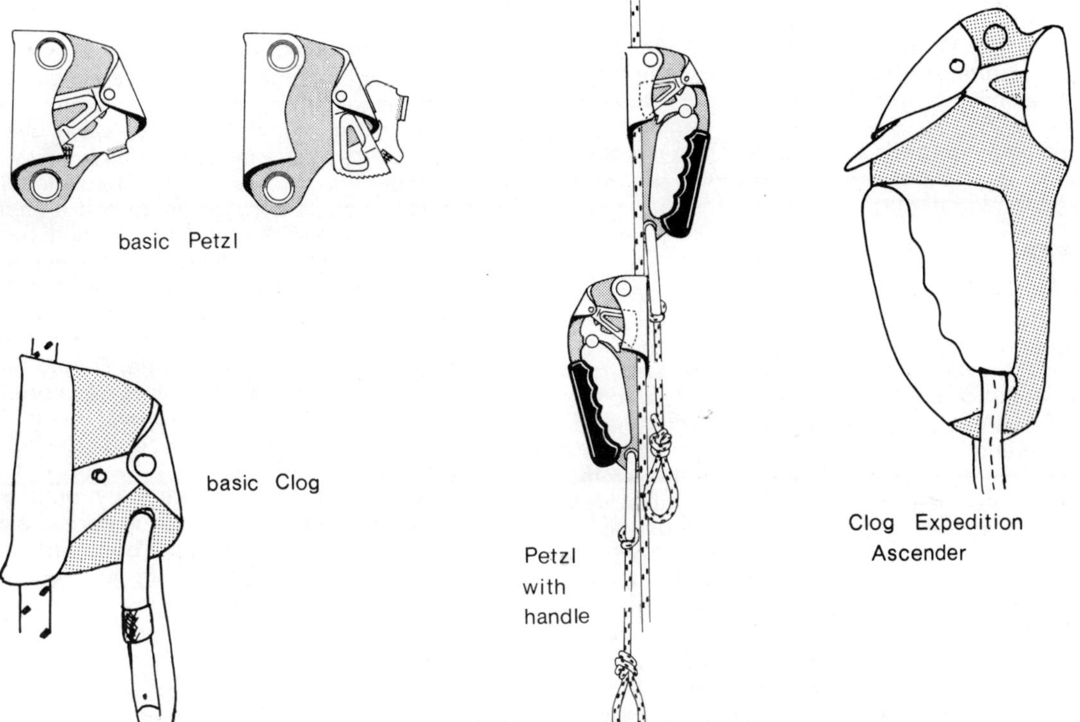

FIGURE 128: Clog and Petzl ascenders. The two Clog ascenders and the Petzl ascender with a handle are supplied in left and right handed pairs. The basic Petzl ascender is available only in a right handed model. The Petzl drawings are from the Petzl Brochure.

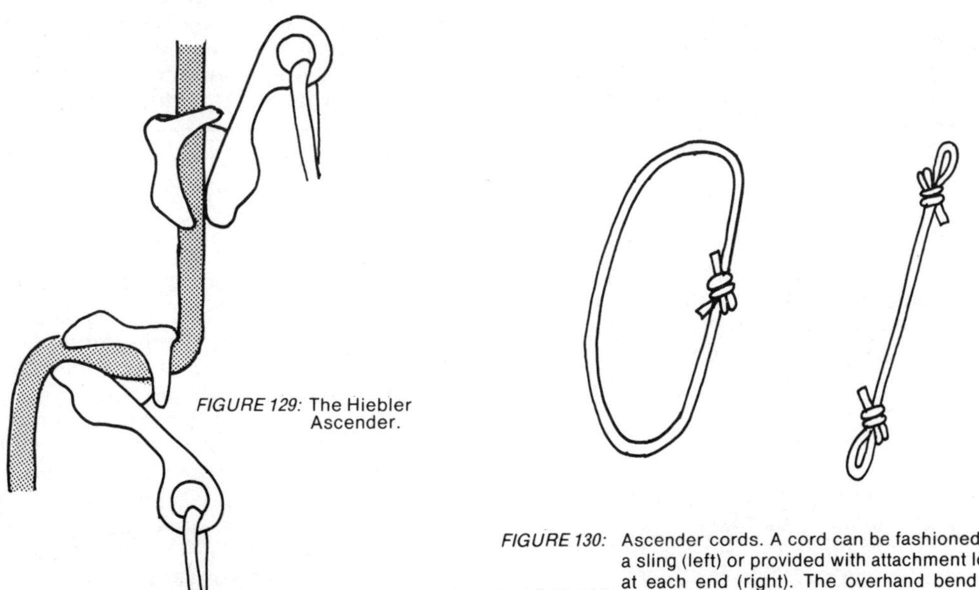

FIGURE 129: The Hiebler Ascender.

FIGURE 130: Ascender cords. A cord can be fashioned into a sling (left) or provided with attachment loops at each end (right). The overhand bend is a good knot to use because of its low bulk.

mend one system over all others. Novices should experiment with a variety of systems and choose that which best suits the style of caving they will pursue, whether it be exploring deep pits or tackling streamways with multiple short pitches. Before describing any systems in detail, some general comments will be made and general comparisons drawn between ropewalking systems and sit-stand systems.

SAFETY

The safety of a prusik system depends on more than a correct choice of harness, ascenders and ascender cords. The system must be fail-safe. This is achieved by having at least two separate points of attachment from the chest or seat to the rope. Since at least one seat attachment is needed for resting, the options are a chest and seat attachment or two seat attachments. All systems have foot attachments, but they are no guarantee of safety because a complete back flip will be taken by the caver before a foot stirrup holds. If the climber is injured or made unconscious by the fall, or if he is too tired to pull himself up, death will quickly occur. In fact, several near accidents and deaths in the USA prompted the Vertical Section of the National Speleological Society (USA) to recommend three points of attachment, though not specifically seat or chest attachments (Smith 1976a, French 1975). In most systems, an extra ascender would therefore need to be added. However, this is at the cost of simplicity which is, in itself, a powerful contributing factor to safety. Accidents with two point systems have occurred, but, to the author's knowledge, have always been due to an unsafe harness, ascender, or ascender cord. Two points of attachment are considered the optimum number. A spare ascender can be carried on a sling, ready to clip on and maintain two point contact if an ascender fails, or is momentarily removed from the rope, such as in crossing a knot.

HANDLING AND COMFORT

Ease of assembly in the cave and low bulk are desirable features of prusik systems, particularly in tight or deep caves. Once on a pitch, comfort depends largely on having an easily attained rest position and in avoiding strenuous use of the arms.

SKILL

Normally people find that sit-stand systems require less skill than ropewalking systems and are therefore easier to learn. This is an attractive feature of sit-stand systems for people who only go caving occasionally.

EFFICIENCY

The efficiency of a prusik system is measured by the amount of energy that is used in climbing a pitch. Ropewalking systems are commonly claimed to be more efficient than sit-stand systems because users of sit-stand systems lose valuable height every time they sit down. The claim is true if consideration is only given to the amount of mechanical work done, but the human body is much too complex to validate such a simple approach. Physiological factors such as strenuousness and frequency of resting must also be included, and on both these points the sit-stand systems have an advantage. During the sitting part of each sit-stand prusik cycle, a brief rest is compulsory. More research will need to be done before systems can be compared for efficiency. What is fairly certain, however, is that in any system efficiency is aided by rigging the system snugly with low stretch materials and, at each prusik step, by keeping the body vertical and pushing straight downwards with the legs, as opposed to pushing outwards.

SPEED

Prusiking speed is of great importance in ascents of deep pits and caves. Speed depends on fitness and expertise, but also on certain qualities of the prusik system in use. One quality is, of course, the efficiency of the system (see above). Another is the distance gained in each step. Any system should be rigged on the body to achieve the maximum gain possible from that system, although in practice it is less strenous to take somewhat shorter steps than the maximum.

A third quality is the natural speed of the climbing motion. Here, ropewalking systems are faster than sit-stand systems because the walking motion is faster to perform than the sit-stand motion. On a free drop, a ropewalking system may be nearly twice as fast as a sit-stand system. The final quality is the ease of crossing overhangs, rope knots, rope protectors, and getting on and off pitches. The best sit-stand systems are faster for these operations because they use simpler rigs. The net result is that pitches of up to about 20m favour sit-stand systems because on-off time is a significant part of total climbing time. If the pitch contains rope knots or rope protectors, this figure may rise to 60m or more. Long, straightforward drops are the domain of the ropewalking systems. For general caving purposes, a compromise choice will need to be made.

Beginning the long prusik out of Kacna Jama, a 213m deep shaft in Yugoslavia. *Andrew Pavey*

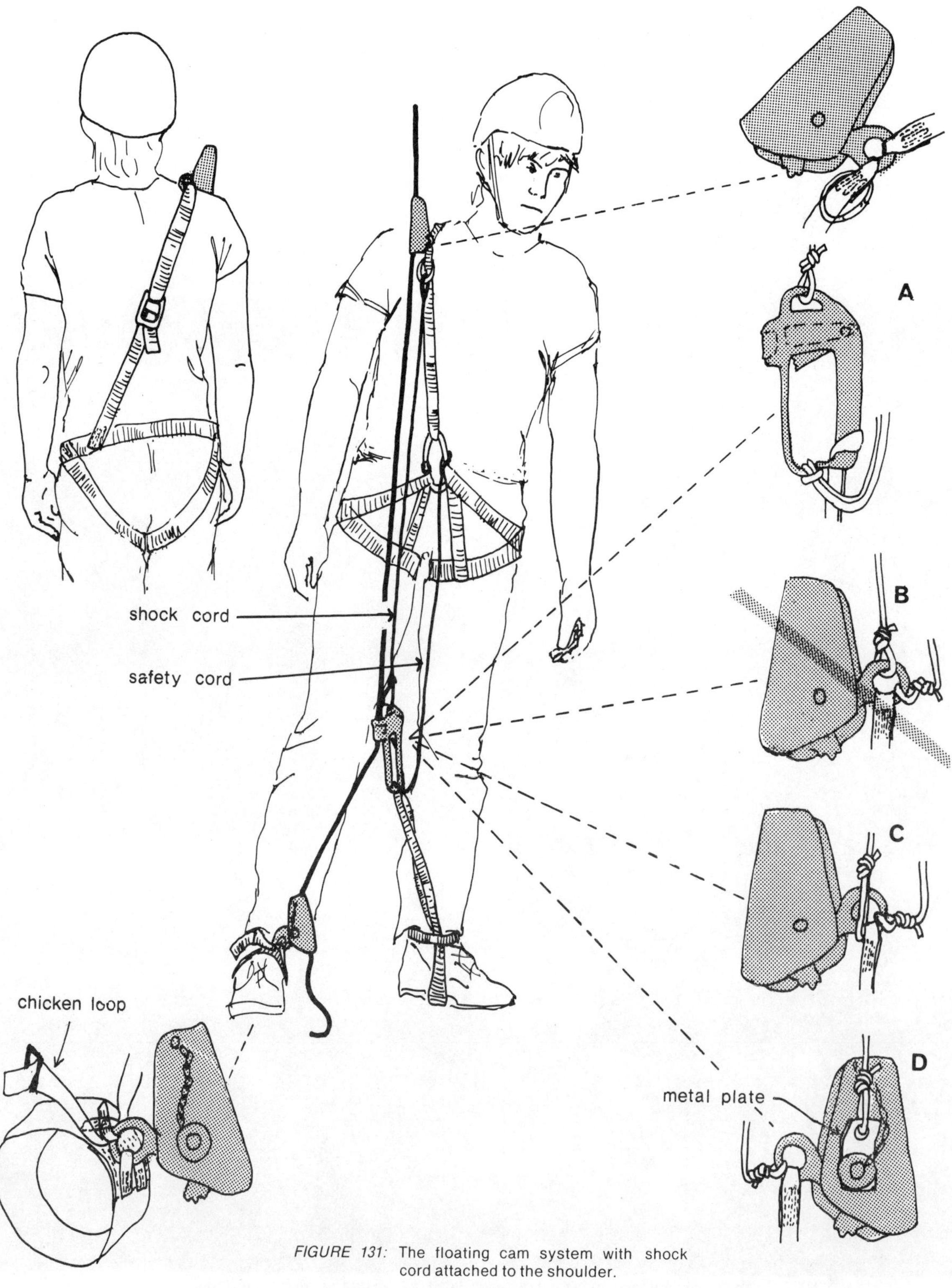

FIGURE 131: The floating cam system with shock cord attached to the shoulder.

VERSATILITY

A prusik system should function well on free drops, against walls, slopes and overhangs, and under waterfalls. It should allow the user to cross rope knots and make a descent.

ROPEWALKING SYSTEMS

The central feature of a ropewalking system is that each leg is attached to a separate ascender, and is thus raised independently. This produces a motion similar to that used in ladder climbing. Efficiency is a function of body stance. The more vertical the body is, the more efficient will be the system. Ropewalking systems differ in the way in which the ascenders are connected to the legs, and the mechanism for holding the body vertical.

THE FLOATING CAM SYSTEM

This popular system uses a Gibbs strapped directly to one foot, a Gibbs strapped to one shoulder and a Gibbs or Jumar which floats in mid-air at knee height attached to one foot by a stirrup and to the waist or shoulder with elastic cord (Figure 131 and 132). The elastic cord pulls the ascender up with each prusik step. The shoulder Gibbs holds the body vertical and is used in resting. The arms are left free to pull on the rope above the head for extra speed and balance or fend away from rock projections. To complete the rig, a safety cord should connect the floating ascender to the waist to give the required two points of seat or chest attachment. A spare Jumar on a sling may be needed for crossing knots or overhangs, and can also be used for resting.

The floating cam was developed by Kirk MacGregor in the USA from an early system which used a Gibbs strapped to the knee. The floating Gibbs proved superior in every way to the knee-strapped Gibbs (Pinchak and Gibbs 1972, Kirk MacGregor, pers. comm.). Five to seven millimetre shock cord (page 21) is the most suitable type of elastic cord. Surgical rubber tubing is another option but is harder to rig and not as durable. Figure 131 shows a number of possibilities for rigging the floating cam. Two decisions are whether to float a Jumar or a Gibbs and whether to attach the elastic cord to the waist or shoulder. A Jumar is easier to float since its lower attachment eye provides a ready placement for the foot stirrup and safety cord, while the upper eye accommodates the elastic cord (Figure 131A). In contrast, the Gibbs only offers one ready point of attachment. It is not satisfactory to simply tie the elastic cord into the top of the eye (Figure 131B) since the rope will tend to spring lever the cam off the rope, possibly resulting in slippage of the Gibbs. Figure 131C shows a good method (Davison 1974). It does not completely eliminate the leverage but should do so enough to prevent slippage. If not, the elastic cord will need to be connected to the cam housing in some way to entirely eliminate the leverage. Figure 131D shows one possibility. Elastic cord leverage does seem to hasten wear of a floating Gibbs, since the foot has to apply more force than usual to the cam in order to overcome the

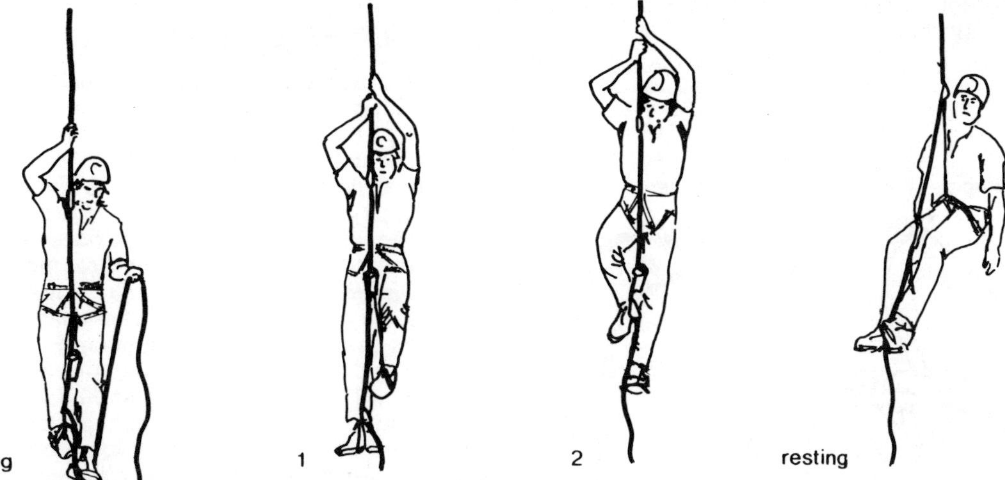

FIGURE 132: The floating cam system in use. To start a pitch it is often useful to draw the rope under the left foot and hold it in the left hand, to prevent the foot Gibbs from hitching up with the rope. Once rope weight becomes sufficient to prevent hitching, both arms are used above the head for balance and the caver "walks" up the rope. To rest, body weight is taken on the shoulder Gibbs.

resistance from the shock cord (Kirk MacGregor, pers. comm.). While the Gibbs is more awkward to rig, it is safer than the Jumar since, if the shoulder Gibbs fails, a shock load may be applied to the floating ascender. A Jumar could break.

The remaining decision is whether to anchor the elastic cord to the waist or shoulder. The shoulder is more effective since it allows a greater length of elastic cord to be used with consequent greater pulling power and a longer step. The merit of the waist rig lies in its neatness and simplicity. The shock cord should be attached to the waist portion of the harness rather than the seat carabiner. This allows a slightly longer piece of shock cord to be used. Even so, the cord will be more highly stretched and thus will abrade faster than a cord to the shoulder. Cavers should try both possibilities and use the one which seems most suitable.

Figure 131 also shows the methods of rigging both the shoulder and foot Gibbs. In rigging the shoulder Gibbs, Smith (1974d) recommends the use of a Gibbs seat harness (page 51) because it allows a firm attachment for the shoulder Gibbs. The Gibbs is positioned on the shoulder away from the collar bone (for comfort) and the back and front straps are sewn to the attachment eye by means of tapered end loops (page 49). The back strap has a buckle for tightening. At pitch tops or on sloping pitches it can be useful to slip off the shoulder Gibbs and move it by hand. (If in use, a floating ascender to the shoulder will then also need to be moved by hand, or else detached.) One problem with the shoulder Gibbs is that the rope drags against the rope housing while prusiking. A solution is to cut a notch in the top of the housing and fit a small pulley wheel (Figure 133) (Isenhart 1974c).

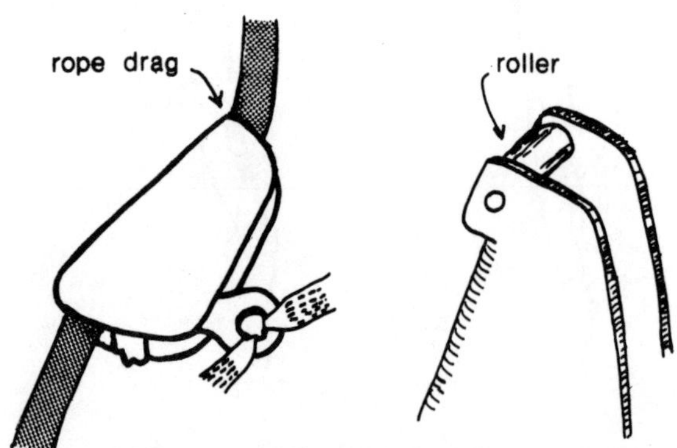

FIGURE 133: The shoulder Gibbs may cause rope drag. A solution is to fit a small pulley wheel in the top of the housing (after Isenhart).

The foot Gibbs is best attached by sewing it onto a band of 50mm tape, which slips onto the boot (Donna Mroczkowski, pers. comm.). The band needs to be custom made for a particular boot size, or an adjustment buckle added. A buckled chicken loop is passed under the cam prior to clipping in the rope and beginning to prusik. Before the invention of this method, cavers had struggled for years with various bandage-like arrangements of 25mm tape.

The hallmark of this system is its prusiking speed, both on free drops and against walls. It is consistently used to win the National Speleological Society prusik contests held annually in the USA, with times for the 30m prusik now less than 30 seconds (Bill Stone, pers comm). Unfortunately, the advantage of high speed on the rope is offset by the bulk of the equipment required, the difficulty of rigging it, and the system's poor performance in crossing rope knots and rope protectors. In fact, rope protectors can create crippling problems because of the difficulty of reaching below the foot Gibbs to replace a protector. Descending is difficult, but can be done by removing both the shoulder and foot Gibbs and attaching the spare Jumar to improvise a Texas prusik (page 94) (Kirck MacGregor, pers. comm.). The system is exasperating in tight caves with many short pitches because, when moving between drops, the rig will often need to be removed if it is not to snag or jam.

In summary, the floating cam system is unequalled on long, straight-forward pitches, but does not perform well on short or technical pitches.

BASIC MITCHELL SYSTEM

In 1967, Dick Mitchell published the description of a simple prusik system which combined the efficiency of the ropewalking method with the versatility of Jumars (Mitchell 1967). The Mitchell system, as it came to be known, has since achieved great popularity because of its good all-round performance. Various refinements have been added since its inception but before mentioning these, Dick Mitchell's basic rig will be described.

The basic rig makes use of a chest harness with a locking carabiner, and two Jumars (Figure 134). Gibbs would also be quite satisfactory, but harder to handle. The chest harness should be placed high on the chest and made as tight as comfort will allow. One Jumar is fixed to a long foot stirrup which passes through the chest carabiner and the other Jumar is fixed to a short stirrup. While standing upright, the upper Jumar should be positioned just above the chest carabiner and the lower one as low as can comfortably be reached (Thrun

1973). The lower Jumar should also be attached to the seat harness for safety purposes. To hold the body as close to vertical as possible, the main rope is passed behind (not through) the chest carabiner. Both hands are used to move up the Jumars. If the upper arm tires on a long drop, the arms can be switched.

Although the Mitchell System cannot compete with the floating cam system on long drops, it does eliminate many of the handling problems of the more complex system. The Mitchell system is light, compact and features fast on-off time. It creates no problems in crossing rope protectors since it is easy to reach below the lower Jumar to replace the protector. Crossing knots is straightforward because of the ease of manipulating Jumars, and since knots will usually slide behind the chest carabiner. Sharp overhangs, requiring one to remove and reattach the upper ascender, are equally simple.

The only difficulties of note are tiring of the upper arm and awkwardness in prusiking against irregular walls. Both hands are occupied and cannot be easily used to fend away from the wall and give balance. The problems are compounded on slopes where the chest harness hunches the body forward. At the cost of a little complexity, the basic Mitchell system can be modified to rectify these problems.

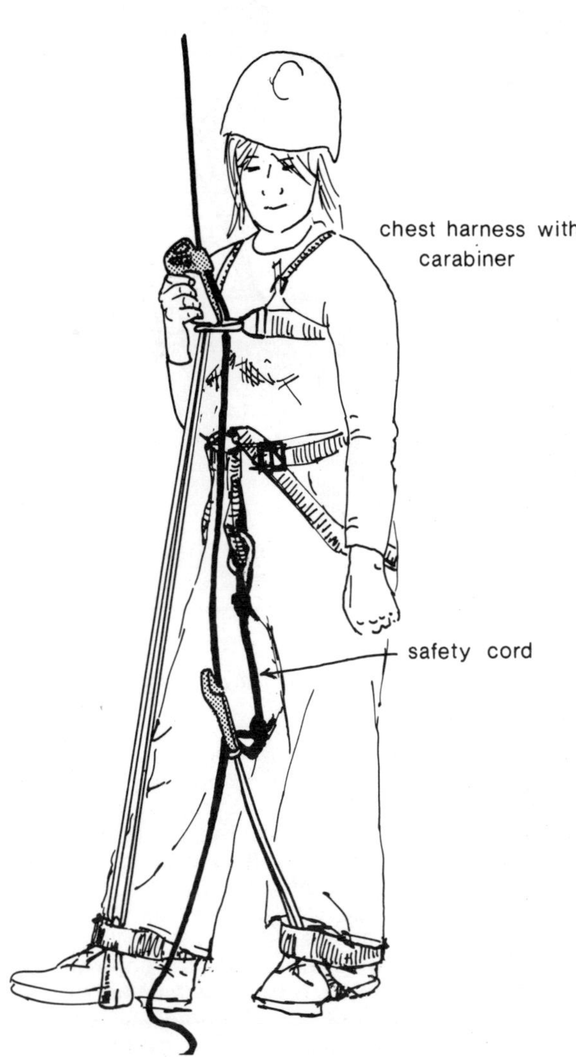

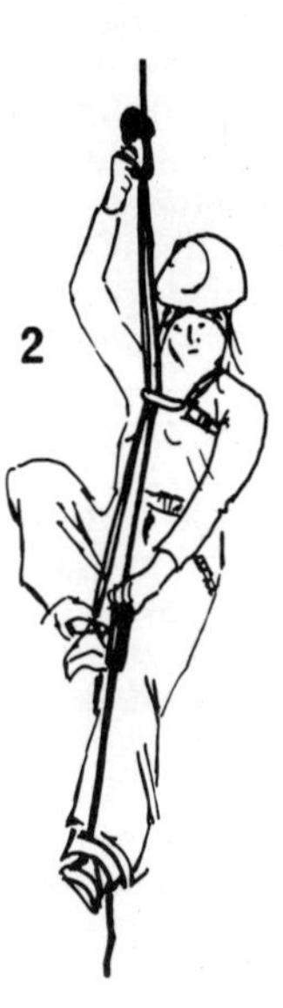

FIGURE 134: The basic Mitchell system.

MITCHELL WITH A THIRD JUMAR

A third Jumar on a sling to the seat is an extremely useful addition. The length of the loop should be chosen to position the Jumar between the chest carabiner and the upper Jumar. The third Jumar provides a safety backup for the other Jumars, an attachment for resting in the seat harness, and can itself be used in prusiking to convert the basic Mitchell system into either the Texas system or the Cuddington Third Phase system.

The Texas system is covered separately on page 94). It is much simpler than the Mitchell system but slower and more strenuous. Nevertheless, it is excellent for short drops where its speed of rigging is a real boon. The Cuddington Third Phase (Figure 135) replaces the Mitchell system on slopes. The chest harness is not required. The third Jumar is attached to the upper Jumar's foot stirrup and its position is adjusted to keep the body upright (Smith 1974e).

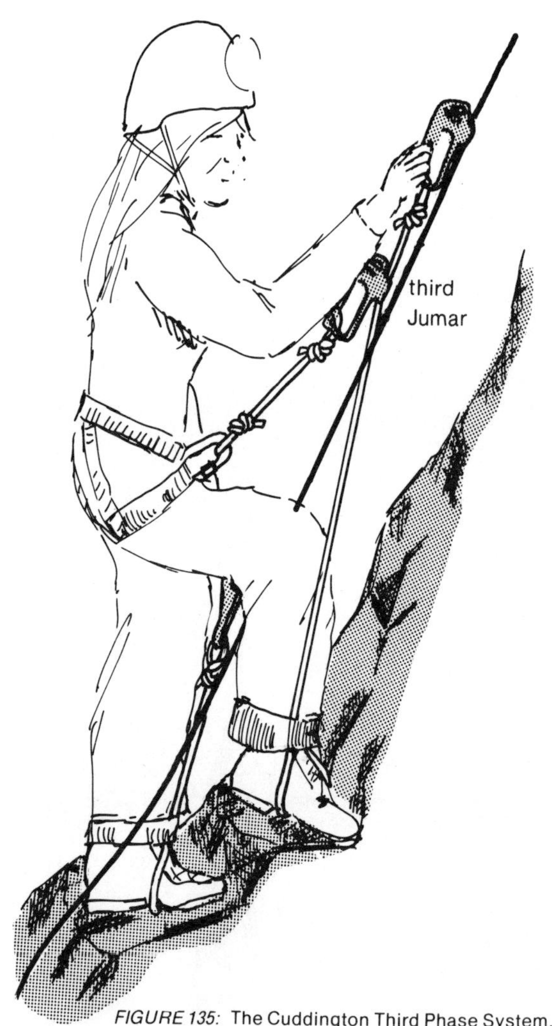

FIGURE 135: The Cuddington Third Phase System.

PYGMY SYSTEM

It is possible to replace the chest harness of the basic Mitchell system with a shoulder Gibbs as used in the floating cam system. This will produce a more upright climbing stance. The Jumar stirrups also need to be shortened a little and this somewhat relieves the problem of arm tiring found with the basic Mitchell system (Smith 1974f). However, the pygmy system is more complicated than the basic Mitchell system and this drawback probably outweighs the advantages (Figure 136).

MITCHELL WITH A FLOATING CAM

It is possible to float the lower Jumar between the foot and waist. The Jumar will need to be placed at knee or calf level to provide a good length of elastic cord. The system is the same as the basic Mitchell except that one hand is now freed to give extra balance by pushing against shaft walls or holding the rope above the chest harness. In deciding whether to use this modification, the value of the floating cam should be weighed against its extra complexity and the handling difficulties created by an ascender placed low on the leg.

For interested readers, Pavey (1972) describes a system similar to the above system except that it is used without a chest harness. It is strenuous on free drops, but a simple conversion to the frog system (page 91) is possible. Another variation is presented by Cowlishaw (1977).

MITCHELL WITH A CHEST BOX

Soon after the invention of the basic Mitchell system, some cavers became dissatisfied with the friction created by passing moving lines behind and through a chest carabiner. An obvious refinement was to replace the carabiner by a two-wheeled pulley. It was found most satisfactory to build the pulley into a rigid box, which became known as an ascender box. At present, ascender boxes are marketed by Blue Water Ltd (Figure 137). The Blue Water boxes are popular, but have a time consuming screw mechanism for rope insertion and do not hold the body as close to the rope as does a simple carabiner. Because of this, their efficiency gain over the carabiner must be fairly

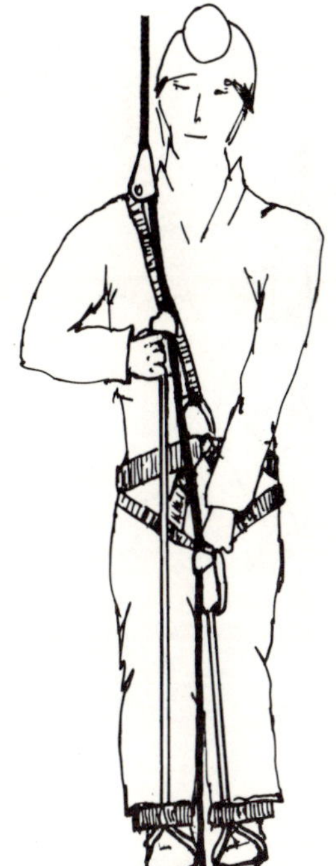

FIGURE 136: The Pygmy System (after Smith).

small. Blue Water boxes are also bulky and can snag when passing overhangs. Prospective users of the Mitchell system would sensibly try the carabiner before purchasing a box.

Other box designs are in existence, including one which snaps open for easy rope insertion (Thrun 1973) and another with a built in cam which replaces the upper Jumar (Donna Mroczkowski, pers. comm.). This latter design then requires a foot Gibbs to involve both feet in climbing. A chest

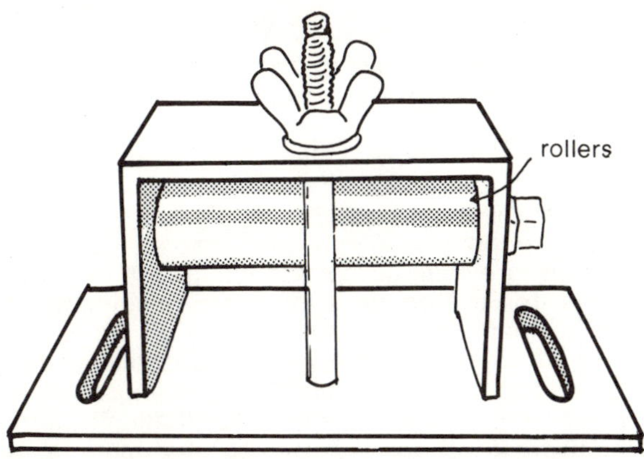

FIGURE 137: Blue Water Ascender Box. The base is connected to a chest harness and the upper Jumar stirrup and abseil/prusik rope are passed through the box (after the Blue Water catalogue).

mounted Jumar (page 92) will do the same job as a cam box, but not as efficiently. It can be hoped that snap open boxes and cam boxes will soon become commercially available.

SIT-STAND SYSTEMS

Whereas ropewalking systems use independent ascenders for each foot, sit-stand systems gain simplicity by using one ascender for both feet. The feet move together and share the load. As remarked earlier, the simplicity of these systems improves their handling qualities and promotes them over the ropewalking systems for short or technical pitches, even though they are not as fast for actual climbing. Other advantages are greater leg comfort (since the legs share the load) and easier resting since one is in the rest position during the sitting part of each prusik cycle. People in poor physical condition often find sit-stand systems less strenuous than ropewalking systems.

Wall climbing may present difficulties for sit-stand systems since both legs are held together. On smooth vertical walls there is generally no problem, but on irregular walls or slopes it is often worthwhile to detach one foot from its stirrup and climb one-legged. The free leg then gives balance. For speedy detachment, the quick release foot stirrup is recommended (page 54).

All sit-stand systems generally use two Jumars with a third Jumar for safety. Gibbs could be substituted.

FROG SYSTEM

The frog system is popular in parts of Europe and Australasia (Caffyn 1974, Courbon 1972, Paul Courbon, pers comm). One Jumar (the upper) is attached by equal length cords to both feet and the other is worn on a chest harness or a tape loop around the neck (Figure 138). Both Jumars are connected to the seat. While climbing, both hands normally move the upper Jumar. The feet are tucked under the body for greatest efficiency (page 92). Stirrup lengths for the upper Jumar should be chosen so that the chest Jumar rises to just below the upper Jumar at each step. The two Jumars should not actually touch because of the high probability of abrading the upper Jumar's stirrups with the chest Jumar. The upper Jumar's seat connection should be of such a length that it is just slack when the Jumar is pushed to maximum reach. Petzl in France markets a device called a Croll Chest Ascender which could replace the chest Jumar. However, Websell (1977) warns of a design fault which can cause slippage.

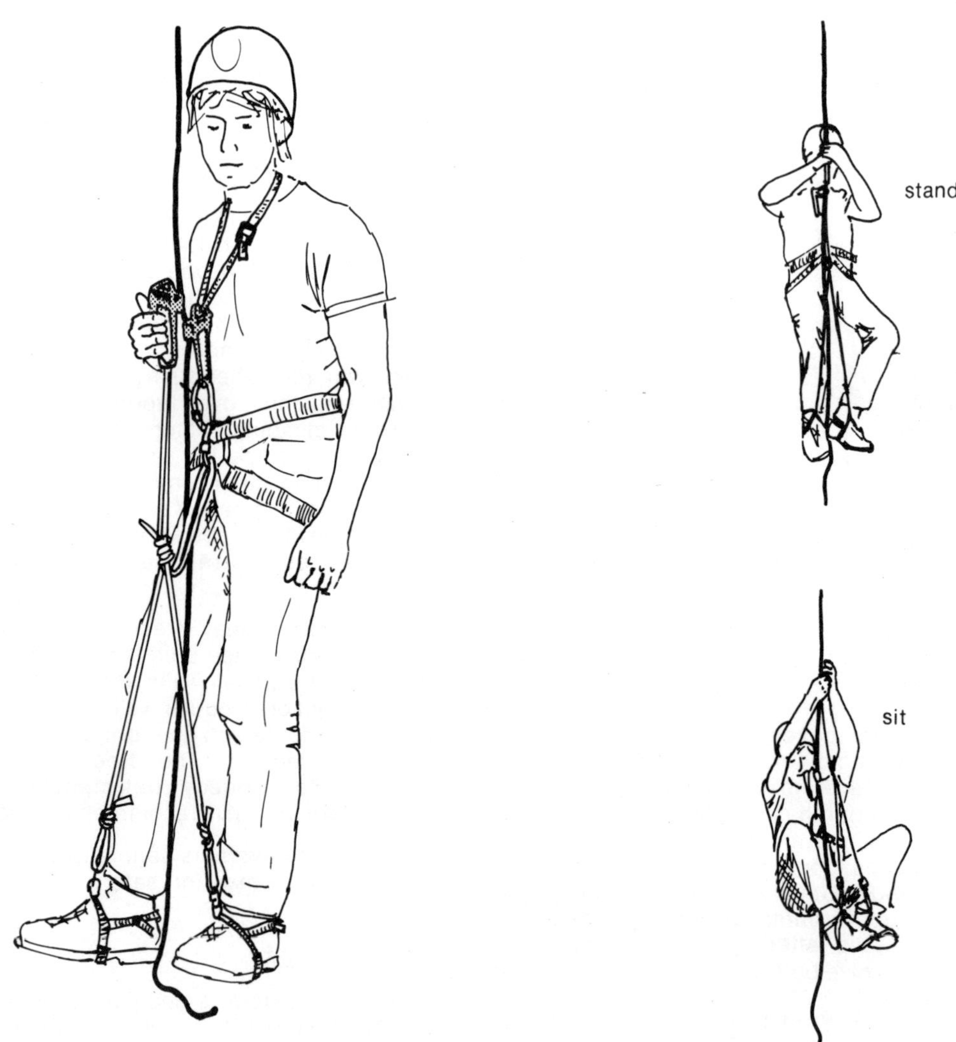

FIGURE 138: The frog system. A third Jumar should be carried on a sling to the seat.

The functions of the chest harness or neck loop are to pull up the chest Jumar with each prusik step and hold the body close to the rope. It is a personal choice whether a neck loop or chest harness is used. The harness gives better support but is bulkier and more complex. Whichever is chosen, it should support the Jumar very tightly. Ideally, the body should be slightly hunched forward when standing upright. This will not cause discomfort while prusiking but, if one is not to suffer discomfort walking between pitches, the rig will need to be loosened. A buckle on the loop or harness will make this possible. A buckle on a neck loop also avoids the need to remove one's helmet to don the loop (Brown 1976). Cavers using the neck loop should note the danger of hanging if the chest Jumar's seat attachment breaks. It may be wise to use a low strength buckle, which will break at about body weight.

The good handling qualities of sit-stand systems are even further accentuated in the case of the frog system because of the positioning of both Jumars above waist level. On-off times and ease of crossing obstacles and descending are exceptional. However, there are problems. One is that it requires practice and concentration to work the system with the legs tucked well underneath the body. It is easy to relax into the more natural procedure of pushing outwards with the legs (Figure 139). A useful aid is to climb with one foot placed behind the main rope. The rope tension then helps to keep the leg push vertical. This is

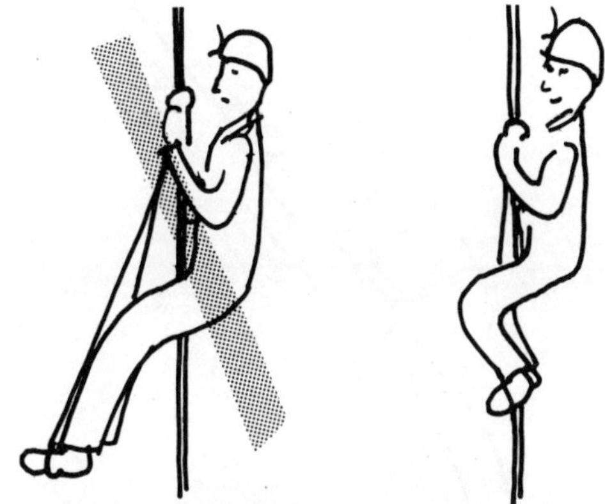

FIGURE 139: The frog system is most efficient when the legs are tucked under the body. Pushing outwards with the legs (at left) wastes energy.

particularly effective on long drops and when tandem prusiking with the weight of another climber below (page 98). A second problem is that the chest Jumar does not keep the body particularly close to the rope. This can prove tiring on long drops. A possible cure is to replace the chest Jumar by an ascender box with a cam (page 91). One could also pass both the upper Jumar's foot stirrups through a chest harness carabiner or pulley arrangement (Figure 140) (Boyd *et al* 1968). This is commonly done in New Zealand.

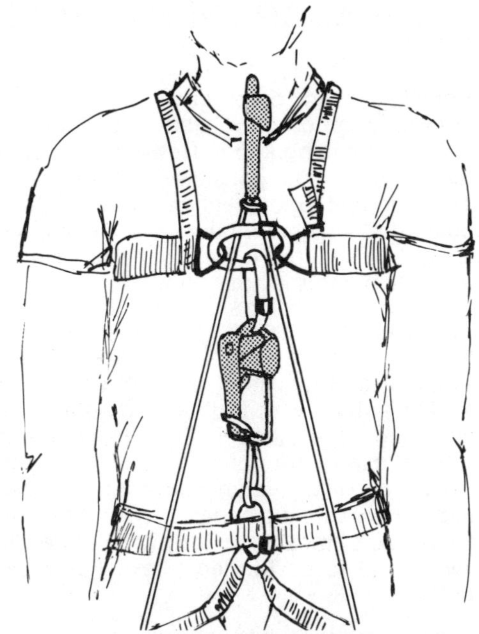

FIGURE 140: A modified frog system. Both foot stirrups are passed through a chest carabiner to produce a more upright stance.

INCHWORM SYSTEM

The inchworm system has achieved some popularity in North America. Its major difference from the frog system is that the upper Jumar of the frog has been replaced by a special Jumar mount at the feet called a Mar-bar (Figure 141). The chest Jumar is exactly the same and can be secured in the same ways. To make the Mar-bar, a piece of aluminium L stock, a U bolt and a short length of tape, cord or garden hose are required (Smith 1976b, Peter Thompson, pers comm). Figure 142 shows the construction details. Garden hose produces the most rigid construction but is not as neat as tape or cord. To tightly affix the tape or cord, measure and secure it before positioning and tightening the U bolt.

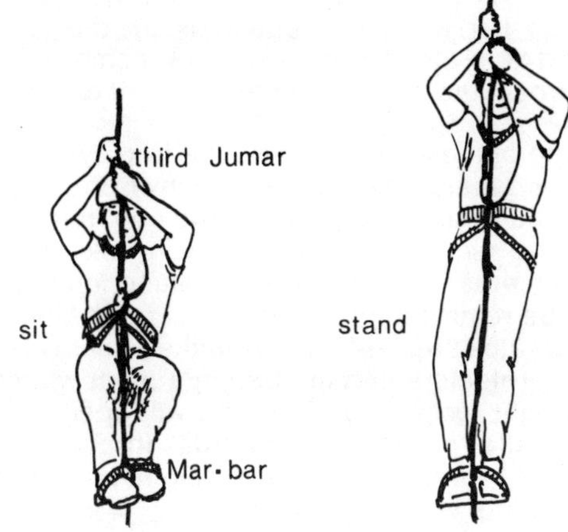

FIGURE 141: The Inchworm system.

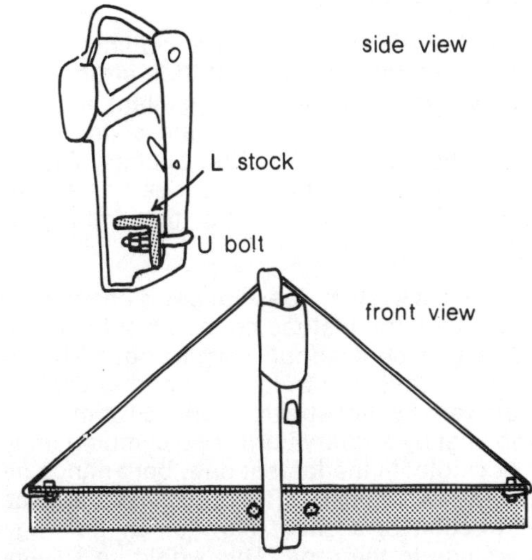

FIGURE 142: Construction of the Mar-bar (after Smith).

To provide two points of seat or chest attachment, an extra ascender must be incorporated at the seat. The options are a Gibbs on a short cord towing below the chest Jumar, or a Jumar on a seat sling above the chest Jumar (Figure 141). The Gibbs has an advantage in that it will tow along of its own accord, whereas the Jumar will need to be moved by hand. However, the Jumar is far more useful for crossing knots and tricky overhangs and climbing off at pitch tops.

The inchworm has an advantage over the frog because the inchworm rigidly holds the feet under the body. This makes it better for deep pit ascents. Another advantage is that the Mar-bar has alternative applications. It can be used for gear hauling and on a sloping pitch may be removed from the feet and used above the head as a pull up bar while the legs walk up the slope (Figure 143) (Peter Thompson, pers. comm.). The same procedure may be helpful in a tight chimney.

In spite of these advantages, the frog system is better for general cave use. The inchworm system is more bulky and necessitates the continual use of a third ascender. The Mar-bar, while giving extra benefits, is restrictive because one foot cannot be removed for fending off on wall climbs. It also creates great difficulties in the replacement of rope protectors and in starting a pitch without rope weight (page 95). The rope will need to be methodically pushed downwards through the Jumar until there is sufficient weight to prevent rope hitching.

TEXAS SYSTEM

The Texas system is the original sit-stand system and still the simplest. It is strenuous, but its very simplicity gives it excellent emergency value and usefulness in certain styles of cave, such as tight caves with short pitches. The Texas system has already been proposed as a suitable emergency system to use with climbing knots (page 76).

The Texas system does not use a chest harness or neck loop but instead connects a Jumar to the seat with a cord about 300mm long. The other Jumar is positioned below this and is connected to both feet by foot stirrups about 600mm long and to the seat by a safety cord. Two climbing motions are possible. In the fastest one, both hands never leave the two Jumars. The upper hand duplicates the function of a chest harness by holding the body close to the rope. This would be strenuous on a long drop and the alternative motions of the Texas system for climbing knots may be found more comfortable (page 76) (Thrun 1973). As for the frog system, prusiking against a wall is often facilitated by removing one foot from its stirrup.

FIGURE 143: Inchworming up a slope. The Mar-bar is removed from the feet and used as a chin up bar. It should be connected to the waist.

A ONE-ASCENDER PRUSIK SYSTEM

Normally, in an emergency situation there would be enough cord available to build a prusik system with climbing knots. However, should the situation arise, it is possible to prusik, albeit slowly, with just one mechanical ascender (or climbing knot) attached to the seat. The ascender would best be secured to a chest harness or neck loop as well, but this is not essential.

There are two techniques for gaining foot purchase on the rope (Figure 144). The foot-lock is the simplest and quickest, but the loop method will allow climbing with a greater weight of rope hanging below the climber. The loop method is thus more useful for long drops. The loop is formed by making a hitch above the head and holding it firmly with the hands. Two or three steps can be gained by moving up the pitch before a new loop will need to be formed (Steve Perry, pers. comm.).

Using the foot-lock, it is possible to climb a rope without any ascender at all by supporting the body with the arms. Taking such a risk may be justified in some circumstances.

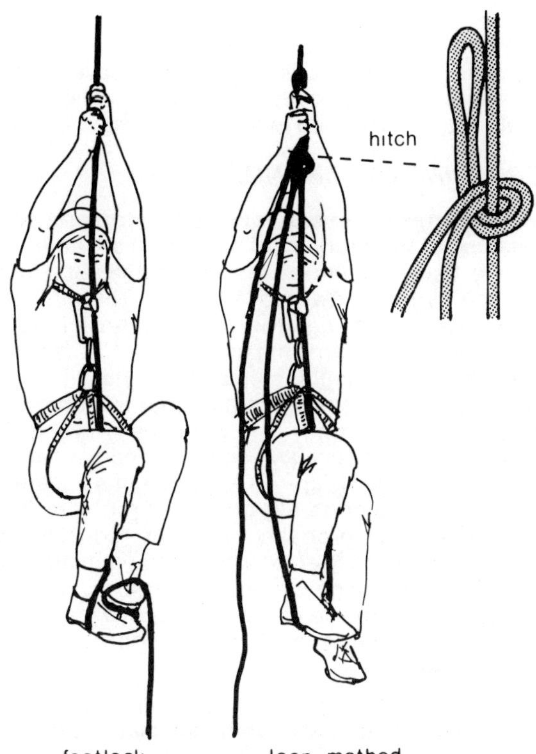

FIGURE 144: One ascender prusik systems. Foot purchase is gained by locking the rope around the feet or by standing in a loop formed by making a hitch above the head.

SAFETY AND TECHNIQUES

LEARNING TO PRUSIK

The basic motions of prusiking can be learned by rigging a rope through a pulley attached to a tree as shown in Figure 145. Rope is fed through the pulley using a descender. This rig allows a prusik of any length to be simulated simply by feeding through sufficient rope. The climber remains almost stationary. The rig also can be used for training purposes prior to expeditions.

Another useful exercise is to rig a short knotted rope and practice crossing the knot during both a prusik and an abseil.

STARTING A PITCH

There is an annoying tendency for the prusik rope to ride up with the lowest ascender when starting a prusik. This is simply due to the friction created by the rope passing through the ascender. The problem will ease when one has climbed far enough for rope weight to overcome the friction. The actual distance which needs to be climbed depends on the type and condition of the ascenders and rope. The distance is greatest using ascenders with spring loaded cams (e.g. Jumars) on furry ropes and it is further lengthened by wet or muddy conditions. Anywhere from 2m to 15m can be expected.

Good general solutions are to have someone hold the rope until the problem stops or tie a pack on the bottom of the rope. The first approach is easiest, but the caver assisting must be careful not to look upwards since he may be bombarded with loose rocks or have dirt dropped

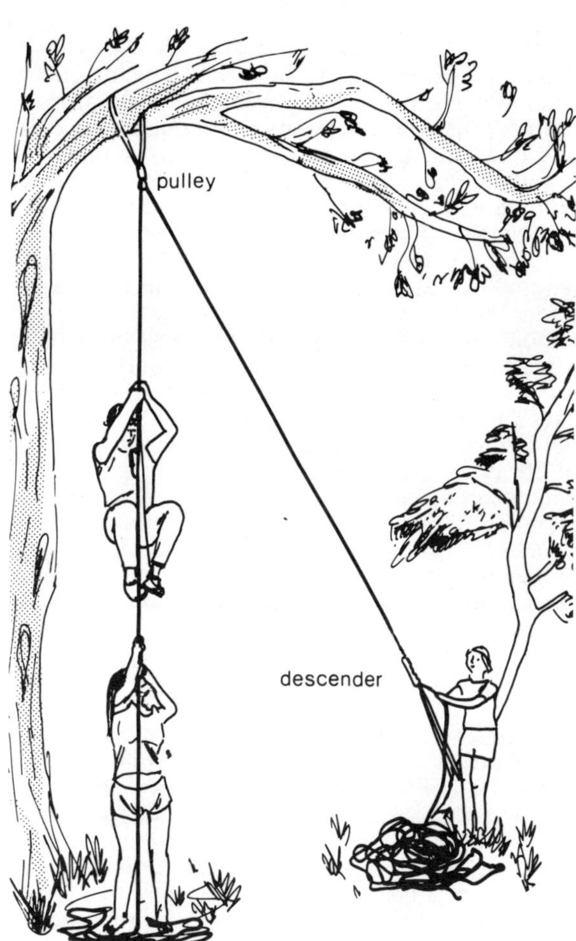

FIGURE 145: Learning to prusik. Rope is let out through the descender at the same rate as the caver climbs. Although the caver remains almost stationary, he must work just as hard as he would during a normal prusik.

into his eyes. A person starting without assistance may use a pack as weight, but he should ensure that the pack will not snag when pulled up afterwards, and that the rope can be dropped back to the bottom for anyone following behind. Often these restrictions will force him to use the alternative procedure of personally pulling the rope below the lowest ascender, or holding the ascender's cam open at each step. This is easy if the ascender is above thigh height, but for an ascender at foot level, it is an awkward process. Users of the floating cam system sometimes pass the rope under one foot and hold it in one hand to give the necessary pull (Figure 132). The inchworm system is even worse as it requires one to slowly push the rope through the foot Jumar from above.

PRUSIK STYLE

During a prusik, each time weight is taken on an ascender the prusik rope stretches a little. In a normal prusik, this happens about once a second and inevitably produces rope bounce. Chapter 2 drew attention to the dangerous tendency of this bounce to cause rope abrasion at sharp rock protrusions. The natural stretch of the rope was highlighted as a factor which determined the length of each bounce stroke and it was underlined that abrasion risk was largely dependent on this length. It must now be added that prusik style also significantly affects bounce length. A smooth, steady prusik style not only saves energy and adds enjoyment to the climb, but also reduces rope bounce and, with it, the risk of abrasion. When learning to prusik, emphasis should be placed on style, not speed. A critical element of good style is to avoid using rope bounce to spring upwards at each step as this enhances bounce without saving any energy. High speed will develop as a natural consequence of good style.

LIFELINING PRUSIKS

Whenever SRT has become popular in a country at the expense of ladder techniques, critics have opposed the innovation on safety grounds, claiming that ladder climbers are safeguarded with a separate lifeline. Experience has shown, however, that a separate line for prusiking is usually just a hazard, contributing little to safety while making life underground more complicated. The same was found to be true for separate lifelines for abseiling (page 67). There is even less of a case for belaying prusiks since it is virtually impossible to fall off the rope or lose control. Even the threat of rope abrasion calls for technical expertise rather than a separate lifeline.

The only application of a lifeline would be in manually assisting an injured caver. There should be little call for routinely belaying cavers up a dangerous pitch because such a pitch should not have been descended in the first place.

CROSSING OVERHANGS

Overhangs present obstacles in prusiking because of the problem of moving an ascender up a rope that is being pushed hard against a rock surface by one's own body weight. The difficulty of crossing overhangs varies with different prusik systems, but the crossing methods are essentially the same. After climbing up as far as possible, the first approach is always to push out from the wall with the feet or arms. This will usually swing the rope clear of the rock and allow the lead ascender to be moved past (Figure 146). Once this ascender is over, there is generally no further problem. This approach will probably fail on square cut overhangs where there is no wall to push against. The procedure is now to attach a spare Jumar for safety, unclip the lead ascender, move it above the overhang and reattach it. Tall people may have an advantage.

On rare occasions an overhang will be met which seems to have been specially designed to foil the unwary caver. It will be square cut below and so smoothly contoured above that the rope hugs the rock for a metre or more, frustrating all normal attempts to reattach an ascender. To make matters worse, it may be on a long pitch where there is a large weight of rope hanging below the caver. In desperation, gymnastics will usually win, but it is better to recognize the problem in advance. Either the rope should be rigged in a different position or a short rope tail should be fixed beside the main rope, extending to just below the overhang with a knot in its end (page 97) (Figure 146). One can then easily clip the lead ascender onto the tail, push it up as far as possible, take weight on it and move up the main rope.

CHANGING FROM ABSEIL TO PRUSIK

In cave exploration, a party descending an unknown pitch will sometimes rig insufficient rope. The first man down will then arrive at a dangling rope end (hopefully a knotted one), with no choice but to prusik back up. He should be thoroughly practised beforehand in the technique of changing from abseil to prusik, and have even performed the operation blindfold to cover the event of losing all his light sources. The technique also has application in crossing rope knots (page 98).

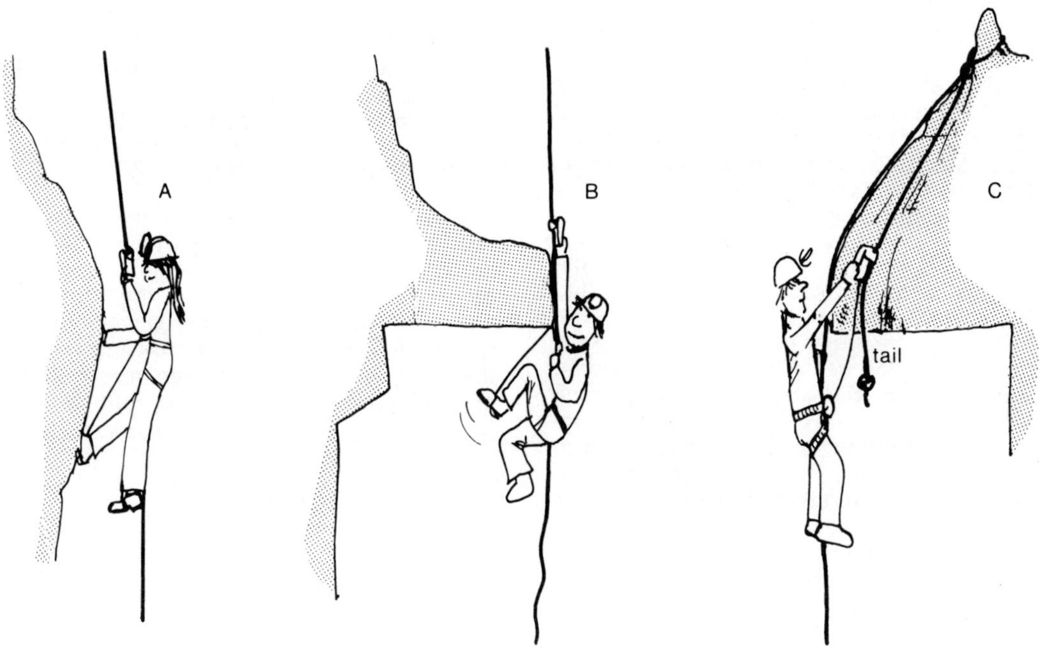

FIGURE 146: Crossing overhangs. Most overhangs can be passed by simply pushing away from the wall (A). If there is no wall to push against, it will be necessary to either remove and reattach the lead ascender (B), or if even this fails, to use a rope tail (C).

No matter which system is in use, the method is to stop several metres before the end knot and attach an ascender above the abseil device. Some systems (eg, floating cam) may require a spare ascender to be carried for this purpose. The abseil is then continued until body weight is taken by this ascender. A second ascender is clipped on for safety before removing the abseil device. Finally, any other ascenders are attached and the prusik commenced.

CHANGING FROM PRUSIK TO ABSEIL

The reverse procedure also has its uses, mainly in crossing rope knots (page 98), but also in the event of injury or flash flooding. If a descender is used, the changeover is aided by clipping the descender to the seat carabiner with a separate carabiner rather than directly. Once again, the technique should be well practised in advance.

The exact technique depends on the actual prusik system in use, but in general it is done as follows. (The explanation will be hard to comprehend unless you are actually on the rope.) Firstly, body weight is taken on an ascender connected to the seat and any ascenders below seat level are removed. There may be none as, for example, in the frog system. During this step, care should be taken to, if necessary, retain two point contact by attaching a safety Jumar. Secondly, the abseil device is attached to the rope as high as possible. The safety Jumar can now be removed. Thirdly, any ascender below the seat is reattached, and standing erect in the foot stirrups, the ascender connected to the seat which supported the body in the first step is detached. Finally, by taking weight on the abseil device and not letting any rope slip through it, all other ascenders are removed and the abseil commenced.

If the technique is unsuccessful, then the ascenders may not have been properly positioned, or one's prusik rig may be equipped with unserviceable cord lengths. A little experimentation close to ground level should identify the problem.

CROSSING ROPE KNOTS

Rope knots are formed when two ropes are joined or a rope is reanchored below the pitch top (page 39). Such knots will need to be crossed when abseiling and prusiking. To do this it is handy to have a ledge just below the knot, but knots cannot often be positioned so conveniently. Safe techniques do exist for crossing knots without any such assistance. The case of a rope join will be considered first.

To abseil past a knot joining two ropes, the usual method uses the techniques for converting from abseil to prusik and prusik to abseil. The descent is stopped a metre or two above the knot and the prusik rig attached. Then one can reverse prusik down across the knot by passing each ascender over it in turn. A Jumar safety may be needed here. The final step is to change back to abseil and continue. Some cavers find it unnecessary to pass all their ascenders over the knot when prusiking down. It depends on the system in use and the person's height. Ascending past the knot on the return trip is much simpler. The ascenders are moved over the knot one at a time, using a safety Jumar if necessary.

Knot crossing is easier in the second case of a knot formed at a position where the rope has been reanchored. Provided that a metre or so of slack has been left at the anchor, the procedure is then to abseil into the slack loop below the knot, change to prusik, attach the abseil device to the rope for the next pitch, prusik down until weight is taken by the abseil device and change back to abseil. It is not necessary to reverse prusik across the knot. On the ascent, the procedure is the same as that just described for rope joins.

HORIZONTAL AND DIAGONAL ROPES

All prusik systems and abseil devices will be subject to difficulties or failure when used on a rope that has been rigged horizontally or diagonally to bypass some obstacle. Abseil devices will twist under body weight and probably jam, especially on low angle ropes. Jumars will behave similarly, unless modified in the way suggested on page 79. Gibbs will probably function normally, but in any event prusiking will be made strenuous and tiresome by the body's awkward reclining position.

The author has devised a system which eliminates these difficulties. With the addition of an extra cord or sling at the seat and two locking carabiners, it can be used with any abseil or prusik rig, though prusik systems with foot mounted ascenders will be slow. A trial run will determine the optimum length for the seat cord for any caver. Probably it will be about 600mm. The system requires an extra line to be rigged below the main rope, as already mentioned in Chapter 4 (page 37). The extra line should be 4m to 5m longer than the main rope and, with discretion, could be a little thinner to save on weight.

Figure 147 illustrates the system in use on a horizontal pitch. Beneath may be a deep shaft or an unnegotiable set of rapids in a streamway. To eliminate excessive stresses, the tighter rope has still been rigged with a certain amount of slack (page 16). The method of crossing it is to abseil down into the centre and then prusik up the other side. Diagonal pitches are generally simpler because only an abseil or prusik will be required.

TANDEM PRUSIKING

The practice of two cavers climbing together on one rope can significantly speed up a cave trip and provide some company in what is normally a solitary activity. Tandem prusiking is useful in deep pits and deep vertical caves where prusiking time forms a large percentage of the total trip time. It works best on free drops, though it is also suitable for walls, provided there are not too many obstacles. Otherwise the top climber will be handicapped by the lower climber's weight. On wall climbs the two should stay close together to minimise the danger of rockfall, and jointly hold themselves away from the rock.

The climbers can decide to climb simultaneously or in separate bursts. Prusiking separately, say 10m at a time, is preferred since it gives frequent rests for each person and eliminates the possibility of the climbers setting up opposing bounces, a common and jarring problem. Also, because each climber moves quickly during his turn, it is not much slower than simultaneous prusiking.

It is often essential to rig a tail (Figure 146c) at the top of the pitch to ensure that the top man can leave the pitch without being hindered by the weight of the lower man.

Cavers considering the use of tandem prusiking should be aware that it imposes higher forces on the rope and its anchor, that it may increase the risk of rope abrasion, and that it increases the chances of ascender slippage for the top man because of the higher tension in the prusik rope. The practice demands an even greater degree of care than usual in all aspects of technique.

PRUSIKING

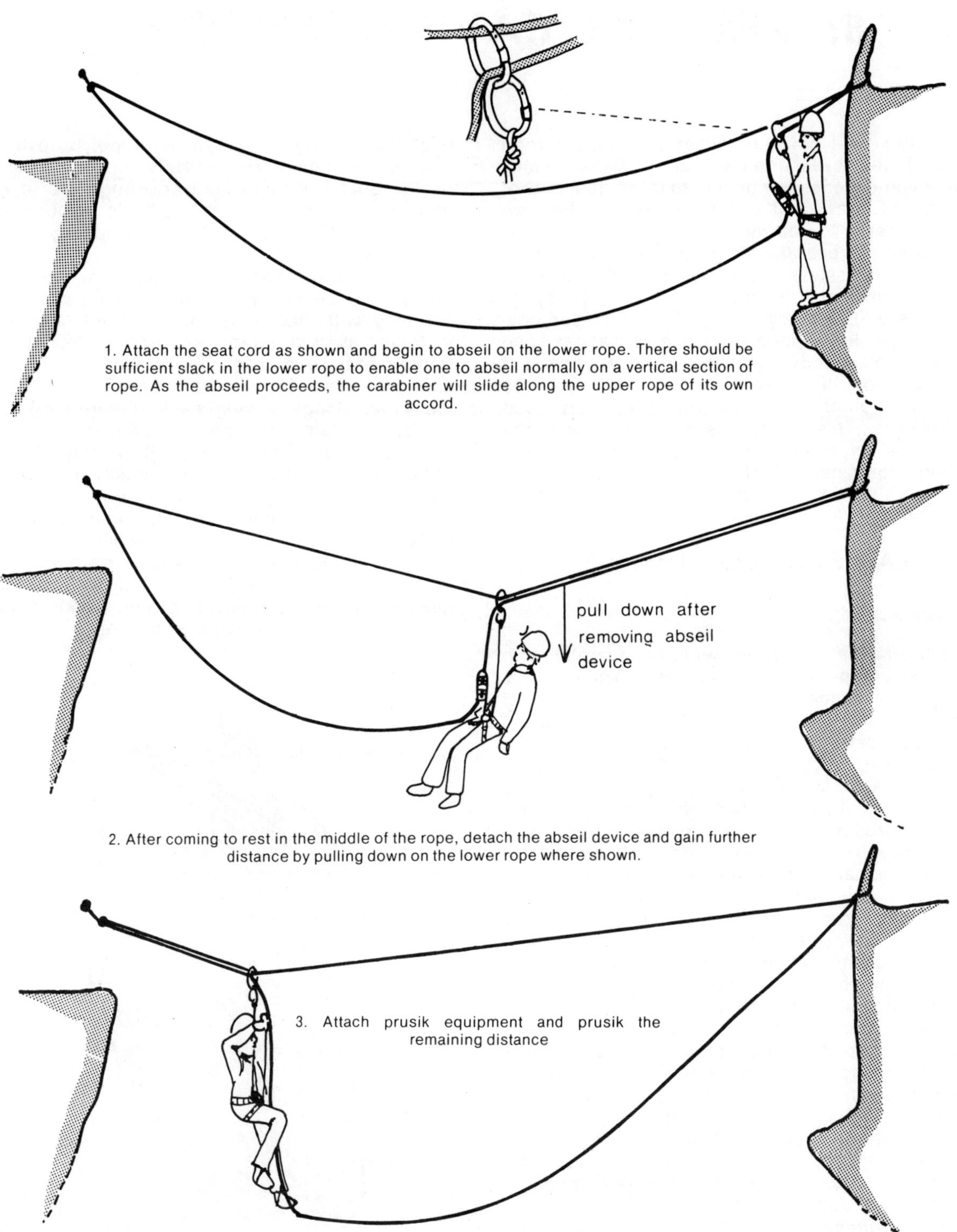

FIGURE 147: An abseil/prusik system for a horizontal rope.

8: VERTICAL CAVING EFFICIENCY

In the best spirit of adventure, single rope techniques have made it possible for small teams of fit and experienced people to make descents of some of the world's deepest caves. Relative newcomers to caving can enjoy a similar challenge by operating in groups of four or five to extend themselves in vertical caves 100m or 200m deep. Efficiency in movement is the key to success. Efficiency involves both personal expertise in negotiating cave passages and shafts, and speedy organisation and movement of equipment. Further to this, it requires coordination of these elements or, in short, good teamwork. This chapter is concerned with the organisation, movement and rigging of ropes and other equipment, and with calls and whistle signals that will be useful for communicating on pitches.

ORGANISING EQUIPMENT

CAVE PACKS

Cave packs protect equipment and contain it in convenient packages for carriage. Their use is highly recommended. There are two types of pack. Small hip or shoulder packs may be carried by each caver to contain personal abseil-prusik equipment, food, spare clothing, and possibly a camera. Army surplus packs or ammunition boxes are the usual choice, although specific packs for this purpose are now manufactured (see Appendix 1). In addition, larger packs will be needed to carry ropes, anchoring equipment, and possibly underground camping equipment.

The underground environment demands special care in the selection of a large cave pack. Commercial mountaineering or walking packs are fairly poor for general cave use since they are usually too large, too weak and too expensive. In addition, they will nearly always have pockets, strings or straps that snag. The framed varieties will be found totally unsuitable for anything but walk-through caves. It is better to either home manufacture cave packs or buy them from a caving store. Unfortunately, at the time of writing, very few caving shops sell packs, although this situation is certain to quickly alter (see Appendix 1). In the meantime, some suggestions on home manufacture are warranted.

The first requirement is tough, waterproof material. Thick tarpaulin canvas is probably the best choice. Nylon, Terylene or polypropylene fabrics as found respectively in commercial packs, boat sails and light coverings are to be generally avoided in the author's experience because of their cost and their tendency to rip when snagged.

Once a material has been chosen, a simple pack design can be sought. It should feature double stitching with heavy synthetic thread, an easy fastening system, straps for carrying, probably a reinforced base, and an eyelet in the bottom to act as a drain hole. These features are illustrated by the Long Range caving pack (Figure 148), an Australian design. The pack is a little smaller in all dimensions than the trunk of the average body. This ensures that the pack will easily fit through any squeeze passages that might be negotiated. It is designed to sit low on the back and so reduce balance problems if it is worn while prusiking. Packs mounted high on the shoulders are tiring. F. Petzl in France markets a pack with similar qualities to the Long Range caving pack, except that it cannot be easily worn on the back.

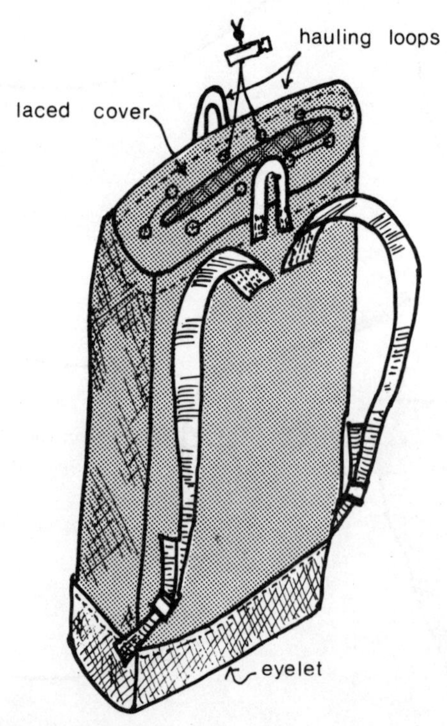

FIGURE 148: The Long Range caving pack.

On first thought, the drain hole may seem a poor feature since, if it will let water out, it will also let water in. In practice, however, the waterproof material will keep the contents dry unless the pack is actually submerged or carried in a waterfall. Under these conditions, water will pour through the top anyway. If there is no drain hole, the pack could become unmanageably heavy and may even burst. A drain hole will also prove useful when dripping wet rope is packed away.

Another feature of interest is the twin hauling loop system. A carabiner is clipped into the two loops to keep the pack closed, serve as a handle when the pack must be carried by hand and provide a ready attachment for a hauling line. During hauling, the twin loops support the pack in a vertical position. This eliminates many of the snagging problems that occur when using a pack with only one loop (Figure 149).

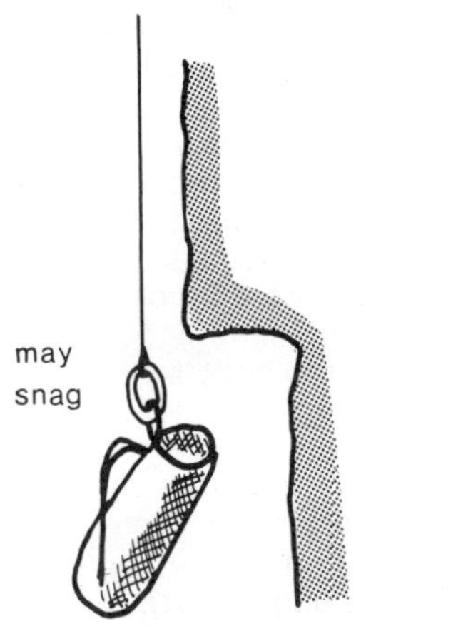

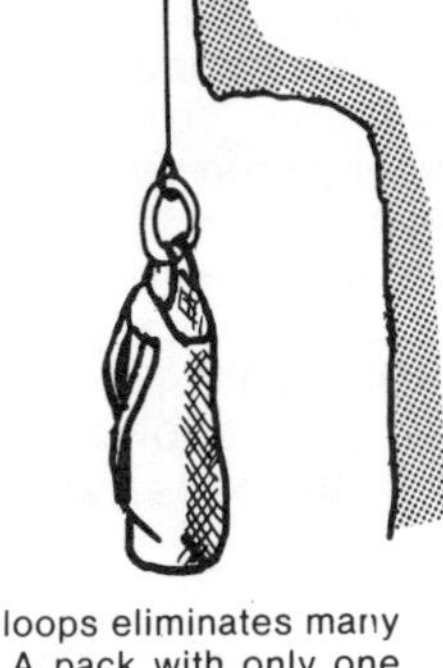

FIGURE 149: The use of two hauling loops eliminates many problems of snagging. A pack with only one hauling loop will tilt forward and catch under overhangs.

To reduce the number of items being handled, some cavers carry their personal equipment, as well as their ropes, in the large packs instead of a separate hip or shoulder pack. This is often worthwhile in tight caves. Each caver must then try to personally carry the pack containing his own equipment as a general safety precaution.

COILING ROPES

Sometimes cavers coil their ropes rather than carry them in packs. This is extensively done in North America where Blue Water rope finds very widespread use. This rope is rather stiff and hard to pack. Coiled ropes must be neat and well secured if they are not to snag and pull apart. Figure 150 shows a good method of coiling.

Donna Mroczkowski

FIGURE 150: Coiling a rope. The final spirals help to prevent the coil from pulling undone. A smaller coil can be obtained by winding the rope around one knee rather than two.

SURFACE PREPARATIONS AND PITCH RIGGING

It is sensible to carry out as much preparation as possible before entering a cave (or leaving an underground camp). The following procedures may be found useful.

Assuming cave packs are to be used, ropes and anchoring equipment should be assembled and checked for their safety and adequacy before packing. Ropes are best stuffed into their packs, rather than first being coiled or chained. If the anchorage requirements for each pitch are known, then the necessary equipment can be attached to each rope end by clipping it to a figure eight loop. Otherwise, it is best to devote one pack to a suitable selection of hardware. Normally, one pack should be carried by each caver, even if the resulting loads are only small. If many ropes are required, then they are best packed in reverse order of use and the individual packs marked in some way. This means that the rope for the final pitch will be packed in the bottom of the last cave pack, the second last rope will be packed on top of it, and so on. The rope for the first pitch will be the last to be packed. Each rope can then be retrieved without sorting through all the packs or digging beneath other ropes.

With this procedure, the team will obviously have to organise itself so that each pack is on hand when needed. This is no problem for groups that move together, but is a problem for groups that spread out and move in ones or twos. Separation often naturally occurs because only one person can descend a pitch at one time. Some discussion of the different role of each team member will therefore be useful. For example, two cavers might opt to move out in front with the first two cave packs and rig the initial bracket of pitches. To allow for the rigging time, a second pair might enter some time later or move at a more leisurely pace with the intention of catching the first pair as they finish their rigging. The second pair could then take the lead position. Others may follow behind.

If ropes are being coiled rather than transported in packs, a similar procedure is advised, still taking care with the order of movement of the ropes. Anchoring equipment would necessarily need to be carried in a separate pack.

DERIGGING PITCHES

The organisation for derigging a cave with many pitches is similar to the one for rigging. A discussion of the role each caver will take can be very helpful. The most efficient approach is to move up through the cave packing gear back into loads of similar proportions to those used for the descent. Unless the group chooses to move as a unit, each time a load is made it is taken by a caver who proceeds ahead of the others to the surface or other prearranged meeting place without causing unnecessary delays for those coming behind. This involves keeping at least one pitch ahead of the next person whenever possible, while still making occasional contact. It is unwise from the safety angle to become completely divorced from the remainder of the party.

MOVING EQUIPMENT

PITCH DESCENTS

Modern abseiling techniques are so close to effortless that it is usually no problem to carry equipment on the body. There is, of course, the proviso that one's abseil device has sufficient friction to facilitate a safe descent with the extra weight. Given this, the only point to watch is that the load does not upset one's balance or become uncomfortable. A small load may be carried on the back, but a larger one should be clipped to the seat harness. Usually it can be swung from the hip, but if balance or comfort problems still occur, the load should be dangled on a cord from the seat carabiner. The load will be unnoticed here because the seat carabiner is the body's centre of balance.

A separate lowering line would only be required for exceptionally heavy items, such as may be carried on a prolonged underground camp. The load can be lowered directly by hand, or with the assistance of an abseil device (Figure 151).

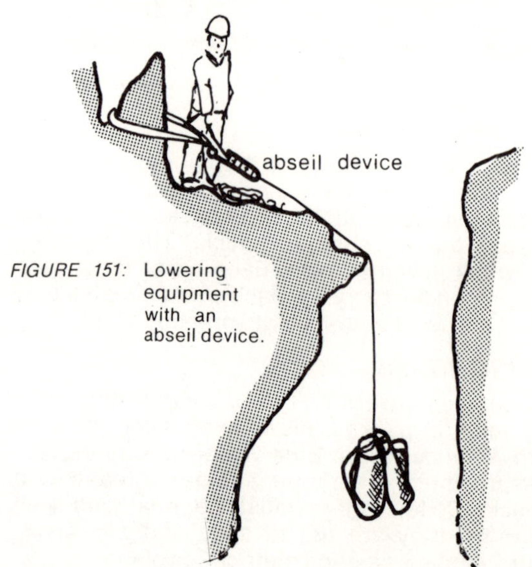

FIGURE 151: Lowering equipment with an abseil device.

ASCENDING PITCHES

On ascending a pitch, group equipment can either be personally carried or hauled separately. Most people find it tiresome to carry a pack or rope coil while prusiking, but often the alternative of gear hauling is less attractive. It is a personal choice.

Balance and comfort are again the key points to consider when carrying a pack. On wall climbs a pack can be carried on the back in the normal way since, with one's feet against a wall, balance problems will not arise. On free drops, even a small load can markedly increase arm strain. In this case, it is better to attach the pack to the seat harness, possibly positioning it on a cord below the feet to keep it out of the way.

Equipment is best hauled if there is too much to be conveniently carried or a long pitch is being prusiked. The prusik rope can be used for hauling but sometimes a separate, lighter line will prove beneficial. Such may be the case on an expedition in a deep cave where many loads need to be hauled. The separate hauling line saves abrasion on the main rope, reduces the weight which must be hauled (assuming a lighter line is used) and leaves the main rope undisturbed, a matter of importance if any rope protectors have been placed. Otherwise, someone may have to abseil down after hauling to relocate dislodged protectors.

The separate line can also be used to alleviate snagging problems. Snagging often occurs when hauling on irregularly shaped or sloping pitches. The problem has a dual aspect since the load may snag as it is being hauled and the hauling rope may snag when it is thrown back down. The solution is to use the main prusik rope for hauling and trail the separate line below the load (Figure *152*). The trailing line is used to direct the load away from snags from below and then pull the main rope back down after hauling. If the separate line is made twice the length of the pitch, then it can be used for both hauling and trailing, leaving the main rope undisturbed.

A polyethylene or polypropylene rope of about 7mm diameter would be a suitable and economical choice for a separate line. In the interests of good abrasion resistance, it should be of stiff construction.

On expeditions in deep caves it may be worthwhile to rig an aerial runway on awkward pitches (Figure 153). This can be used for lowering as well as hauling. The equipment is clipped to the runway with a carabiner and hauled or lowered with a separate line. For this purpose, a wire rope is fixed in the entrance series of the Gouffre

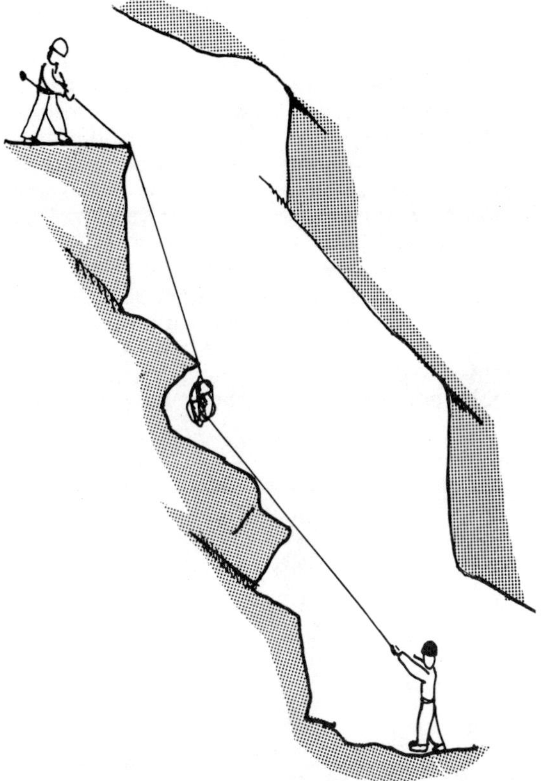

FIGURE 152: Use of a trailing line in hauling.

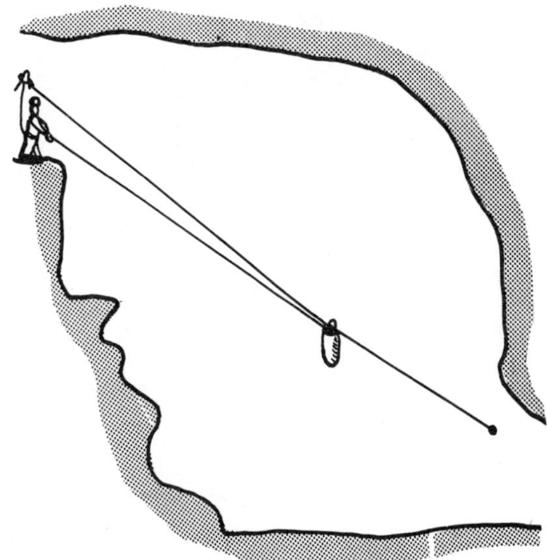

FIGURE 153: An aerial runway. A load is attached to the runway with a carabiner and it can be hauled or lowered without any possibility of snagging.

Berger, a vast and deep cave near Grenoble in France.

In most instances, it is easiest and fastest to haul gear directly by hand, preferably using a Jumar as a grip. Only for large hauling efforts is it desirable to rig something more sophisticated. American rock climbers developed a hauling technique for use on big wall climbs at Yosemite, California, that has application for cavers (Figure 154) (Robbins 1973, Wade 1972). It is efficient because it uses the legs rather than the arms. As originally devised, the technique uses a pulley and two Jumars, one for pulling the load and one for holding it. The holding Jumar must be weighted to prevent it from riding up with the rope. A Gibbs could be used without weighting, but it would then be more difficult to clip the rope in or out (Humphrey 1973). The pulley should have swing open cheeks for easy rope insertion (Figure 155). A number of specialist climbing and caving pulleys are available (see Appendix 1). A foot sling is attached to the hauling Jumar and the load is raised with a pumping motion of the foot. Alternatively, a foot Gibbs could be used (page 86). Light loads can still be pulled by hand.

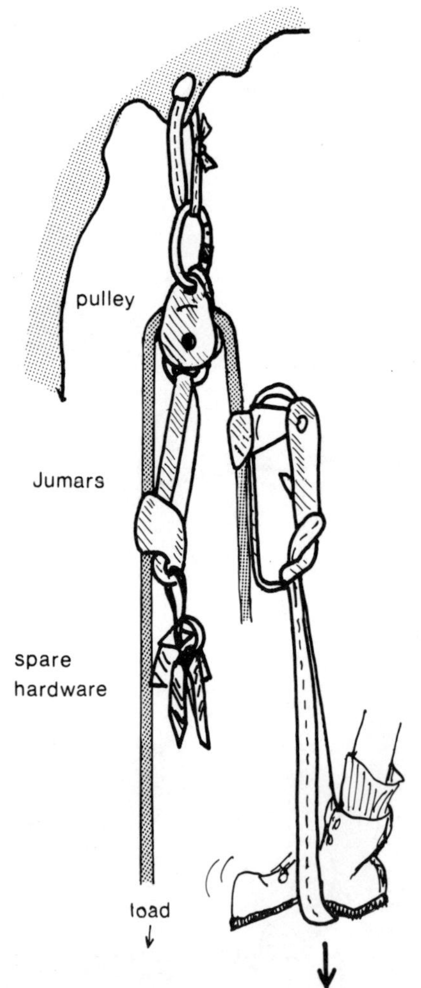

FIGURE 154: The Yosemite Lift. The load is pumped up by foot. The weighted Jumar holds the load after each step.

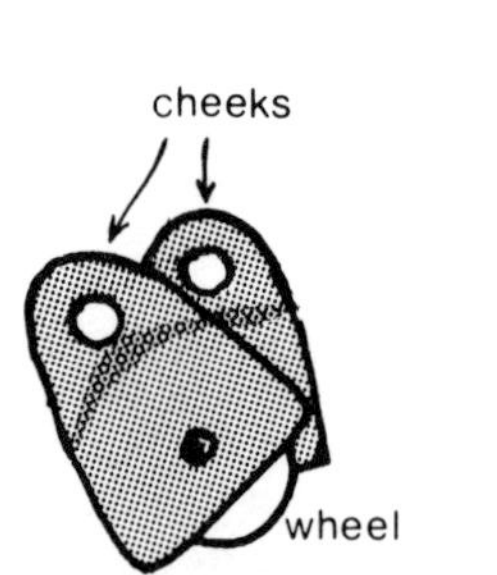

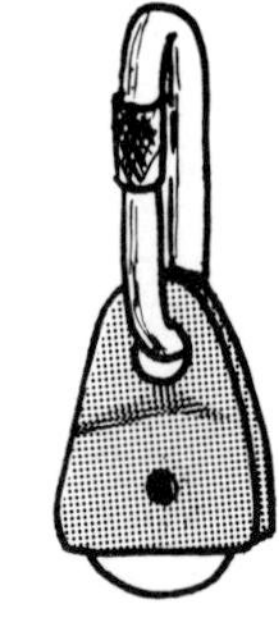

FIGURE 155: A swing open pulley.

There are also hauling rigs which offer a mechanical advantage. A number of the rescue rigs treated in the next chapter are of this kind, but they would only rarely be useful for equipment hauling because of their complexity.

CARRYING EQUIPMENT BETWEEN PITCHES

Carrying equipment between pitches is rarely a technical problem, but more a skill that is acquired through experience. Technical problems only arise in chimneys, where the arms and legs cannot generally be spared for pack movement. A procedure that often helps is to clip the equipment to the seat harness so that it dangles beneath the feet. One is then free to concentrate on the climbing.

CALLS AND WHISTLE SIGNALS

Communication is the foundation of good teamwork. It is especially critical on pitches where cavers at the pitch top and bottom need to know of each other's movements. As a general policy, verbal statements should be brief, unconfusing and clearly spoken. Best clarity is often achieved by speaking at a normal level rather than shouting. If, because of a waterfall or poor pitch acoustics, it is impossible to give a verbal call, then a whistle signal should be used. Should even a whistle signal fail, a field telephone or walkie talkie or a prearranged system of rope tugs can be considered.

Listed below are a number of standard calls and whistle signals to cover most situations. Note that each one is distinctly different so that it may not be confused with some other call. It would be a poor choice of calls that included such combination as belay and below or rope and rock.

CALL	SIGNAL	MEANING
"STOP"	One Whistle Blast	Used to stop all movement until further instructions. It is especially useful in hauling.
"UP"	Two Whistle Blasts	Means something or somebody is moving up or requires to be moved up. It is most commonly used while hauling or when a snag occurs during lowering and a brief lift is required.
"DOWN"	Three Whistle Blasts	Means something or somebody is moving down or requires to be moved down. It has a similar field of use to "UP".
"ROPE FREE"	Four Whistle Blasts	Used at the end of an abseil or prusik to communicate that one is off the rope, has found a safe stance, and that the next person can immediately begin to descend or ascend.
"BELOW"		Means stand clear below, something is falling. There would be insufficient time to give whistle blasts. The call "BELOW" should be given immediately by anyone who drops a rock, rope or anything down a pitch at any time. After a time, this call will be learnt automatically.
"HELP"	Continuous Whistle Blast	Probably the best emergency call. On an abseil, it would include the need for a bottom belay. The call alerts others to come to the aid and, if necessary, work quickly and safely to effect a rescue.

9: SELF RESCUE FROM A VERTICAL CAVE

Should an accident occur underground, those in the caving party who are uninjured immediately become the rescuers until such time as outside help arrives. In those cases where outside help is not or can not be called, the caving party will assume entire responsibility. Accordingly, a small emergency kit should be carried by every caving party. Important items might be First Aid supplies, spare food, a writing pad and pens, at least two light pulleys and, in cold caves, space blankets or bivouac sacs. The space blankets or bivouac sacs give good protection against hypothermia during prolonged periods of waiting. Cavers can curl up inside, insulated from the cold, and even use a carbide lamp for warmth. The pulleys are all that are needed in addition to normal SRT equipment to arrange systems for hauling or lowering. They should be of the swing open type illustrated in Figure 155 (page 104).

In any rescue, the first line of action is to quickly assess the victim's situation and condition, bring him to safety (if necessary), and render First Aid. Any caver may be called upon to do this and thus all cavers should attend a First Aid course or study a book and practise the necessary skills. It is also wise to keep abreast with the caving literature on First Aid, since basic First Aid courses may not give an adequate coverage of certain special dangers in caving, such as hypothermia.

SELF-RESCUE OR OUTSIDE RESCUE?

Once the victim's condition is in control, decisions should be made concerning the cave rescue. Possibly after treatment, the victim will be able to move out by himself under the supervision of others. But, if not, the crucial decision has to be made whether to move the victim using the resources of the caving team (self-rescue) or call in a fully equipped outside rescue group. If the caving team is capable of it, self-rescue is likely to be faster and cause less inconvenience to others, but for a patient in a critical condition, inexpert attention and lack of a stretcher could prove fatal or permanently disabling. A well organised outside rescue gives the advantage of expert medical attention, a stretcher, and the support of a strong and experienced crew. However, it may take from several hours to several days to arrive, depending on the difficulty of the cave and its location. During this time, hypothermia and weakness from lack of food are very real dangers. British cavers have extremely efficient rescue groups, but cavers in other countries are generally less fortunate.

Whatever the proximity of a rescue group, the decision to wait will usually be made in cases of unconsciousness, serious hypothermia, or severe injury. If a rescue group is close at hand, it will obviously be made in many milder cases as well. Two people (or one if two cannot be spared) should go *carefully* out of the cave for help with a clear and, if possible, written message of the facts of the accident and an estimate of the equipment and personnel requirements. Meanwhile, the victim should be kept under the care of someone who will do all that is possible to alleviate injury and shock, guard against hypothermia, and provide reassurance if the victim is conscious. Some additional supplies sent down from the surface may help in this task.

Advanced rescue techniques as used by a fully equipped rescue group are beyond the scope of this book. Robinson (1969) gives details. Attention will be turned instead to the problem of self-rescue since this is the area of importance to every vertical caver.

Self-rescue will be appropriate in most cases where a rescue group is remote and the victim can move by himself. Often it will be wise for one or two people to go immediately to the surface and arrange for additional warm clothing, high energy food, hot drinks, and perhaps a sleeping bag with a bivouac sac or space blanket to be brought down, if these are not already on hand. There may also be additional cavers on the surface who can be asked to provide assistance. In a self-rescue attempt, the victim should be persuaded to help himself as much as possible. This will speed the rescue, provide a confidence boost to the victim, and lessen the risk of hypothermia (Frankland 1973).

The remainder of this chapter will be concerned with hauling and lowering techniques which may be needed for moving the victim up or down pitches. In the simplest case, the victim will have been easily reached by his rescuers after the accident and these techniques will only be needed to get him out of the cave. The rescue becomes more complex when the accident has taken place on a pitch and the victim is hanging on the rope, unable to move. Speedy removal from the rope will be necessary regardless of whether a self-rescue or an outside rescue will ultimately be arranged. Injury may have been caused by rockfall or the victim may have succumbed to exhaustion or hypothermia. If not quickly brought to safety, he may die because of an obstructed airway (resulting from unconsciousness) or from blood loss, shock, or hypothermia. Hauling and lowering techniques are again used, but they will be complicated by the need for fast action and the lack of any prior preparations. The basic hauling and lowering techniques will be presented before this special problem is considered.

HAULING SYSTEMS

Self rescues from a vertical cave will normally involve a good deal of hauling and little (if any) lowering to get the victim to the surface. A number of hauling systems have been developed for rescue use, some offering a mechanical advantage, others not. Systems giving a mechanical advantage use arrangements of pulleys supporting two or more moving lines. The victim's weight is shared between these lines and can be raised by pulling with a force less than that needed for a direct pull with no mechanical advantage. A technique with a 2:1 mechanical advantage ideally requires a lifting force equal to half the direct pull force, a 3:1, a third, and so on. However, the ideal is never realised because of friction imposed on the system at each pulley and at any point where the rope rubs against the rock. In practice, there is little sense in using a system with an ideal advantage of greater than 4:1. It is even less advisable to rig systems with carabiners instead of pulleys or to attempt to haul a victim with the rope angling sharply over a rock edge, though, of course, both may need to be done if pulleys are not available. A further point is to use flexible ropes if available. Schermerhorn and Taylor (1967) tested a 2:1 hauling system with a 70kg victim and a Samson rope (very flexible) and a Goldline rope (very stiff) as the hauling line. The Samson rope required a 40kg pull for lifting and the Goldline a 48kg pull. Friction is the enemy of hauling rigs and must be eliminated in all possible ways.

Key features of a good hauling system for cave rescue are simplicity and versatility. Those systems with no advantage or a 2:1 advantage always win on these points. The effort of rigging and operating a 3:1 or 4:1 system would usually only prove worthwhile on a pitch of over about 40m.

Finally, it must be remembered that the victim will be in a delicate state and that the hauling rig should be arranged and operated with his comfort and safety foremost in mind. Where practicable, it is essential to use a lifeline from above to give extra security and assist the victim in getting off the rope at the pitch top, and also to have someone prusik beside the victim on a separate rope to watch his progress and help fend him away from the walls. A trailing line from below may also be useful for guiding the victim. For the sake of simplicity, these additions have not generally been shown in the figures in this chapter.

A number of hauling systems will now be described, beginning with the simplest ones. No single system will suit all situations so it is wise to have knowledge of a variety of them and apply the one which seems most suitable. Often the number and position of available anchor points will be a large deciding factor. The common features of all systems are that pulleys are used where possible to guide the rope where it takes sharp turns and than an ascender is always incorporated to capture the victim's upward progress and allow rests. In each figure Jumars have been shown, but any other ascender could generally be substituted.

THE YOSEMITE LIFT

The system for equipment hauling described on page 104 also has application in rescues, but since there is no mechanical advantage, it will not work well unless the person hauling is at least about 10kg heavier than the victim. Even so, the rescuer will need to stand entirely in the stirrup at each step. A possible improvement is to have two people hauling. They can each use a foot stirrup or else pull down heavily with their arms using Jumars as hand grips. The method requires at least a 3m high roof above the top of the pitch.

THE COUNTERWEIGHT SYSTEM

The counterweight system is a simple extension of the Yosemite Lift. It again relies on using the weight of a rescuer to lift the victim, but this time the rescuer prusiks or hangs below the pulley (Figure 156). Little space is required at the pitch top, because if necessary the rescuer can position himself below the edge of the drop. The rescuer will ideally be about 10 to 15kg heavier than the victim to make the victim rise. It is important to try to incorporate a lifeline and trailing line to guide the victim and keep him moving at a controlled, steady speed. If he tends to go too fast, he is held back by the trailing line and if he does not move at all (because the rescuer is too light), he can be partly pulled with the lifeline (Adamson 1965).

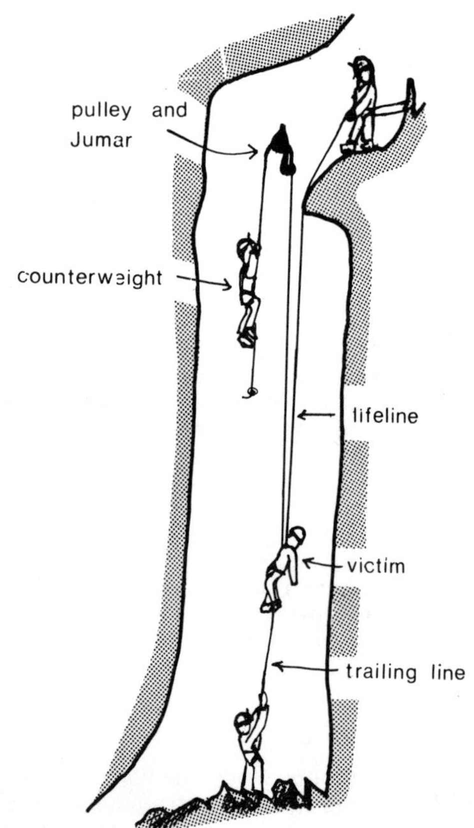

FIGURE 156: The Counterweight system. To enable the victim to be taken off the rope at the pitch top, the counterweight man must clip himself into the anchor for the pulley.

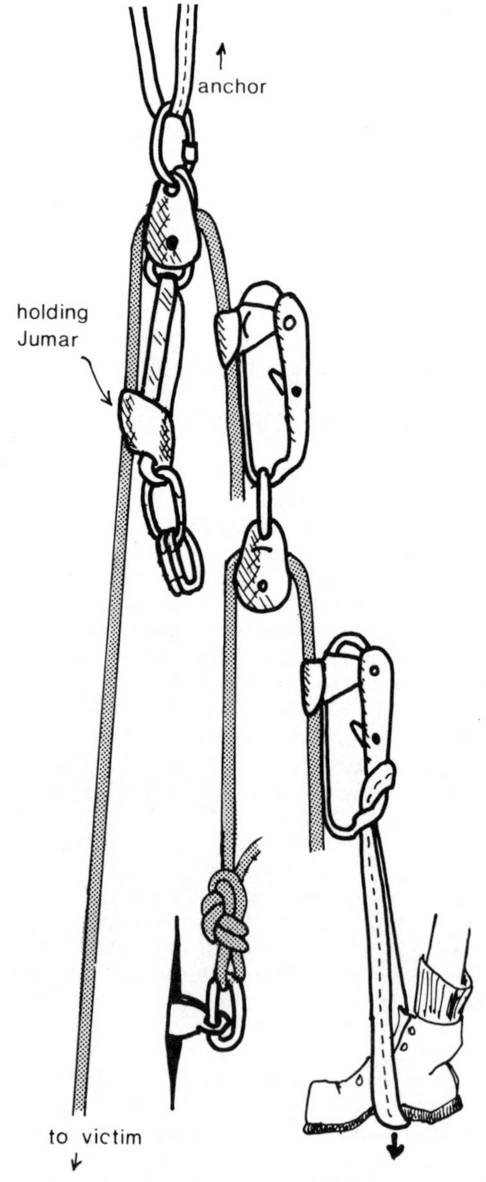

FIGURE 157: 2:1 hauling system based on the Yosemite Lift.

2:1 HAULING SYSTEM

A hauling system giving an ideal 2:1 mechanical advantage can be easily rigged in various ways to suit different pit geometries and rescue situations. There are three main arrangements.

The first is another extension of the Yosemite Lift. A 2:1 system is clipped into the hauling side of the basic Yosemite rig and worked with a foot stirrup (Figure 157) (Wade 1972). After each step the system must be reset. This is a good system when only one person is available for hauling.

Alternatively, the 2:1 system can be arranged to allow a horizontal pull along a passage above the drop (Figure 158). Two or three people can do the hauling and again the system must be reset after the pulley stops against the anchor.

Another arrangement is possible which does not require any resetting of the system. The victim can then be pulled up non-stop. It works by actually clipping the victim to the hauling pulley and hauling him up on a loop of rope (Figure 159). The holding ascender is worn on the victim's chest. One or two people can do the hauling. Very little preparation is required at the pitch top, but there must be available at least enough rope to cover the pitch twice (Bill Stone and Tracy Johnston, pers. comm.). This system is well suited to short drops.

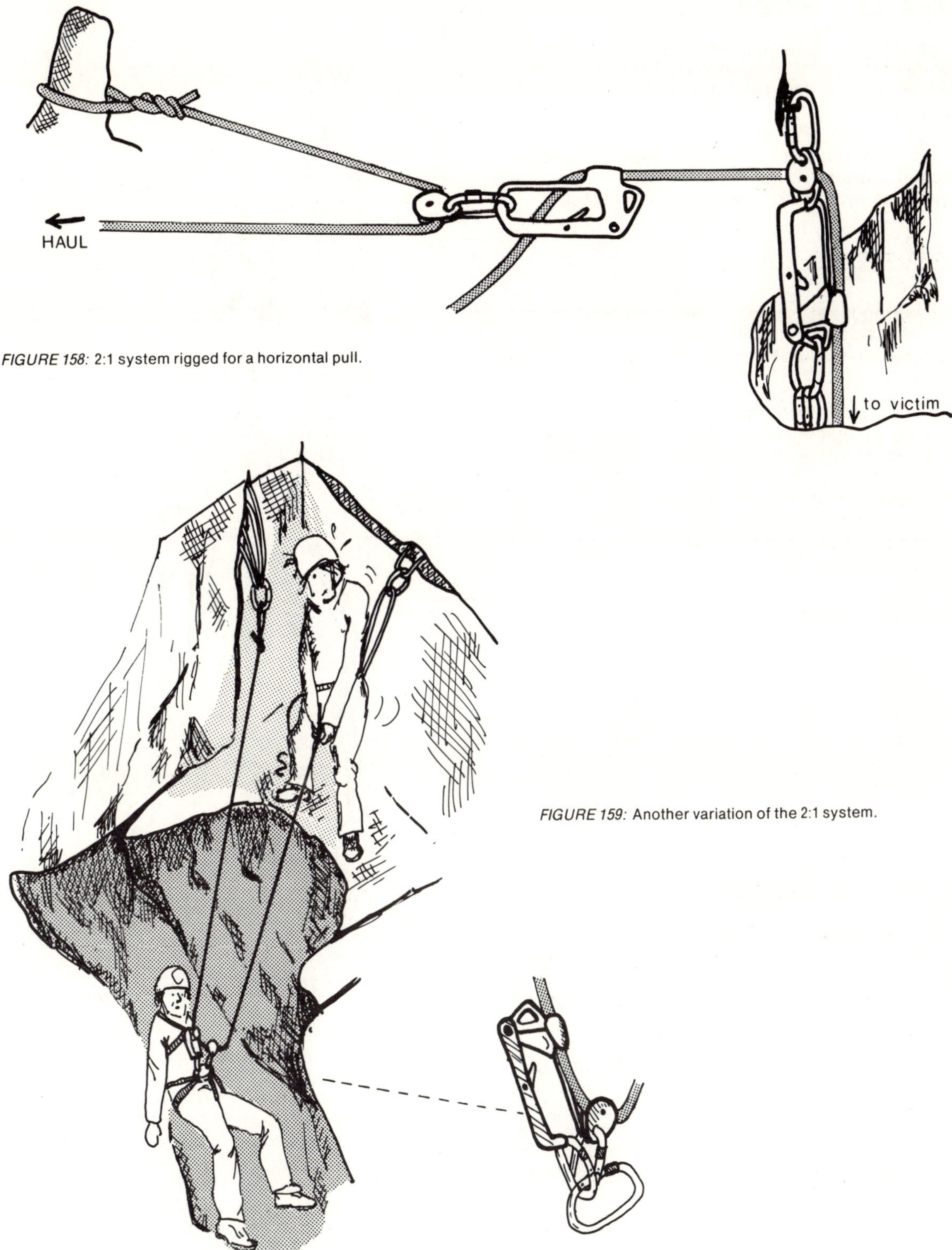

FIGURE 158: 2:1 system rigged for a horizontal pull.

FIGURE 159: Another variation of the 2:1 system.

4:1 HAULING SYSTEM

The 2:1 Yosemite system (Figure 157) can be modified to give a mechanical advantage of 4:1. This is called the Crowther Lift (Figure 160) (Cosbey 1968).

For a horizontal pull, two 2:1 systems can be stacked together to give a 4:1 system called the piggy back system (Figure 161) (Smith 1976c).

LOWERING

Lowering is, of course, easier than hauling, but will only be infrequently used in cave rescue because the way out of most vertical caves is an upward one.

The lowering technique is simple. Just as for lowering equipment (page 102), an abseil device is anchored at the pitch top and the victim's rope is threaded through it. The victim is helped over the edge and someone wearing gloves can then pay the rope out slowly. If possible a person should abseil beside the victim and the victim should be lifelined as well.

PITCH ACCIDENTS

It is now appropriate to consider the case of a pitch accident where a hauling or lowering system will need to be quickly set in operation without any advance preparation and possibly without cavers in favourable positions. The general action taken by the caving party will depend on whether they are all on the bottom of the pitch below the victim, all on the top above him, or scattered between both places.

CAVING TEAM ABOVE THE VICTIM

This is the most likely case. Typically the first member of a team will have descended a pitch, experienced difficulties, and been unable to return to his companions. A case example occurred in 1965 when a caver had trouble returning up a very cold waterfall pitch in Schroeders Pants Cave, New York State, USA. Only about 4m from the top of the pitch and both his companions, he became too weakened to prusik (presumably from hypothermia), lost consciousness, and died. His two companions were unable to pull him to safety (Boston Grotto 1975, Hartline 1965).

While this accident seems to have been caused primarily by the jamming of wet prusik knots, other circumstances such as injury or the presence of foul air could result in exactly the same situation.

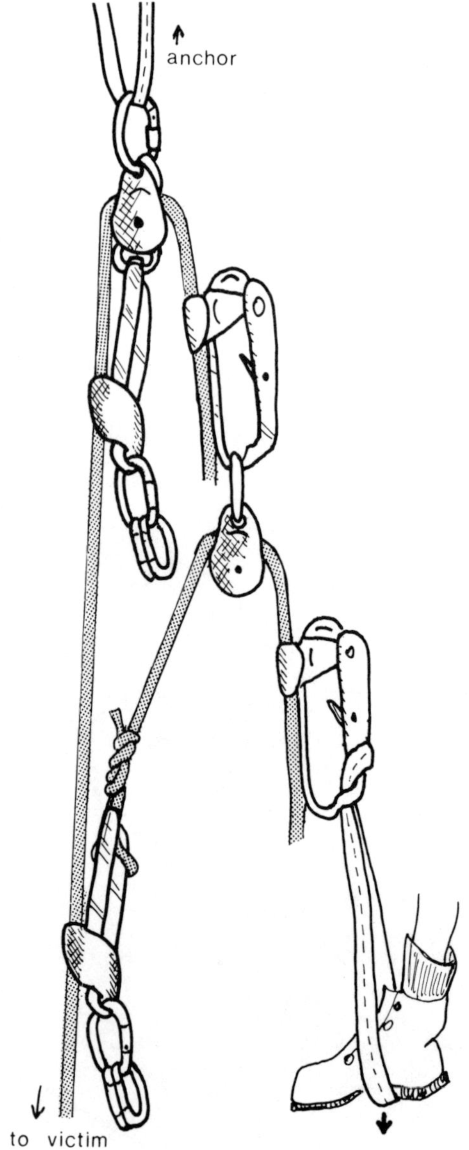

FIGURE 160: The Crowther Lift.

Fast action will usually be required. Probably it will be unsafe for anyone to abseil down to the victim on a separate rope and render assistance, because this person could easily become a second victim. Usually, assistance will better be given from the pitch top. It will be necessary to either lower or haul the victim. Where practical, hauling is better because it starts the victim on his

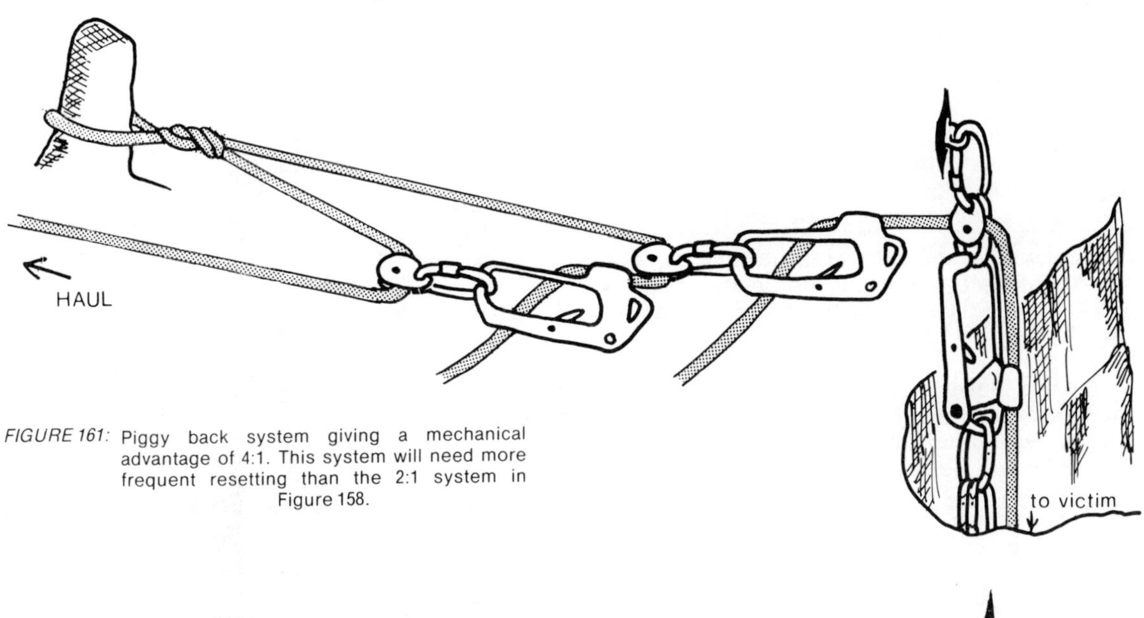

FIGURE 161: Piggy back system giving a mechanical advantage of 4:1. This system will need more frequent resetting than the 2:1 system in Figure 158.

way out of the cave. However, if his condition is very serious, lowering may be faster and more comfortable. It will help if the victim is conscious and able to advise on the relative merits of hauling or lowering. If he is unconscious, there will probably be little choice but to haul as lowering could cause the victim to drop into a pool and drown or otherwise land in a very awkward position. The hauling method will depend on the available manpower and equipment, and the urgency of the situation. For accidents requiring immediate assistance, a "brute force pull" will probably be best if there is sufficient manpower. A holding ascender will be all that is needed. Otherwise, a hauling system will need to be rigged. Figure 162 shows a method of coupling any system to a taut line in a way which eliminates friction at the pit edge. In addition, if no spare rope is available to rig a mechanical advantage system, the method can be used with a Yosemite Lift to haul up sufficient rope.

If the victim is to be lowered, a spare rope will need to be threaded through an abseil device and tied to the victim's rope. The victim's rope will then need to be released from its anchor. This is simple if it has been secured by winding it around the anchor (page 15), but otherwise it will need to be cut, or briefly hauled to take the weight off the knot.

FIGURE 162: A method of coupling a hauling system to a taut rope.

CAVING PARTY BELOW THE VICTIM

The other main category of pitch accidents is that where the accident victim has been the last to descend a pitch or the first to ascend it. The whole party is then beneath him, faced with a difficult rescue problem. The case of a caver injured while ascending will be considered first.

The first step is again for a rescuer to reach the victim, this time by prusiking up on the victim's rope. A decision can then be made to haul or lower. Hauling will require at least one person to prusik past the victim and rig a hauling system at the pitch top. However, this is a relatively lengthy procedure, and there may be insufficient time. Lowering will often be safer. The general procedure is for the rescuer who has prusiked to the victim to detach the victim from the rope and abseil back down with him. This may sound impossible but, with the right technique, it can be done. The rescuer need only carry a spare ascender, a pulley, a cord about 2m long, and a few spare carabiners. Figure 163 illustrates the method, which is based on a similar method by Dobrilla and Marbach (1973). It definitely requires practice if an unbelievable tangle is to be avoided.

The method may be simplified if a spare rope is available. The spare rope could then be threaded through the pulley and operated by cavers on the ground to first support the victim while his ascenders are released and then to lower him with an abseil device anchored at the bottom of the pitch.

Simpler versions of the same techniques can be applied to rescue a caver who has been the last to abseil down a pitch and has had an accident. Normally, he will slide all the way down to the ground but, if using excessive friction in his abseil device or, if using a trailing ascender belay, he may be left hanging on the rope.

DIVIDED CAVING PARTY

The simplest situation in a pitch accident is generally that where the caving team is divided between the pitch top and bottom. The two groups can then communicate and decide on the best procedure, which may make use of any of the methods described above.

The important point with all rescue techniques is to practise them thoroughly in simulated rescue situations. Then in an actual emergency, the rescue effort can be mobilised with a sense of confidence and efficiency that will save invaluable time and calm the victim and the rescuers alike.

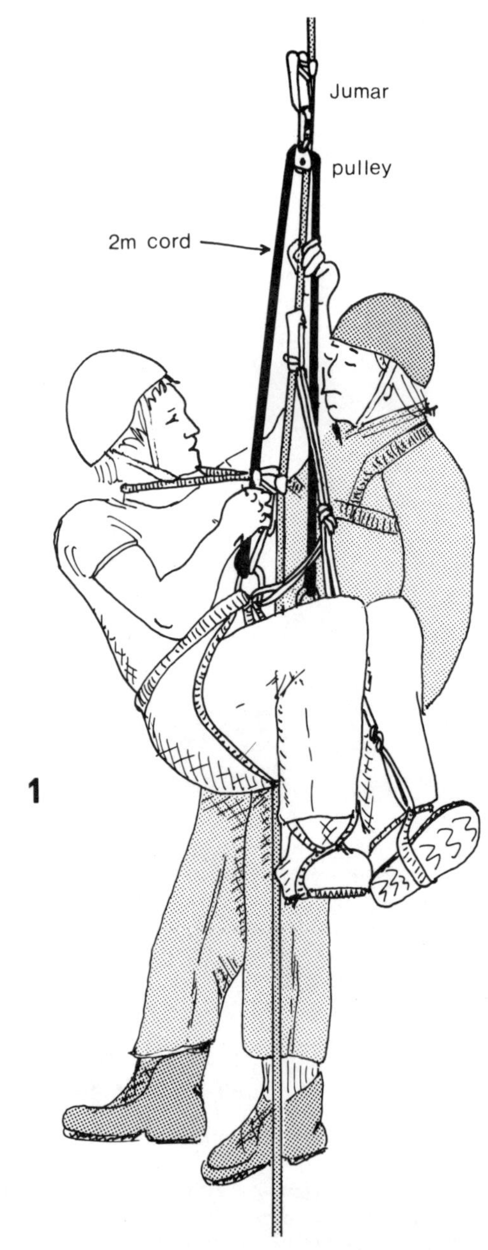

FIGURE 163: Removing an accident victim from a rope. The first step is to prusik up beside the victim, remove as many of his ascenders as possible, and attach the Jumar, pulley and cord arrangement as shown. The rescuer can then act as a counterweight and lift the victim slightly so that the victim's remaining ascenders can be removed. The victim will then be supported solely by the weight of the rescuer. (Figure continued over page.)

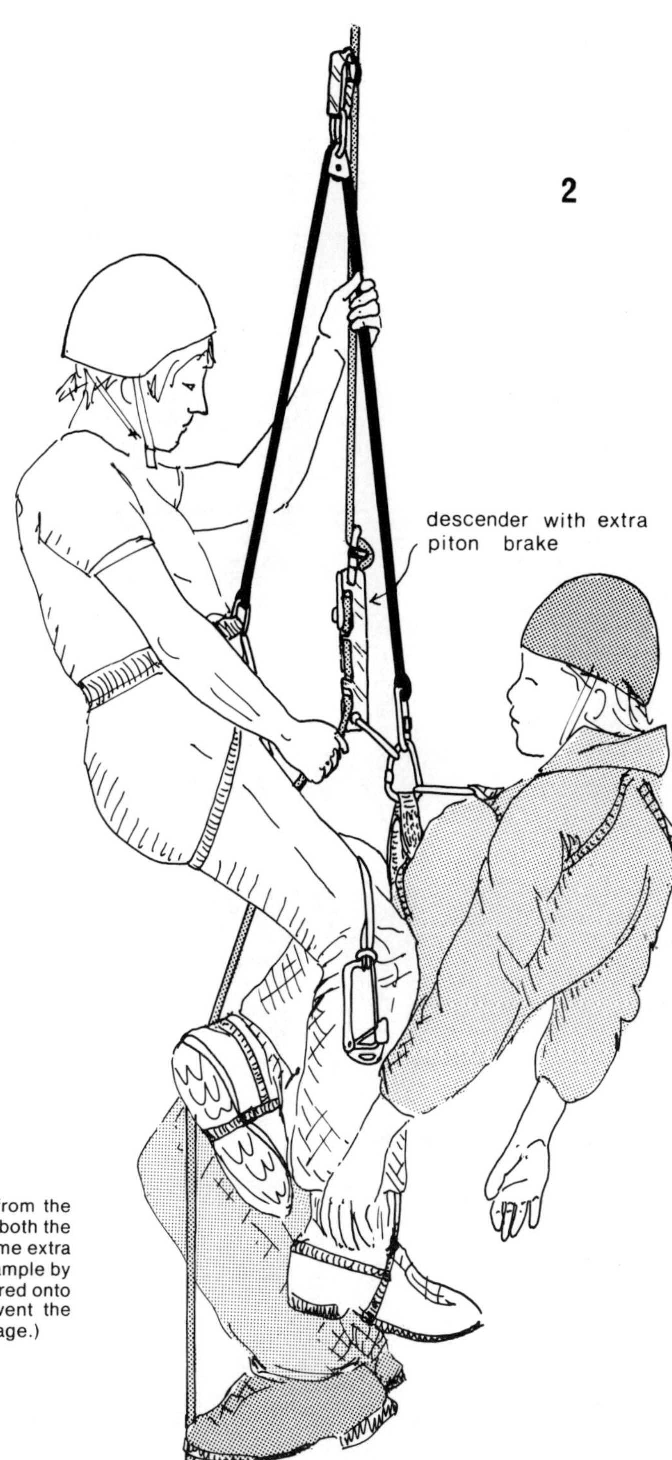

FIGURE 163 (continued).

The rescuer must then remove his own ascenders from the rope, thread a descender and clip the victim to it. Since both the rescuer and victim will abseil on this one descender, some extra friction will probably be required, as provided in this example by a single piton brake. The victim's weight should be lowered onto the descender and the descender locked off to prevent the victim from sliding downwards. (Figure continued over page.)

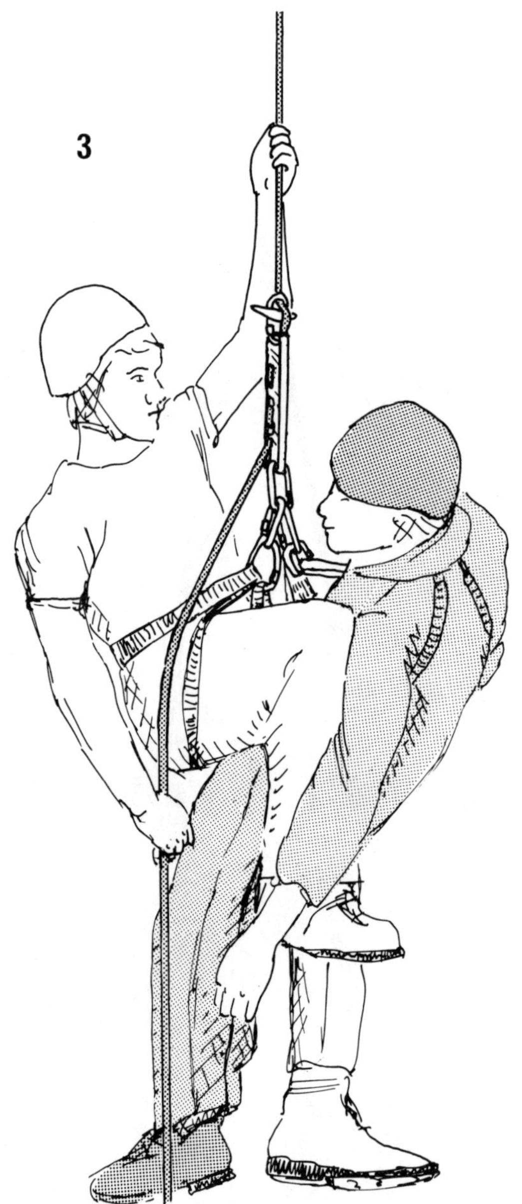

FIGURE 163 (continued).

The Jumar, pulley and 2m cord must then be removed. To do this, the rescuer must reclip an ascender to the rope (one with a foot stirrup) and stand in the stirrup. After removing the Jumar, pulley and 2m cord, it should be possible for the rescuer to squat down and clip into the descender. The rescuer can then remove his ascender and start the abseil.

APPENDIX 1: SOME MANUFACTURERS AND SUPPLIERS OF EQUIPMENT FOR SRT

Below are listed some manufacturers and suppliers of equipment for SRT. The list covers nearly all of the equipment described in this book, although doubtlessly some companies have been neglected. Companies are invited to contact the author, so that details might be included in a second edition of this book.

MANUFACTURERS

Most manufacturers will supply to individuals as well as retailers.

BLUE WATER LTD, PO Box 6276, Fort Lauderdale, Florida 33310, USA — Blue Water II and Blue Water III nylon ropes, ascender box, rappel rack.

BRIDON FIBRES AND PLASTICS, Condereum House, 171 West Road, Newcastle-upon-Tyne NE991AE, Britain — Marina (Braidline) nylon, Terylene and Polypropylene ropes.

CLOG CLIMBING GEAR, Clwty Bont, Deiniolen, Gwynedd, North Wales LL553DE, Britain — Clog ascenders, figure eight descender, chocks, pitons.

COLORADO MOUNTAIN INDUSTRIES (CMI), PO Box 44179, Cincinnati, Ohio 45244, USA — Chocks.

CORDAGE GROUP, THE, Divison of Columbian Rope Company, Auburn, N.Y. 13021, USA — Goldline nylon rope.

DONAGHYS INDUSTRIES, Stanley Street, Auckland, New Zealand — Nylon and Teryiene ropes.

DOWNS AND SON PTY LTD, 24 Meeks Road, Marrickville, NSW, 2204, Australia — Terylene ropes.

FORREST MOUNTAINEERING LTD, 1517 Platte Street, Denver, Colorado 80202, USA — Chocks.

GIBBS PRODUCTS CO, 854 Padley Street, Salt Lake City, Utah 84108, USA — Gibbs ascender.

GREAT PACIFIC IRONWORKS, PO Box 150, Ventura, California 93001, USA — Chouinord chocks, pitons and other climbing equipment.

KINNEARS ROPES, 16 Bunn Street, Pyrmont, NSW 2009, Australia — Terylene and polypropylene ropes.

MARLOW ROPES LTD, Marlow House, Hailey Road, Thamesmead, Erith, Kent DA184AL, Britain — Terylene and polypropylene ropes.

MOUNTAIN SAFETY RESEARCH, 1100 East Pike Street, Seattle, Washington 98108, USA — Longhorn Ring, helmets, climbing equipment.

PETZL, F., 38 St Ismier, Nr Grenoble, France — Ascenders, Shunt, bobbin, pulleys, hanger, climbing platform.

RAWLBOLT CO LTD, Rawbolt House, London Road, Kingston-upon-Thames, Surrey, Britain — Bolts.

SPELEAN, PO Box 230, Milsons Point, NSW, 2061, Australia — Whaletail descender, Long Range cave packs, rope protectors, pulleys.

SPELEOSHOPPE, PO Box 8044, Louisville, Kentucky 40208, USA — SupeRack.

TROLL PRODUCTS, Spring Mill, Uppermill, Nr Oldham, Lancs, Britain — Whillans Sit Harness, Troll waist belt, cave packs, tape.

WALTER MARTI APPARATEBAU, CH-3713 Reichenbach, Switzerland — Jumar ascender.

SUPPLIERS

Bridon, Donaghys, Downs, Kinnears and Marlow ropes are available from boating shops, though possibly only in their country of manufacture. Climbing equipment by Clog, CMI, Forrest and Great Pacific Ironworks is available from many climbing shops. Bolts from Rawbolt and other companies are available from large hardware shops. The suppliers listed below will forward a catalogue on request.

Australia

BONWICK, J. H. and CO., Russell St, Emu Plains, N.S.W., 2750 — Supplier and manufacturer of cave ladders, scaling poles, rescue stretchers and caving equipment.

BUSHGEAR PTY LTD, 46 Hardware St, Melbourne, Victoria, 3000 — Jumars, climbing equipment.

CAVING EQUIPMENT, 10 Binda Street, Merrylands, NSW 2160 — Gibbs, Jumars, Blue Water rappel racks, whaletails, Blue Water and Marlow ropes, pulleys, cave packs, climbing equipment.

MOUNTAIN EQUIPMENT PTY LTD, 17a Falcon St, Crows Nest, NSW, 2065 — Jumars, Edelrid static rope, climbing equipment.

PADDY PALLIN PTY LTD, 69 Liverpool St, Sydney, NSW, 2000 — Jumars, Clog equipment, climbing equipment.

SOUTHERN CROSS EQUIPMENT PTY LTD, 33 King St, Sydney, NSW, 2000 — Gibbs, Jumars, climbing equipment.

SPELEO ENTERPRISES, PO Box 230, Milsons Point, NSW, 2061 — Blue Water ropes and racks.

Britain

CAVING SUPPLIES, 84 Chatsworth Rd, Cheam, Sutton, Surrey — Gibbs, ascender box, rappel rack, Bridon ropes.

ROCKSPORT, Bus Station, Wells, Somerset — UK Ropewalkers, Jumars, Clog, Petzl and Troll equipment, rappel racks, Blue Water, Bridon, Edelrid Static, Interalp Static and Marlow ropes, climbing equipment.

WHERNSIDE MANOR, Retail Dept, Dent, Sedbergh, Cumbria LA105RE — Petzl equipment, Blue Water rope.

New Zealand

ALP SPORTS, Box 553, Christchurch — climbing equipment.

U.S.A.

BILL CUDDINGTON, 4729 Lumary Drive, NW, Huntsville, Alabama 35810 — Gibbs, Jumars, Blue Water equipment.

BOB & BOB, Bob Liebman, PO Box 441, Lewisburg, West Virginia 24901 — Gibbs, Jumars, Blue Water equipment, seat harnesses, Goldline ropes.

RECREATIONAL EQUIPMENT INC, 1525 Eleventh Ave, Seattle, Washington, 98122 — Gibbs, Jumars, Goldline rope, climbing equipment.

SPELEOSHOPPE, PO Box 8044, Louisville, Kentucky 40208 — Gibbs, Jumars, Blue Water equipment, SupeRacks, carabiner brake bars, climbing equipment.

REFERENCES

ADAMSON, S., 1965. Cave Rescue Technique. **The Guacharo, 6**(1):23-6. Reprinted in **Speleo Digest, 1965**:.73-9.

AMERICAN ALPINE CLUB, 1967. **Accidents in North American Mountaineering, 1967**:4-5.

ARMITAGE, J., 1966. What is a "Safe" Piton? **Summit**, July-August, 1966, pp 24-27+.

ARMITAGE, J., 1967. What is a Safe Piton? **Summit**, June 1967, pp 10-13.

BAGULEY, F. S. S. and BRANDON, D. P., 1969. Ladders. (In) Cullingford, C. (Ed), **Manual of Caving Techniques** (Routledge and Kegan Paul, London) pp 57-108.

BAZ-DRESCH, J., 1974. Whaletail Versus Rappel Rack. **Descent**, 30:33-5.

BEDFORD, B., 1977. Recommendations on Using a Shunt. **Descent**, 35:30.

BERTULIS, A., 1976. CCCP Spells Friendship. **Off Belay**, 25:19-24.

BORWICK, G. R., 1974. Mountaineering Ropes. **Off Belay**, 15:5.

BOSTON GROTTO, 1965. Boston Grotto Report on the James Mitchell Accident. **Massachusetts Caver**, 4(1). Reprinted in **Speleo Digest, 1965**:3.106-9.

BOYD, R. J., POSTER, C. and OLMSTEAD, B., 1966. Parachute Harnesses and the Jumar Ascender: A New System. **The Wisconsin Speleologist**, 5(2):49-55. Reprinted in **Speleo Digest, 1966**:3.69-75.

BOYD, R. J. and FRATER, N. K., 1968. The Strength of Brake Bar Systems. **The Wisconsin Speleologist**, 7(4):133-6. Reprinted in **Speleo Digest, 1968**:3.62-6.

BREW, B., 1976. How Strong are Tape Slings? **Descent**, 34:46-9.

BROOK, A., 1972. Artificial Belays Underground. **Technical Aids in Caving Symposium** (Cave Research Group) pp 13-15.

BROOK, A., 1974. Artificial Anchors. **Brit. Assoc. Caving Instructors Bulletin**, 2(1):6-14.

BROWN, A. L., 1976. Frog Prusik Technique. **Down Under, 15**(4):105.

BUNNING, P., 1974. The Chock Wrench. **Summit**, June 1974, pp 8-9.

CAFFYN, P. H., 1974. Deep Caving Techniques and Equipment Used by the New Zealand Speleological Society 1971-72 Mt Arthur Expedition. **J Syd Speleol Soc, 18**(4):83-99.

CHEVALIER, P., 1948. **Subterranean Climbers** (Translated by Hatt, E. M. Faber and Faber, London).

CHILDS, J. J., 1976. The Strength of Bolt Belays. **BRCA Trans.**, 3(2):100-9.

CHOUINARD, Y. and **FROST, T.**, Undated. **Great Pacific Ironworks Catalog** (Great Pacific Ironworks, Ventura, Calif).

COLE, J., 1966. New Rappel Device. **NSS News**, **24**(6):154-5.

COSBEY, B., 1968. More Rescue Techniques. **The Massachusetts Caver, 7**(4):74-7.

COURBIS, R., 1976. Utilisation d'un Mat en Escalade Souterraine. **Spelunca, 1976**(2):81-2.

COURBON, P., 1972. **Atlas des Grands Gouffres du Monde** (Courbon).

COWLISHAW, M., 1977. APS: Another Prusiking System. **Descent**, 36:39-42.

CUDDINGTON, B., 1966. Brake Bar Rappel Caution. **Speleo Digest, 1966**:3.79.

DAVIS, J., 1969. Rockclimbing. (In) Davis, J. (Ed), **Rope and Rucksack** (Angus and Robertson, Sydney).

DAVISON, D. Jr, 1974. The Davison System. **Nylon Highway**, 2:12-19.

DAVISON, D. Jr, 1975. Beyond the 7th Tooth. **Nylon Highway**, 4:11-12.

DAVISON, D. Jr, 1976a. Dear STC. **NSS News, 34**(9):160-1.

DAVISON, D. Jr, 1976b. Hits and Near Misses. **NSS News, 34**(5):80-1.

DAVISON, D. Jr, 1976c. Safety Rappel Cam. **NSS News, 34**(8):140-3+.

DAVISON, D. Jr, 1977a. Safety Techniques. **NSS News, 35**(5):92-4.

DAVISON, D. Jr, 1977b. **Dear STC. NSS News, 35**(4):73.

DEAL, D., 1968. How to Kill Your Friends Or: Don't Use Bolts Unless You Know What You Are Doing. **The Texas Caver, 2**(10):122-4. Reprinted in **Speleo Digest, 1966**:3.57-60.

DOBRILLA, J. C. and MARBACH, G., 1973. **Techniques de la Speleogie Alpine** (Marbach, Paris).

DRESSLER, B. and CHAZALET, M., 1966. "L'Araignee". **Spelunca, 6**(4):269-70.

DUNSTER, J. A., 1976. Karabiners. **BCRA Trans.**, **3**(1):43-7.

EAVIS, A., 1974. The Rope in Single Rope Technique Caving. **BCRA Trans., 1**(4):181-98.

EAVIS, A., 1975. Gaping Ghyll: Why did the Rope Break? **Descent**, 31:5-6.

EAVIS, A., 1976. Equipment Report. **BCRA Trans, 3**(3 and 4):223-7.

EAVIS, A., 1977. Observations on the Use of SRT in Australasia. **Descent**, 36:33-6.

ELLIS, I. G., 1977. An Open Letter from the Speleoshoppe. **NSS News, 35**(5):109-10.

ERRINGTON, A., 1972. Piton Removal Techniques. **Off Belay**, 2:38-9.

EYRE, J., 1969. Use of Ladders and Ropes. (In) Cullingford, C. (Ed), **Manual of Caving Techniques** (Routledge and Kegan Paul, London), pp 109-26.

FRANK, B., 1975. A Rebolting Experience. **Inner Mountain News, 7**(2):8.

FRANKLAND, J. C., 1973. Exposure Underground. **Brit. Assoc. Caving Instructors Bulletin**, 7:1-7.

FRENCH, J., 1975. Letter to the Editor. **NSS News, 33**(6):107.

GRIFFITHS, J., 1976. Letter to the Editor. **Descent**, 33:48-9.

GOULBOURNE, A., 1974. Abseiling Devices. **ULSA Review**, 13:4-7.

GRAHAM, D., 1969. Caving with the Ascender Knot. **Huntsville Grotto Newsletter**. Reprinted in **Speleo Digest, 1969**:2.09.

HAARR, A., 1962. Scaling Pole. **The Netherworld News, 10**(10):189-90. Reprinted in **Speleo Digest, 1962**:3.16.

HAARR, A., 1968. Scaling Pole. **The Netherworld News, 16**(4):40-2. Reprinted in **Speleo Digest, 1968**:3.83-6.

HARTLINE, D., 1965. James Mitchell Accident — Analysis. **Massachusetts Caver, 4**(1). Reprinted in **Speleo Digest, 1965**:3.109-15.

HENSLER, E., 1969. Miscellaneous Mechanical Aids. (In) Cullingford, C. (Ed), **Manual of Caving Techniques** (Routledge and Kegan Paul, London) pp 176-94.

HOFFMANN, P., 1975. What Makes a Rappel Rack Work. **The Speleograph, 11**(4):35-7.

HOWIE, W., 1975. In Search of a Better Seat Sling. **Nylon Highway,** 4:2-3.

HUMPHREY, N. H. Jr, 1973. The Versatile Gibbs Ascender. **Off Belay,** 11:37-41.

ISENHART, K., 1974a. The Super Rack. **Nylon Highway,** 1:30-7.

ISENHART, K., 1974b. How to Rig a Vertical Pitch. **Nylon Highway,** 2:21-2.

ISENHART, K., 1974c. Roller Cam. **Nylon Highway,** 1:22.

ISENHART, K., 1974d. The Care and Feeding of Nylon Rope. **Nylon Highway,** 1:4-10. Reprint from **Georgia Underground.**

ISENHART, K., 1975. Temperature Studies of Rappelling Devices. **Nylon Highway,** 4:20-3.

ISENHART, K., 1976. Bolt Installation Made Easy. **Nylon Highway,** 5:11-2.

ISENHART, K., 1977. SupeRack. **NSS News, 35**(5):109.

JAMIESON, R. and FRIEND, J., 1977. Technical Note. **Thrutch,** 70:17.

KNUTSON, S., 1973a. Rope Ascending Systems and Methods. **The Speleograph, 9**(1):12-9.

KNUTSON, S., 1973b. The Penberthy (Path) Knot. **The Speleograph, 9**(2):31-2+.

KNUTSON, S., 1975. The Strength of Stitched Splices in Nylon Webbing. **The Underground Express, 1**(2):37-9.

KOON, A. W., 1973. **Product Bulletin R5 of the Cordage Group.** Reprinted in part in **Off Belay,** 22:3.

LEEPER, E., 1963. Testing Drills and Anchors in Granite. **Summit,** April 1963, pp 18-23.

LINK, C. H. Jr, 1958. Rope Notes. **The Southeastern Caver, 3**(4):50. Reprinted in **Speleo Digest, 1958**:3.7-3.8.

LUCAS, J. M., 1973. Large Differences between Partial Correlation Coefficients. **The American Statistician, 27**(2):77-8.

MacGREGOR, K., 1975. Mud-Proofing Quick Release Pins. **Nylon Highway,** 4:4-6.

MAGNUSSEN, C., 1972. How Strong is a Stitched Splice in Nylon Webbing? **Off Belay,** 5:6-8.

MASKASKY, J. E., 1977. A Safer Rappel. **NSS News, 35**(5):103.

MITCHELL, D., 1966. An Accident in Fern. **Potomac Caver, 9**(5):34-5. Reprinted in **Speleo Digest, 1966**:3.84-5.

MITCHELL, D., 1967. Fastest Method with Jumars. **NSS News, 25**(12):211-12.

MIXON, B., 1966. Deterioration of Climbing Rope. **The Windy City Speleonews, 6**(6):42-3.

MONCRIEFF, R. W., 1970. **Man Made Fibres,** Fifth Edition (Heywood, London).

MONTGOMERY, N. R., 1974. Equipment and Techniques. (In) James, J. M. (Ed), **Papua New Guinea Speleological Expedition** (Speleological Research Council, Sydney) pp 55-9.

MONTGOMERY, N. R., 1976. Protecting Ropes from Abrasion in Single Rope Techniques. **Helictite, 14**(2):49-62.

MONTGOMERY, N. R., 1977a. A New Look at the Whaletail Descender. **Nylon Highway,** 7:2-6.

MONTGOMERY, N. R., 1977b. Australian Foot Harness. **Nylon Highway,** 6:7.

MONTGOMERY, N. and MONTGOMERY, G., 1972. The Whaletail Descender. **J Syd. Speleol. Soc., 16**(7):185-90.

MOOREHOUSE, D., 1976. Letter to the Editor. **Off Belay,** 30:54-5.

MOSS, L., 1977. A Tension Sensitive Gibbs. **Nylon Highway,** 6:8-10.

NEWELL, J. R. Jr, 1969. A New Rope for Caving. **Huntsville Grotto Newsletter.** Reprinted in **Speleo Digest, 1969**:2.14-5.

NEWELL, J. R. Jr, 1976. Development of Caving Rope. **Nylon Highway,** 5:5-8.

PADGETT, A. and PADGETT, K., 1975. A Guide to Rappelling. **Nylon Highway,** 3:2-5.

PATTEN, J., 1966. Tensions in Cave Ropes. **The Huntsville Grotto Newsletter, 7**(10):24-5. Reprinted in **Speleo Digest, 1966**:382-3.

PAVEY, "Pooh", 1972. Pavey's Premier Perspicuous Perfected Personal Perambulating Prancing Prusiking Procedure, Presages Precession, Provoking Profane Professions, Promoting Positive Progressive Propulsion, Provided Prudent Prowess Predates Primary Precipe Practice ... Precluding Potential Plumline Plummets. **Spar,** 19:7-10.

PENBERTHY, L., 1971. Some Facts about Nylon Ropes. **Summit,** January-February 1971, pp 14-15.

PENBERTHY, L., 1972a. Life of Climbing Ropes. **MSR Newsletter,** May 1972, pp 6-14.

PENBERTHY, L., 1972b. Climbing Helmets. **MSR Newsletter,** May 1972.

PETERS, E., 1976. Wedging Action of Chocks. **Off Belay,** 29:18.

PLANINA, T., 1975. Contribution to the Knowledge of Climbing Ropes Wearing Out. **Nase Jame,** 17:101-9.

PIERSON, R., 1975. A No-Tie Ascender. **Off Belay,** 23:2.

PINCHAK, A. C. and GIBBS, C. H., 1972. A Rope Ascender Field Test. **Climbing,** May-June 1972, pp 21-4.

POPE, J. F., 1972. Tests on Knots. **Summit,** April, 1972, pp 6-7.

PLYMOUTH CORDAGE CO, 1958. Note in **Summit,** November 1958, p 24.

PUCKETT, B. C., 1976. Chicken Loops. **Off Belay,** 25:8.

QUIGG, G., 1976. Effects of Whaletail and Brake Bar Rack Descenders. **Bulletin New Zealand Speleol Soc, 5**(97):513.

RAINES, T. W., 1968. **Sotano de las Golondrinas, Bulletin 2, Assoc. Mex. Cave Studies.**

RAINES, T. W., 1972. Preliminary Report on the Exploration of El El Sotano. **Assoc. Mex. Cave Studies Newsletter, 3**(5):107-12.

RECKERT, N., 1977. Letter to the Editor. **Descent,** 35:51.

RICHARDS, J. and HOSELY, B., 1965. Some Problems in the Use of Jumar Ascenders for Rope Climbing. **CIG Newsletter, 9**(1):10-14. Reprinted in **Speleo Digest, 1965**:3.28-3.31.

RICHINGS, G., 1977. Letter to the Editor. **Descent,** 35:51-2.

INDEX

ADDENDUM:

RECENT DEVELOPMENTS IN S.R.T.

I attended the Seventh International Speleological Congress in Sheffield England (September 1977) and obtained some important new information on ropes for abseiling and prusiking, and on ascender boxes.

ROPES

In the last year in Europe and America about ten new ropes have appeared for SRT. They are all made especially for caving. Also, it is certain that several more will become available in the next year. The new ropes have yet to be subjected to extensive underground use. In addition there has recently been some valuable research done on ropes.

NEW ROPES

1. Most of the large manufacturers of mountaineering ropes in Europe now produce 'Speleo Ropes' which are similar to static mountaineering ropes but are generally less stretchy. They are of braided nylon and are 10-11mm in diameter. Initial testing by Andy Eavis (soon to be published in the British Cave Research Association Transactions) shows these ropes to be promising for SRT, with the possible exception of the Edelweiss rope, which is rather too stretchy. All British caving shops sell at least one brand of speleo rope.

2. The 16 plait staple braided Terylene rope by Marlow Ropes, which has been popular for SRT for many years, has now been discontinued as a boating rope and is being produced solely for cavers. A new rope has taken its place for boating. The new rope outwardly has exactly the same appearance as the caving rope but has a different core. The boating rope is unsuitable for SRT and care must be taken to select the correct rope. The caving rope has a **parallel core** and this should be specified at the time of purchase. Any rope bought at a boating shop would require checking (Marlow Ropes, personal communication).

3. A competitor to Blue Water rope has appeared on the American market. It is made of nylon and is called Pigeon Mountain rope. The new rope has less static stretch and is probably more abrasion resistant than Blue Water, but this is at the expense of a tighter construction which may result in very poor handling qualities after a period of use. There is also the worry that a rope with so little stretch may be dangerous if a fall should occur on it during use, such as may happen if a rope snags on a pitch and suddenly gives way, or an anchor fails.

RECENT RESEARCH ON ROPES

1. There is now irrefutable evidence that Terrylene ropes commonly lose 25-50% of their new strength after just a few trips underground. The cause of this is unknown, but research is under way. Nylon has yet to be thoroughly tested but should only Terylene suffer from this dramatic strength loss, nylon would be clearly favoured as the best fibre for SRT ropes (Marlow Ropes, personal communication).

2. It has been demonstrated that nylon is a significantly better fibre than Terylene for absorbing the heat that builds up in an abseil device during abseiling (Eavis, A., 1977. Thermal Properties of Abseil Devices. In: Ford, T.D. ed. *Proceedings of the 7th International Speleological Congress, Sheffield, 1977* (BCRA) pp. 165-7).

3. Mike Cowlishaw in Britain (personal communication) has examined the forces that SRT ropes may be subjected to under shock loads, such as might be sustained by ropes in falls. The most significant result at present is that 10mm Terylene ropes may break under falls that could realistically occur while caving. Special care should be taken with these ropes.

4. Sheath slippage is noted in Chapter 1 of *Single Rope Techniques*, as being a particular problem with loose sheathed braided ropes. Testing has now shown this to be only a significant danger with new ropes. After a rope has been used and washed a few times, slippage should be only slight (article by Paul Ramsden, soon to be published in *Descent*).

ASCENDER BOXES

Two new models have recently appeared on the market, one from the USA and one from Britain. The Gosset Box from the USA differs from the Blue Water box mentioned in Single Rope Techniques, in having two rollers for each of the two ropes which pass through the box and in having a different mechanism for rope insertion. It is still a screw mechanism however, and thus is fairly time consuming to operate. The British designed Niel Box seems to have a quicker and simpler method of rope insertion, except perhaps on long pitches where a large weight of rope hangs below the box. The rope needs to be slightly lifted for insertion in and removal from the Niel Box.

ANCHORS

For some time cavers in Britain have been making artificial jughandles as alternatives to the placement of permanent bolts or pitons. To make an artificial jughandle a hole is simply drilled through a narrow rib of rock (should one be suitably positioned) and the edges of the hole rounded off. If the hole is over 14mm diameter it should be possible to thread the abseil/prusik rope through. In some caving areas suitable ribs will abound, in others they will be almost absent. In any event it is an excellent practice which deserves more attention than it has had in the past.

ABSEILING

Spelean in Australia are now making a variation of the Figure-Eight descender which can be used either like the standard figure-eight or the MSR Longhorn Ring. It is called the Harpoon.